Publisher and Creative Director:
B. Martin Pedersen

Chief Visionary Officer:
Patti Judd

Design Director:
Hee Ra Kim

Designers:
B. Martin Pedersen
Hee Ra Kim
Hiewon Sohn

Associate Editor:
Colleen Boyd

Contributing Editor:
Patti Judd

Publisher's Assistant /Designer:
Claire Yuan Zhuang

Interns:
Lauren Letarte
Kaitlyn Morrison
Kaitlyn Richardson
Ella York

Japanese Advisors:
USA: Toshiaki & Kumiko Ide
Japan: Taku Satoh
Sakura Nomiyama

Chief Executive Officer:
B. Martin Pedersen

Cover Image:
"AIGA Boston, Honoring Matthew Carter Poster, 2010" by Skolos-Wedell

Published by:
Graphis Inc.
389 5th Ave., Suite 1105
New York, NY 10016
Phone: 212-532-9387
www.graphis.com
help@graphis.com

ISBN 13: 978-1-954632-46-2

Dear Graphis Readers,

Welcome to *Graphis Journal 386*—a place where art and design speak louder than words, and creativity never stands still. In this issue, we highlight the artists, designers, educators, and thinkers shaping the future across continents and disciplines. Their work doesn't just impress—it resonates.

DESIGN: Nancy Skolos, one half of the celebrated duo **Skolos-Wedell** (US), shares how early exposure to art led both her and **Tom Wedell** to Cranbrook and eventually to teaching at the Rhode Island School of Design. Their poster designs, rich in structure and typographic rhythm, blur the line between art and communication. In Australia, **Toben** (AU) crafts bold brand experiences for clients like QT Hotels and McGrath Estate Agents, drawing from the contrast of vibrant local art and refined German minimalism.

ADVERTISING: At **Nikkeisha, Inc.** (JP), advertising is more than messaging—it's emotional motivation. Their creative process is rooted in empathy and bold proposals, always asking, "Would this move me?" as both creators and consumers.

PHOTOGRAPHY: Robert Seale (US) elevates the industrial and everyday with authenticity and insight. With a background in photojournalism, he prepares multiple lighting setups in advance to maximize time and impact. **Tim Tadder** (US) got his start with a Gatorade campaign and has since worked with brands like Nike, Amazon, AT&T, McDonald's, and Reebok. For him, trust and collaboration matter more than the logo.

ART/ILLUSTRATION: This issue includes a dynamic selection of winning illustrations from our New Talent competition, showcasing a range of styles—from detailed and haunting to whimsical and raw. Each artist reminds us of the unshakable power of pure visual storytelling.

EDUCATION: At **Brigham Young University** (US), educator **Linda Reynolds** encourages students to create work that fosters contemplation, connection, and cultural elevation. She integrates AI tools into her curriculum—ethically and effectively—to help students shape the future of design with intention.

PRODUCTS: Cars: The **La Rose Noire Droptail** (UK) is a bespoke masterpiece where every curve is artfully rendered. The **Owlet One** (US) modernizes e-bikes with style, multiple speeds, and a sleek folding frame.
Planes: The **Midnight** (US) flying taxi hints at a near future of urban air mobility, while the **NISUS Gyroplane** (SK) introduces Slovakian engineering to personal aviation.

ARCHITECTURE: Sky Base One (PT) merges sci-fi aesthetics with Taoist philosophy for a striking yet serene living space. **Projekt Datscha** (AT) redefines small-space living with its minimalist mobile cabin—now a symbol of collaborative, creative freedom.

We're proud to bring you this collection of groundbreaking work. May it fuel your own vision, challenge your process, and inspire you to keep asking what design—and creativity—can really do.

Warm regards,

B. Martin Pedersen
Publisher & Creative Director

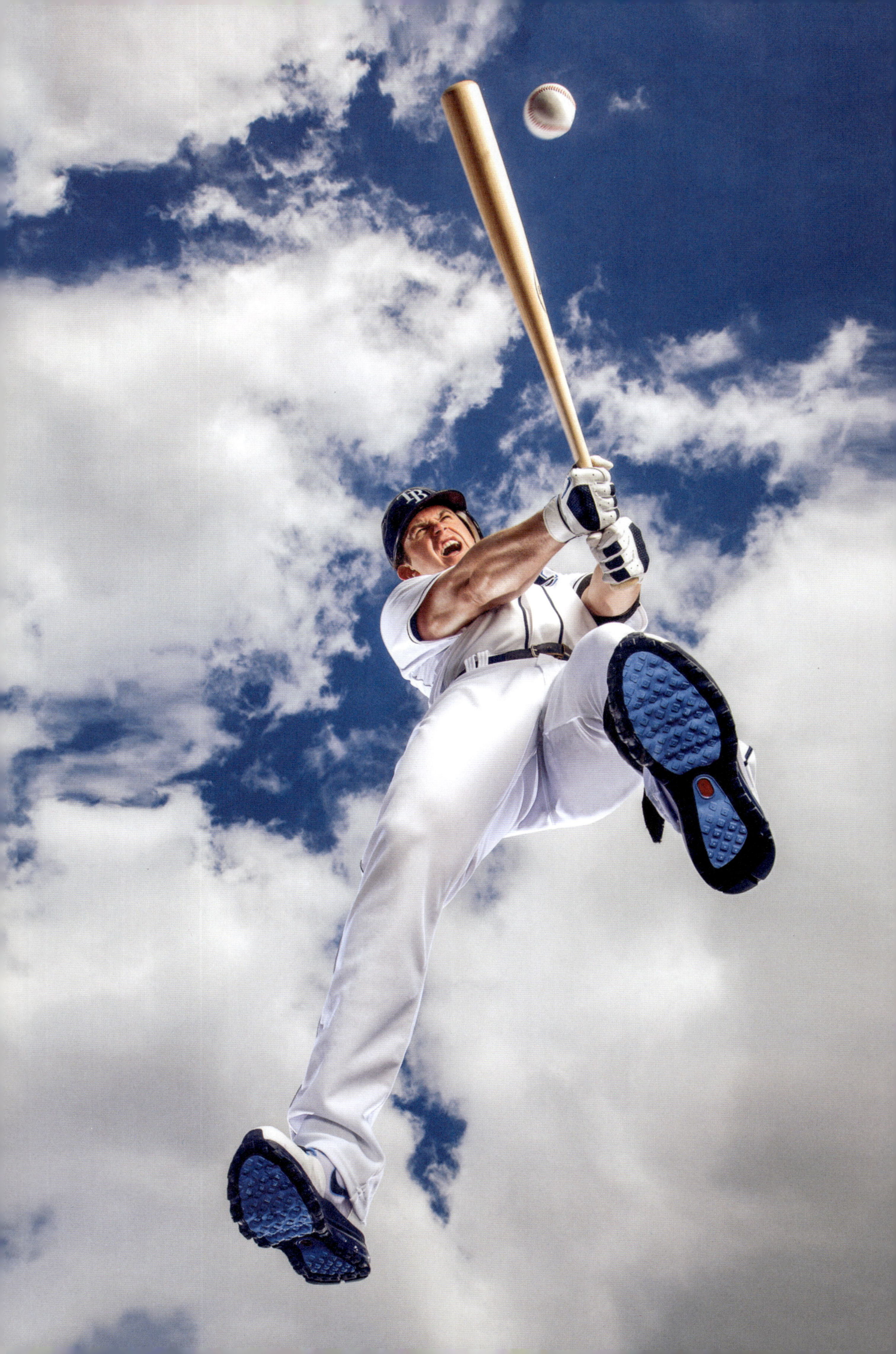

Contents

(Opposite page) Evan Longoria on Plexiglas, Pt. Charlotte, Florida. Photo by Robert Seale.

PHOTOGRAPHY:

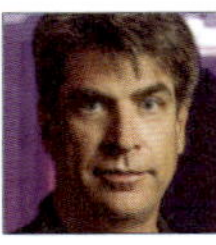

64 Robert Seale / USA

Robert Seale is a Houston-based commercial photographer known for his heroic portraits and striking industrial imagery. A native of the Texas Gulf Coast, he studied journalism and art at Stephen F. Austin State University before beginning his career as a newspaper photojournalist. He transitioned to sports magazines, first at the *Sporting News* and later at *Sports Illustrated*, photographing Super Bowls and World Series games while honing his lighting skills on cover portraits of famous athletes. Robert started his own studio in 2006, and today, he works for a diverse clientele in the sports/fitness, oil and gas, aviation, and healthcare industries. His clients include ExxonMobil, Phillips 66, Atlas Air, SLB, Aramco, the MLB, the NBA, Pepsi, Gatorade, Mattress Firm, Methodist Hospital, UT Health, Memorial Hermann, the MD Anderson Cancer Center, Under Armour, *Sports Illustrated*, ESPN, *Businessweek, Forbes, Fortune, Barron's, GOLF Magazine, Smithsonian,* and *Air & Space*.

Introduction by Quinn Stewart

Quinn Stewart is a multimedia specialist at W. R. Grace based in Maryland, where she specializes in video editing and in-house photography. She has worked within the public and private sectors in the US and Japan, creating business showcase videos, tourism publications, and designs for merchandising. She is very interested in 2D and 3D feature animation production, along with international marketing for feature films. She received her BA in international business from Towson University in Maryland, with an additional certification from Kansai Gaidai University in Japan, and with additional education at the Maryland Institute College of Art and CG Master Academy.

82 Tim Tadder / USA

Tim Tadder is a visual artist and photographer whose work bridges the worlds of fine art, commercial creativity, and experimental digital media. A graduate of the Ohio University School of Visual Communication, Tim began his career in photojournalism, driven by a deep interest in narrative truth and human emotion. That foundation evolved into a distinctive visual style—bold, surreal, and conceptually charged—that has become instantly recognizable across both artistic and commercial spheres. Based in Southern California, Tim has spent the past two decades crafting imagery that challenges perception and defies categorization. His work is known for its vibrant color palettes, hyper-real compositions, and seamless integration of emerging technologies such as AI and generative design. Through this evolving approach, he explores themes of identity, culture, and futurism with a visual language that feels both cinematic and deeply personal. Tim's images have been exhibited internationally, collected by art patrons, and commissioned by global brands seeking to break from the expected. His practice continues to push the boundaries of what photography can be—not just a tool for representation but a medium for reinvention. Tim's work lives at the edge of imagination—bold, unapologetic, and always reaching forward.

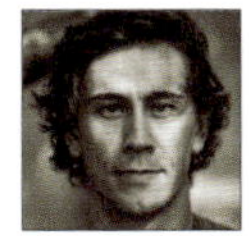

Introduction by Michael Christopher Brown

Michael Christopher Brown is a photographer, filmmaker, and author. Above all, he is an artist and storyteller who passionately explores the human experience through all media, including artificial intelligence. A former photographer at Magnum Photos, he has worked as a *National Geographic* photographer since 2004. His current creative projects include a book collaboration with Palestinian poet Mosab Abu Toha and designer Ramon Pez in order to raise money for Doctors Without Borders (MSF) and their ongoing efforts in the Gaza war. He speaks at institutions, festivals, and organizations worldwide, offering personal insights and lessons from the frontlines of human experience. You can see his work at www.instagram.com/michaelchristopherbrown or www.michaelchristopherbrown.com.

ART/ILLUSTRATION:

99 New Illustrators (Selected Award-Winning Work from Graphis 2024-25 New Talent Competitions)

PRODUCTS:

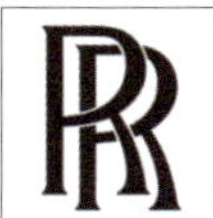

110 La Rose Noire Droptail by Rolls-Royce Motor Cars Limited / UK

In 1904, Charles Rolls and Henry Royce, two visionaries from vastly different backgrounds, forged an unlikely partnership with a shared ambition to make motoring extraordinary, which led to the creation of one of the world's most prestigious brands in 1906. Since 2003, Rolls-Royce Motor Cars Limited has operated as a wholly owned subsidiary of BMW AG. Iconic models like the Rolls-Royce Phantom and Ghost continue to carry the impressive legacy started all those years ago. The La Rose Noire Droptail is the first of four Droptail Coachbuilt commissions, inspired by the Black Baccara rose and offering a unique combination of roadster and coupe styles.

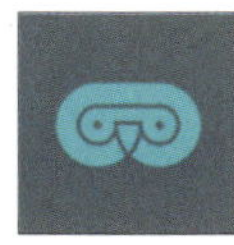

114 Owlet One by Owlet Bikes / USA

At Owlet Bikes, living in style means more than just looks. It's about embracing an inner vibe, caring for the planet, and changing how people move around cities by getting out of cars, connecting with nature, and bringing back forgotten values for more fulfilling lives. Drawing inspiration from aerospace, UAV technology, art, fashion, jewelry, and energy sectors, the company has crafted utterly stylish designer e-bikes that are not just vehicles but pieces of art, exemplifying a perfect blend of form and function.

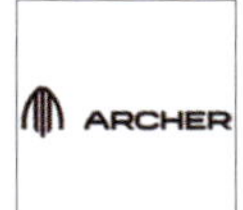

116 Midnight by Archer Aviation / USA

Archer Aviation was founded in 2018 by Adam Goldstein and Brett Adcock and is a publicly traded company designing and developing electric vertical takeoff and landing aircraft (eVTOL) for use in urban air mobility networks. Archer's mission is to unlock the skies, freeing everyone to reimagine how they move and spend time by providing rapid and affordable travel in and around cities, helping to alleviate traffic congestion and reduce carbon emissions. Archer has formed strategic partnerships with industry leaders such as Stellantis, United Airlines, and Southwest Airlines that are supporting its path to commercialization and operational readiness.

(Opposite page) Nothing To See, Untitled #2 2017. Photo by Tim Tadder.

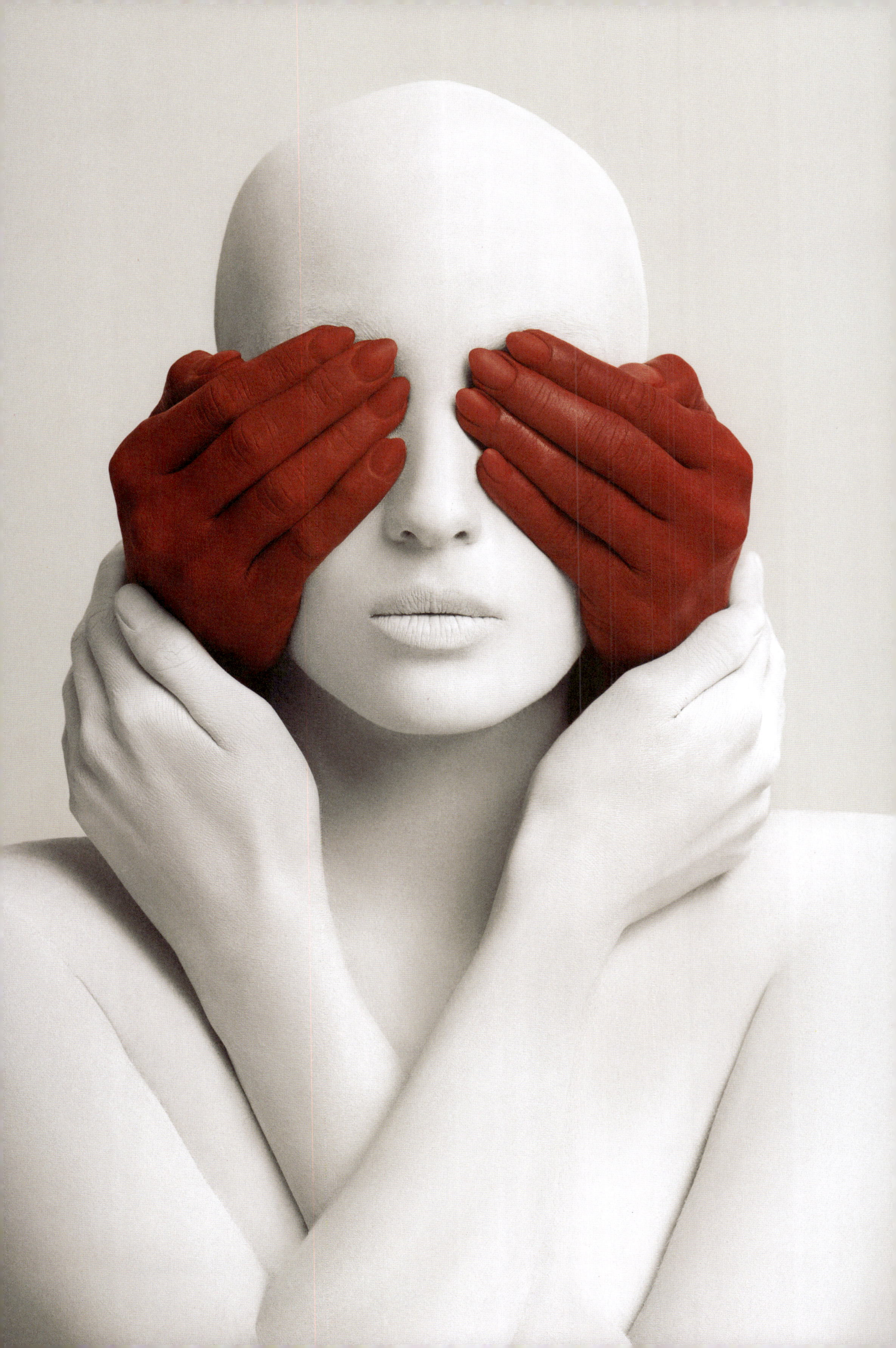

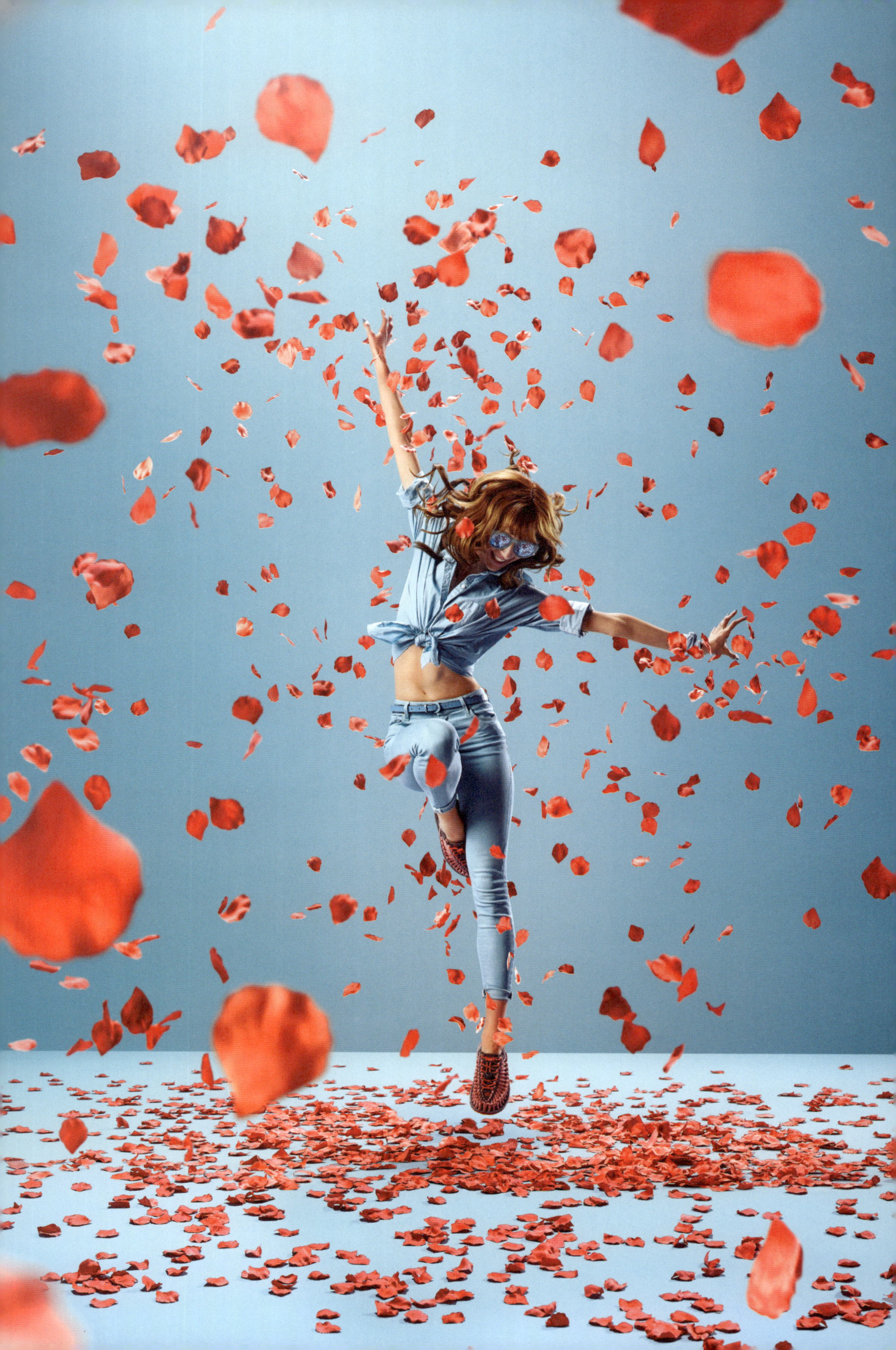

(Opposite page) KEEN Flowers. Photo by Tim Tadder.

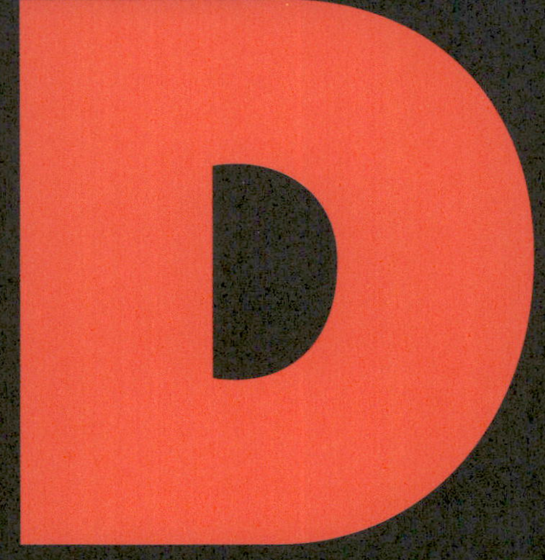

DESIGN

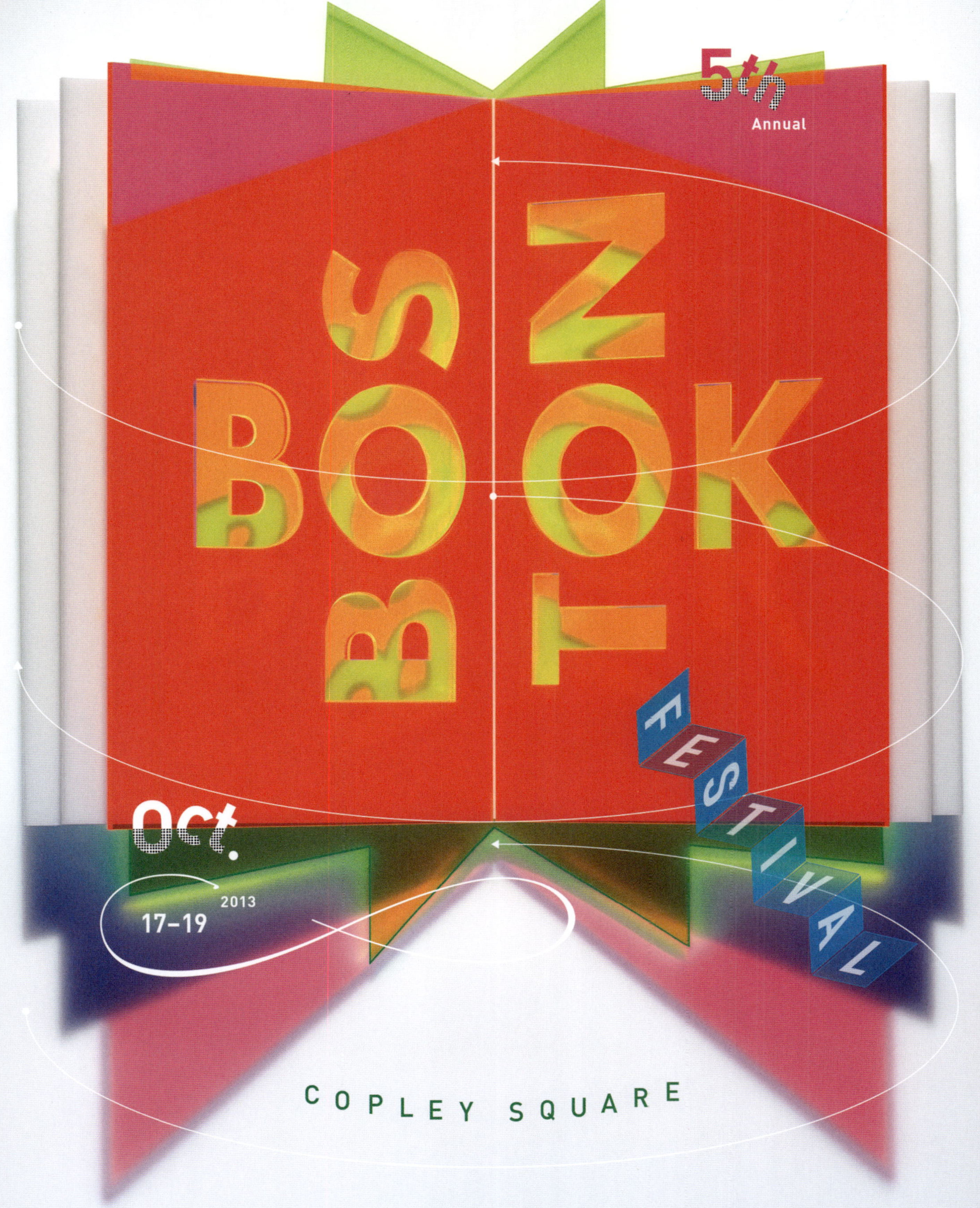
5th
Annual
BOSTON
BOOK
FESTIVAL
Oct.
2013
17–19
COPLEY SQUARE

Skolos-Wedell: The Scale of a Poster

NANCY AND TOM COMPOSE IMAGES LIKE MUSIC. THEIR WORK BALANCES PRECISION AND BREADTH, STRUCTURE AND LYRICISM, IN A WAY THAT FEELS ARCHITECTURAL AND ALIVE.

Anette Lenz, *Graphic Designer, Atelier Anette Lenz*

SKOLOS-WEDELL REDEFINED WHAT'S POSSIBLE AT THE INTERSECTION OF IMAGE AND TYPE. AS TEACHERS, NANCY AND TOM'S WARMTH, GUIDANCE, AND ENCOURAGEMENT HAVE SHAPED HOW I SEE DESIGN AND THE WORLD AROUND ME.

Shuixin Wang, *Former Student & Freelance Graphic Designer*

NANCY AND TOM EMBRACE THE CHALLENGE OF DESIGNING FOR DESIGNERS WITH INSIGHT AND BOLDNESS, TURNING THE PROCESS INTO A RICH LEARNING EXPERIENCE FOR EVERYONE INVOLVED.

Chris Pritchett, *Collegiate Associate Professor, School of Architecture at Virginia Tech*

NANCY AND TOM'S WORK IS AN IRIDESCENT AMALGAM OF PHOTOGRAPHY AND GRAPHICS. THEIR POSTERS HAVE THRILLED ME FOR DECADES. THEY ARE SHINING DIAMONDS OF POSTER HISTORY. THEY APPEAR LIGHTER THAN LIGHT.

Ralph Schraivogel, *Graphic Designer, Atelier Schraivogel*

NANCY TAUGHT US TO TRUST THE PROCESS, EXPLORE, AND HAVE FUN—LESSONS I STILL TRY TO CARRY INTO MY DESIGN WORK TODAY. HER ENCOURAGEMENT PUSHED US FURTHER —THANK YOU FOR LEAVING A MARK ON US.

Adèle Roncey, *Former Student & Graphic Designer, Saint-Lazare*

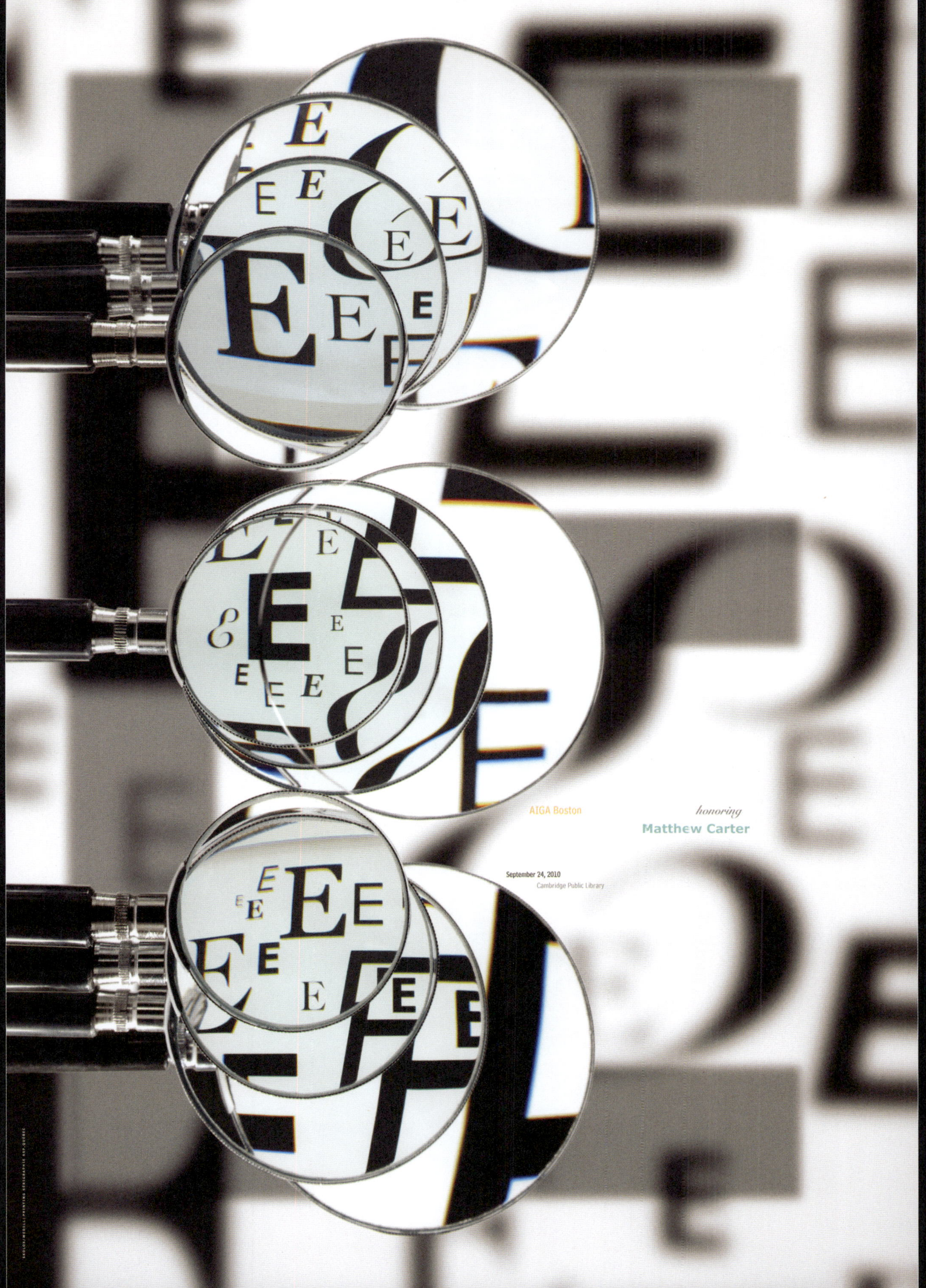

(Page 9) Boston Book Festival Poster, 2013, Fuji OnSet S-20 print, 50 1/2 × 35 1/2 in.
(Above) AIGA Boston, Honoring Matthew Carter Poster, 2010, Fuji OnSet S-20 print, 50 1/2 × 35 1/2 in.

Introduction by Ramon Tejada *Graphic Design Dept. Head & Associate Professor, Rhode Island School of Design*

Nancy Skolos and Tom Wedell are consummate designers. They are deeply thoughtful and inquisitive and make work that is distinctly conceptual and beautifully crafted. Their work expresses the high value they place on collaboration, their immense curiosity, and their rich love of process. Nancy and Tom are also exceptional teachers, mentors, and colleagues. We are indeed fortunate that they are members of the design community in the Graphic Design Department at the Rhode Island School of Design (RISD). Each plays a key role in the strength, vitality, and versatility of the department. Together, they enrich our community with their creative spirits—creating in collaboration with students and colleagues with joy, playfulness, and a deep love of the craft of design.

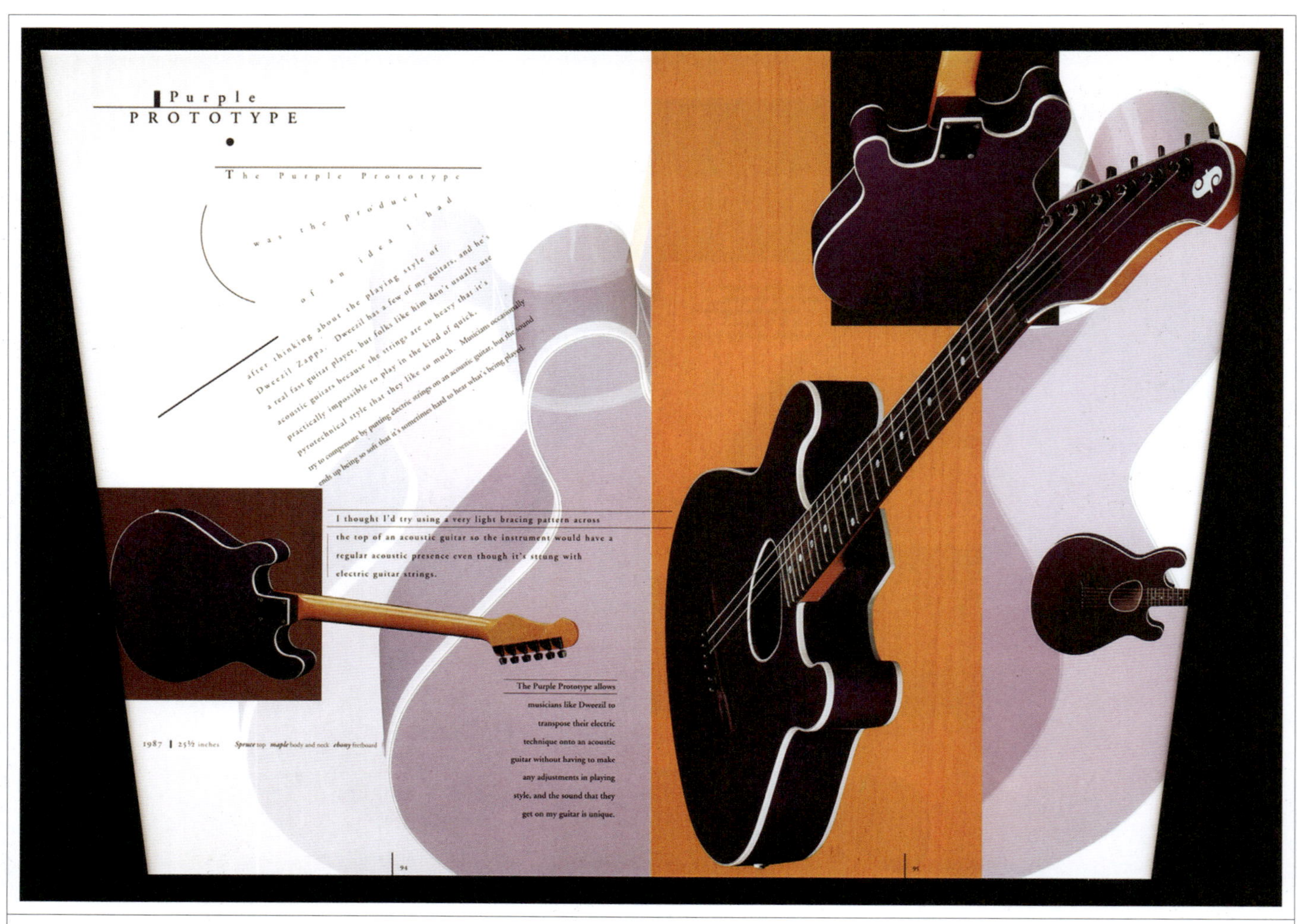

Ferrington Guitars, Callaway Editions, 1992, offset lithography, 13 1/2 × 10 in.

WHETHER IT'S A POSTAGE STAMP, A POSTER, OR A BRANDING CAMPAIGN, DESIGN SPARKS IDEAS, EVOKES EMOTIONS, AND PLAYS A PIVOTAL ROLE IN SHAPING CONTEMPORARY CULTURE.

Nancy Skolos, *Professor & Designer, Skolos-Wedell*

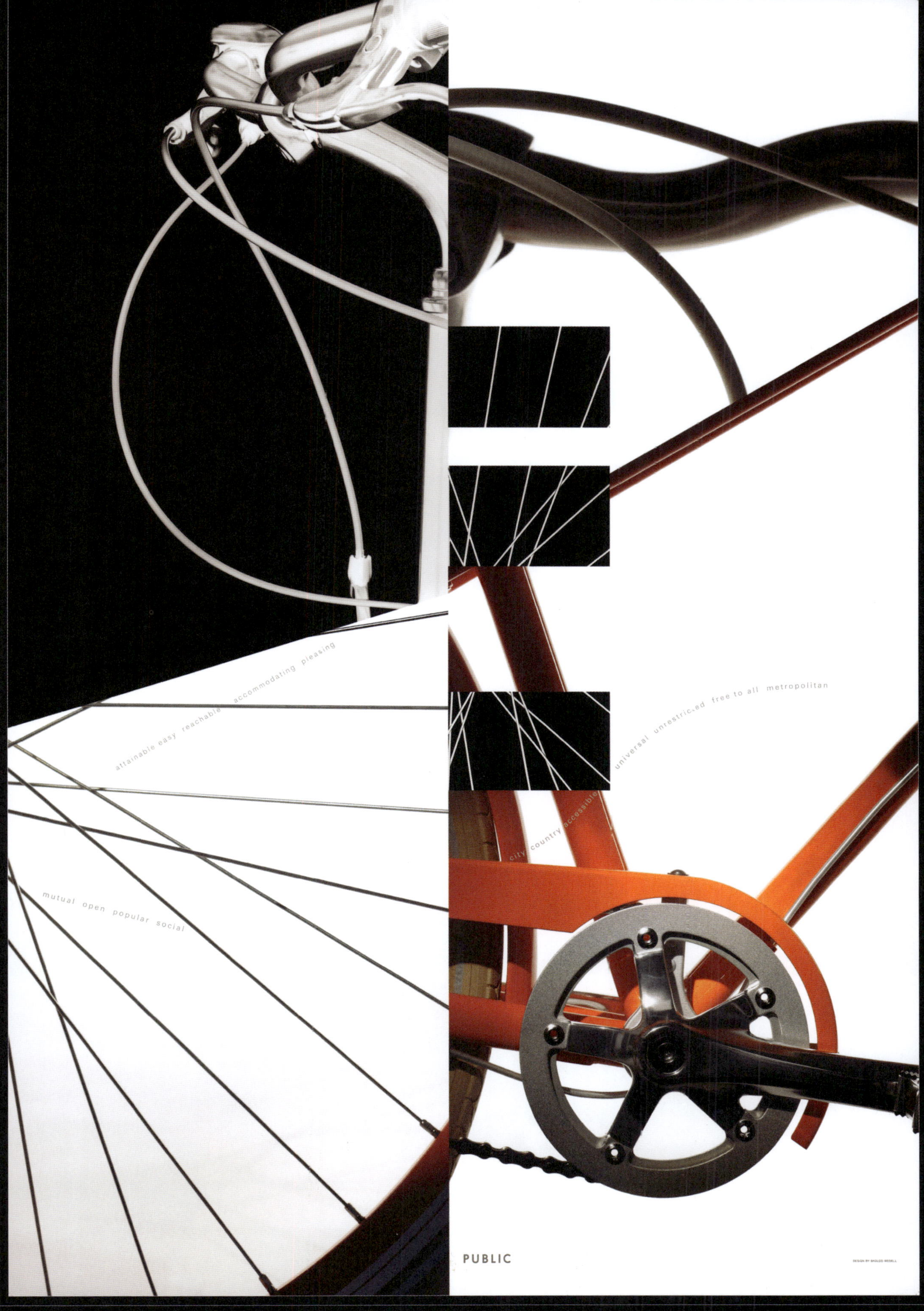

Public Bike Poster, Public Works Poster Series, commissioned by Public Bike, 2012, Fuji OnSet S-20 print, 50 1/2 × 35 1/2 in.

What motivated you two to have a career in design?

My father was an industrial designer, so I grew up surrounded by design—everything from designer objects and spaces to the tools and materials that create them. I don't think I ever had conventional crayons, but I was offered gouache, pastels, colored pencils, Magic Markers, and even an airbrush from my father's studio. Tom was always the artistic one in his family, spending his childhood drawing, painting, and crafting elaborate scale models with his brother. In high school, he became interested in architecture, but everything changed one day at a beach on Lake Michigan. He was painting the breakwater with his friend, who was photographing it, and at that moment, he realized the unique power of the camera to capture time in a way that painting could not.

Looking back, it seems as if both of our educations were carefully planned, but the truth is we both meandered through multiple institutions and majors. I began studying industrial design at the University of Cincinnati but eventually switched gears and earned my Bachelor of Fine Arts in interdisciplinary design from Cranbrook. I then pursued a Master of Fine Arts in graphic design at Yale. Tom's path was even more winding: He started in photography at the Layton School of Art, then moved to the University of Michigan to study fine art before completing his MFA in photography at Cranbrook. He stayed at Cranbrook for another year to focus on graphic design.

We met on my first day at Cranbrook. I had just parked my car and was walking toward the dorms with my suitcases, feeling rushed and frazzled after scrambling to pack because I'd mixed up the school start date. That's when Tom approached me and, with a grin, said, "Cheer up; it will get worse."

Who is or was your greatest mentor?

In our first years of art school, we both had highly technical, craft-driven training, each mentored by groups of faculty—Tom in photography at Layton and me in industrial design at the University of Cincinnati—who instilled in us a dedication to perfection. While this didn't directly inform our creativity, it laid a foundation for understanding the critical role precision plays in execution.

Our time at Cranbrook was by far the most formative period in our design careers. Under the guidance of Katherine and Michael McCoy, co-chairs of the design program, and Carl Toth, chair of photography, we were immersed in an experimental environment that encouraged interdisciplinary thinking. The McCoys' interdisciplinary approach taught us the value of integrating diverse media—photography, typography, and three-dimensional forms—into cohesive and complex designs.

Carl's influence was particularly crucial in helping Tom develop the ability to design photographs, where the interplay of form and light went beyond aesthetic considerations to become a means of communicating through symbols. Carl fostered an expressive, idea-driven process that deeply resonated with Tom and later shaped our collaborative work, where we layered images with typography to invite deeper meaning and storytelling.

What is it about design that you are most passionate about?

Our passion lies in exploring the intersection of art and design. While we've always pushed design toward the conceptual realm of fine art, we chose design because of its ability to bring art into everyday life. In a way, it subversively reaches millions, engaging people in shared visual experiences. Whether it's a postage stamp, a poster, or a branding campaign, design sparks ideas, evokes emotions, and plays a pivotal role in shaping contemporary culture.

What are some of your greatest past influences?

Our greatest influences have evolved over time, particularly as contemporary art and design education shifts away from a Eurocentric focus to embrace a broader range of global influences. But in the late 1970s, when we were art and design students, we were deeply immersed in Modernist principles. We were taught to see design through a Modernist lens that emphasized clean lines, form, and function—ideas that shaped our foundational thinking.

As we began working in Boston with emerging high-tech companies, we felt a connection to modern artists whose work, a century earlier, had been inspired by technological innovations of their time. The inner workings of computers and the geometric purity and dynamic movement of laser discs evoked ideas of the Futurist aesthetic. Electronics and circuitry, often explained through diagrams, had an elemental energy that reminded us of Constructivism. The complexity of new technologies, with their multilayered structures, echoed the simultaneity of Cubism and the paradoxical nature of Surrealism.

A key influence was the Russian Constructivist movement, which emphasized geometric forms, bold typography, and the fusion of art with industry and technology. We were inspired by El Lissitzky and Alexander Rodchenko, whose dynamic compositions pushed design into new realms. As our work grew more layered, we were drawn to Cubism, particularly its deconstruction of objects into geometric fragments. This led us to explore nonlinear perspectives and simultaneity, capturing multiple viewpoints and moments in time through techniques like multiple photographic exposures. Our use of collage as a generative technique was also deeply influenced by the Cubists, including Pablo Picasso and Georges Braque, and the Dadaists, like Hannah Höch. For us, collage became a way to create meaning by juxtaposing disparate visual elements, whose proximity formed a new visual grammar that we could further manipulate by substituting intentional elements.

The work of photographers and filmmakers like Man Ray and Sergei Eisenstein expanded our imagination about photography and its malleability. Man Ray's experimental techniques and Eisenstein's theories of montage helped us evolve the potential for photography and graphic elements to come together to create layered, cinematic narratives—stories that unfold not just through linear progression but through the interplay of images, symbols, and time.

You are primarily known for your poster design. What draws you to that type of design?

The most distinctive characteristic of poster design is scale, which accommodates many of our interests. A good poster makes you feel as though you are walking through a threshold and stepping into an altered world. The scale of a poster gives it a loud voice, but more importantly, it allows meaning to play out over time, guiding the viewer through its vast space to reveal the relationships between type and image. We love how posters work on multiple levels. From afar, the large shapes, colors, and bold elements catch your eye. As you move closer, the message becomes more legible, and you begin to understand how the visual and textual details fit together. At the closest level, the finer details, often unnoticed from afar, reveal even more depth and nuance.

Type and image play a central role in this experience, and we're passionate about experimenting with how they interact. In our 2006 book *Type, Image, Message*, we explored distinct ways that text and visuals can relate:

- Separation: Type and image operate independently, each

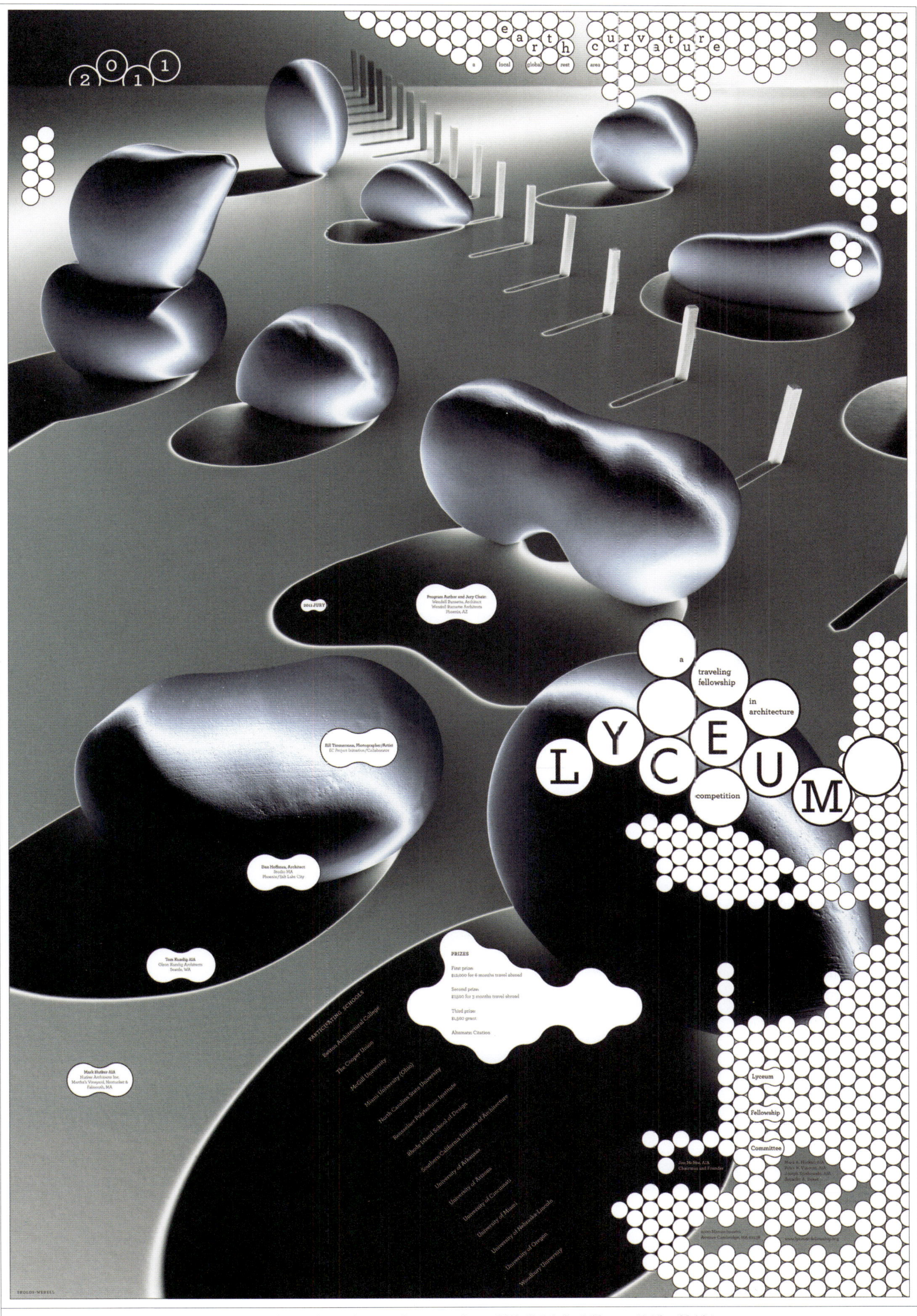

Lyceum Fellowship, Student Architecture Competition Poster, 2011, Fuji OnSet S-20 print, 50 1/2 × 35 1/2 in.

maintaining its autonomy within a defined space, often using frames or layers.

- Fusion: Type and image merge into a single entity, unified by optical effects, surface treatment, or perspective.

- Fragmentation: Type and image disrupt one another, creating a sense of tension or change.

We often incorporate many of these relationships in each poster to further enhance meaning.

Who among your contemporaries today do you most admire?

We are naturally drawn to designers whose sensibilities align with ours, those who share a Modernist influence and an emphasis on structure and composition, particularly in the way they integrate type and image. Two designers we admire greatly are Anette Lenz and Ralph Schraivogel, both of whom came to our attention in the mid-1990s. They had a significant impact on how we thought about the poster as a form, and their work continues to inspire us.

Anette's approach is systematic, with incredible attention to detail. She often works on large-scale design campaigns for theater and performance festivals, where every element—posters, programs, and environmental graphics—harmonizes, yet each piece can stand on its own. She also draws on the site-specific context of each festival, whether it's a rich natural setting or an iconic performance hall. Even when her posters are placed in more utilitarian spaces, like subway tunnels, she considers the relationships among them, often creating playful juxtapositions that invite discovery.

Ralph's work is more immersive and tactile. His posters engage the entire picture plane, blending type and image into a unified whole. He often uses silkscreen printing techniques, incorporating metallic inks and unusual paper to emphasize the printmaking process. His optical effects, created through materials like water and acetate, bring a magical, almost physical quality to his designs. Even as digital tools have evolved, Ralph has maintained his unique vision, continuously pushing the boundaries of visual form in fascinating ways.

Both Anette and Ralph have invigorated our understanding of the poster as a medium, and both continue to shape how we approach design today.

Who have been some of your favorite people or clients you have worked with?

One of our longest and most cherished clients has been the Lyceum Fellowship, founded by architect Jon McKee in 1985. It grew out of Jon's own experiences as an architecture student, where his travels profoundly impacted his education. He created the program to offer undergraduate students a competition with travel prizes, providing them the chance to broaden their horizons. We've had the privilege of designing the annual call for entries for the Fellowship for 38 years. Each year, a renowned architect writes a unique program for the students, reflecting their own area of expertise. As architecture has always been one of our biggest influences, this collaboration is a true highlight for us. Our role is to design a poster that sparks interest in the program without giving away any hints or solutions, keeping the creative challenge fresh every year.

When we first began working with Jon, he likened the process to diving off a high dive, unsure if there was water below. Over time, however, trust was built, and that trust has allowed us to push ourselves creatively, producing some of our best work year after year.

In addition to the Lyceum Fellowship, we've also had the pleasure of working with various art-related clients and institutions such as design organizations, schools, museums, printers, and art and entertainment companies like EMI Music. These projects have always been rewarding because of the shared passion for creativity.

On top of being designers, you two also work at the Rhode Island School of Design. How does your employment there influence your work?

Teaching at the Rhode Island School of Design has profoundly influenced our design work, especially through the faculty we've had the privilege of working with. Their expertise spans a wide range of disciplines—communication theory, history, typography, information design, type design, color theory, systems design, and more—and their diverse interests complement each other in ways that constantly challenge and inspire us.

The students have also been a huge source of creativity. They're incredibly talented and full of passion, and their enthusiasm always reignites our own. Whenever our interest in design starts to wane, we're reminded of the excitement of the field by the spark in their eyes. As Tom puts it, teaching has helped him think in new, flexible ways: "When you teach, you have to stay intellectually agile. You're constantly thinking about how what you say will affect students, how they might interpret it, and what they'll do with it. You need to come up with multiple solutions for every question a student might suggest. That process trains your mind to be more flexible, and I believe it makes us better designers. It certainly helps our creative process."

What is the greatest satisfaction you get from your work?

The greatest satisfaction we get from our work comes from the dynamic back-and-forth of the creative process. We love how the work evolves, starting with early collages and sketches, progressing to small paper models, and finally translating everything into a finished image. The real magic happens when we bring these three-dimensional forms into photography, where lighting plays a crucial role in amplifying structure and texture. At that point, the challenge is to preserve the model's structural integrity while still leaving space for typography and graphic elements to complete the composition. The most rewarding part is achieving a balance between image and text that communicates a holistic and compelling message.

What advice would you give to students starting out today?

I always think of the advice my mother, Marge, instilled in me: "Think for yourself." Over the 50 years since I went to design school, I've seen countless trends come and go. It can be tempting to feel the pressure to align with each one, but over time, you learn that some trends resonate with you and some don't. What's most important is maintaining your own convictions and staying true to your vision, even when it's not the most popular or in sync with the latest movement.

I know that may sound counterintuitive, especially as a student, because you're in school to learn from others. But part of that learning process is discovering and trusting your own instincts. It takes trial and error, and there will be some moments of uncertainty, but with each project, it becomes easier to trust your own path.

Skolos-Wedell www.skolos-wedell.com

See their Graphis Master Portfolio at graphis.com.

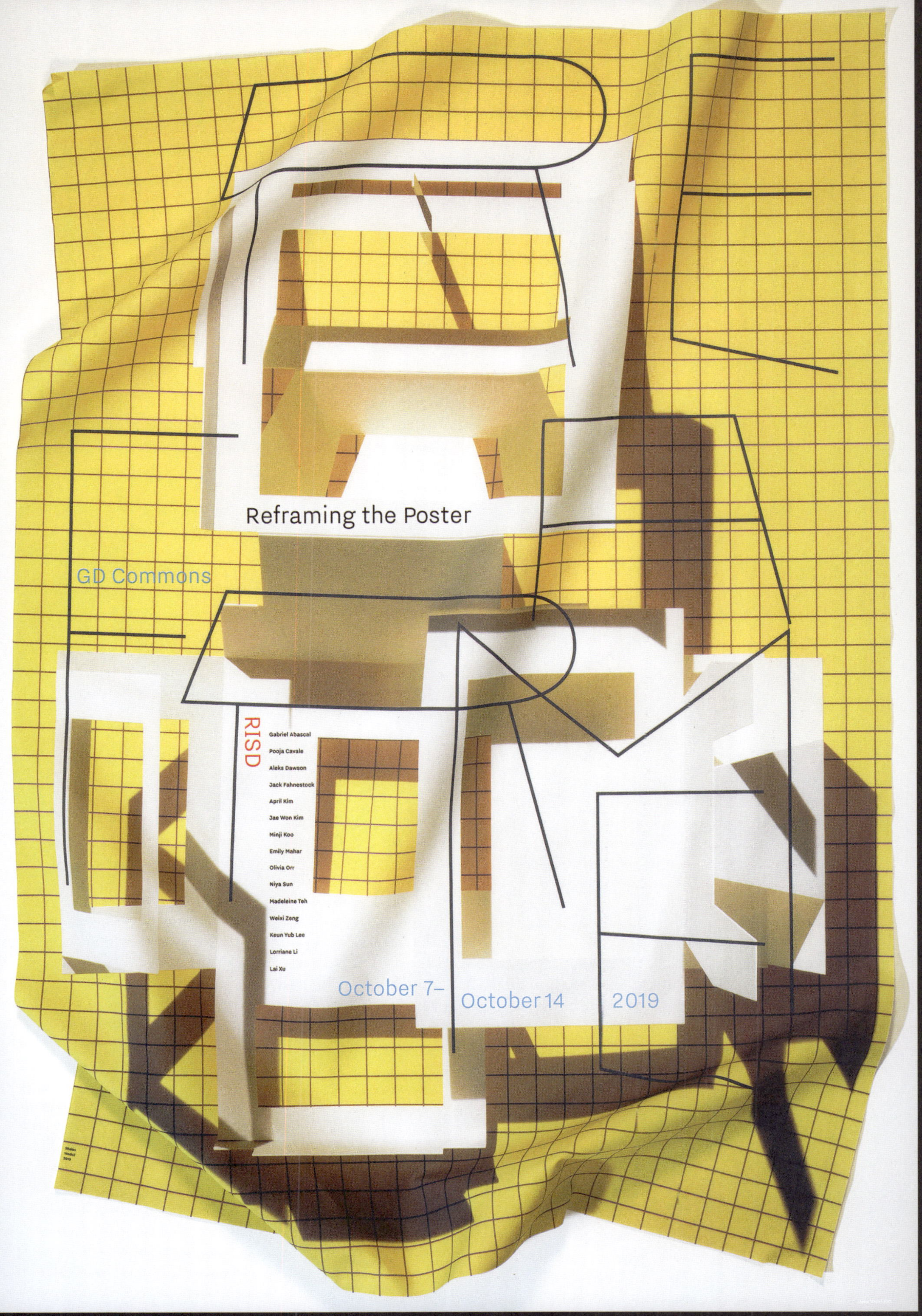

Reframing the Poster Exhibition Poster, Rhode Island School of Design, 2019, Fuji OnSet S-20 print, 50 1/2 × 35 1/2 in.

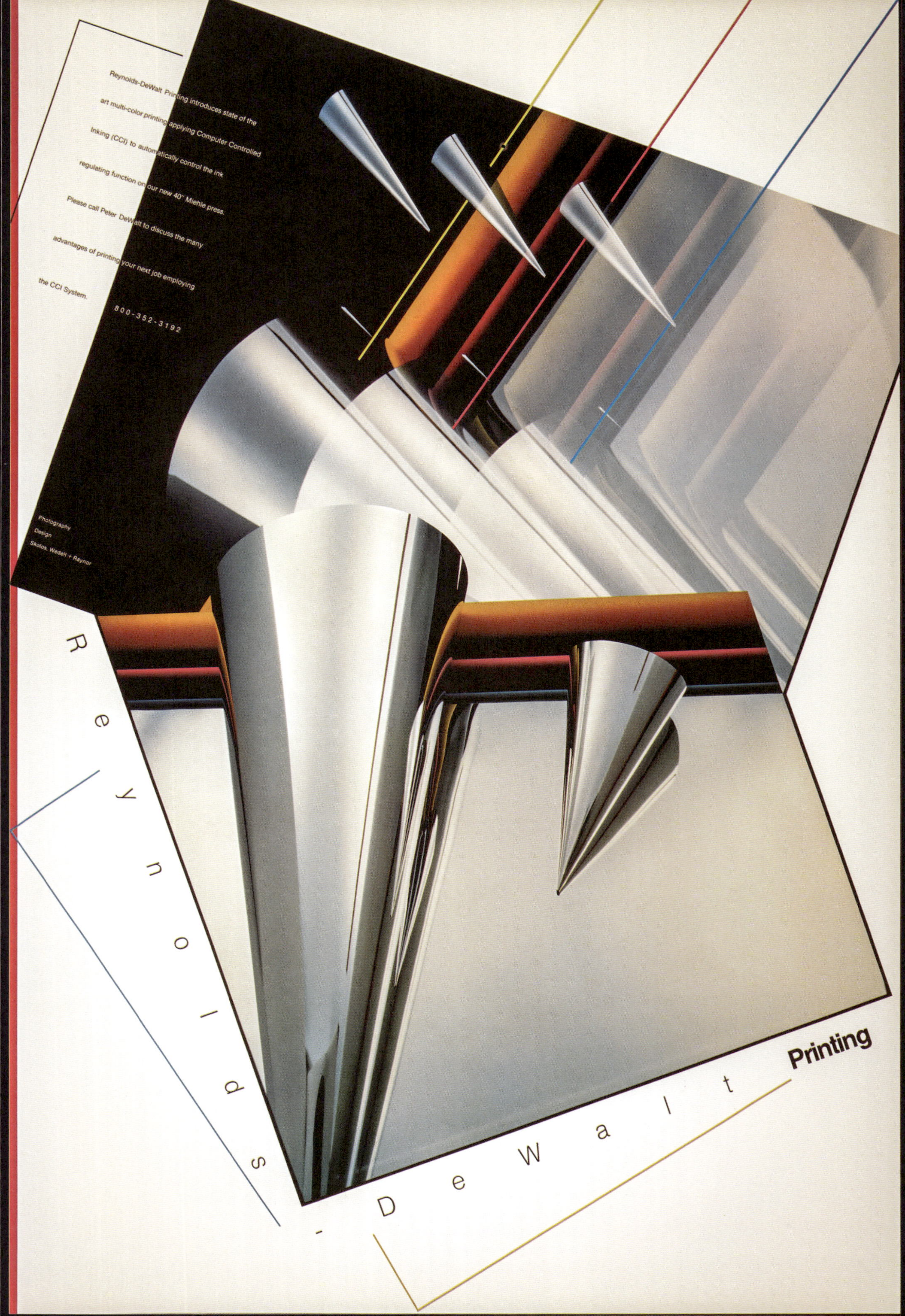
Reynolds-DeWalt Printing introduces state of the
art multi-color printing applying Computer Controlled
Inking (CCI) to automatically control the ink
regulating function on our new 40" Miehle press.
Please call Peter DeWalt to discuss the many
advantages of printing your next job employing
the CCI System.
800-352-3192
Photography
Design
Skolos, Wedell + Raynor
Reynolds-DeWalt
Printing

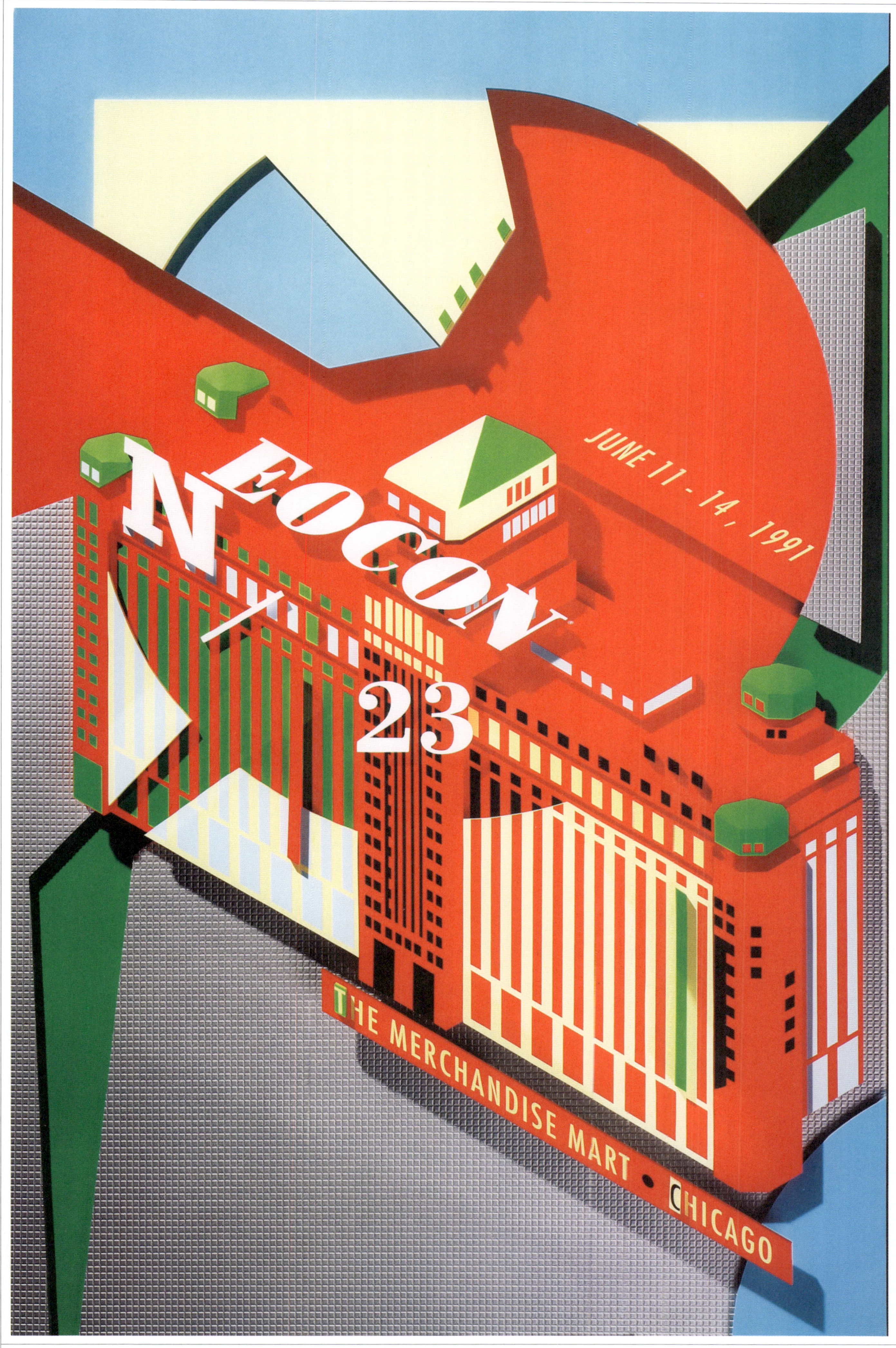

NeoCon 23 Poster, 1991, offset lithograph, 36 × 24 in.

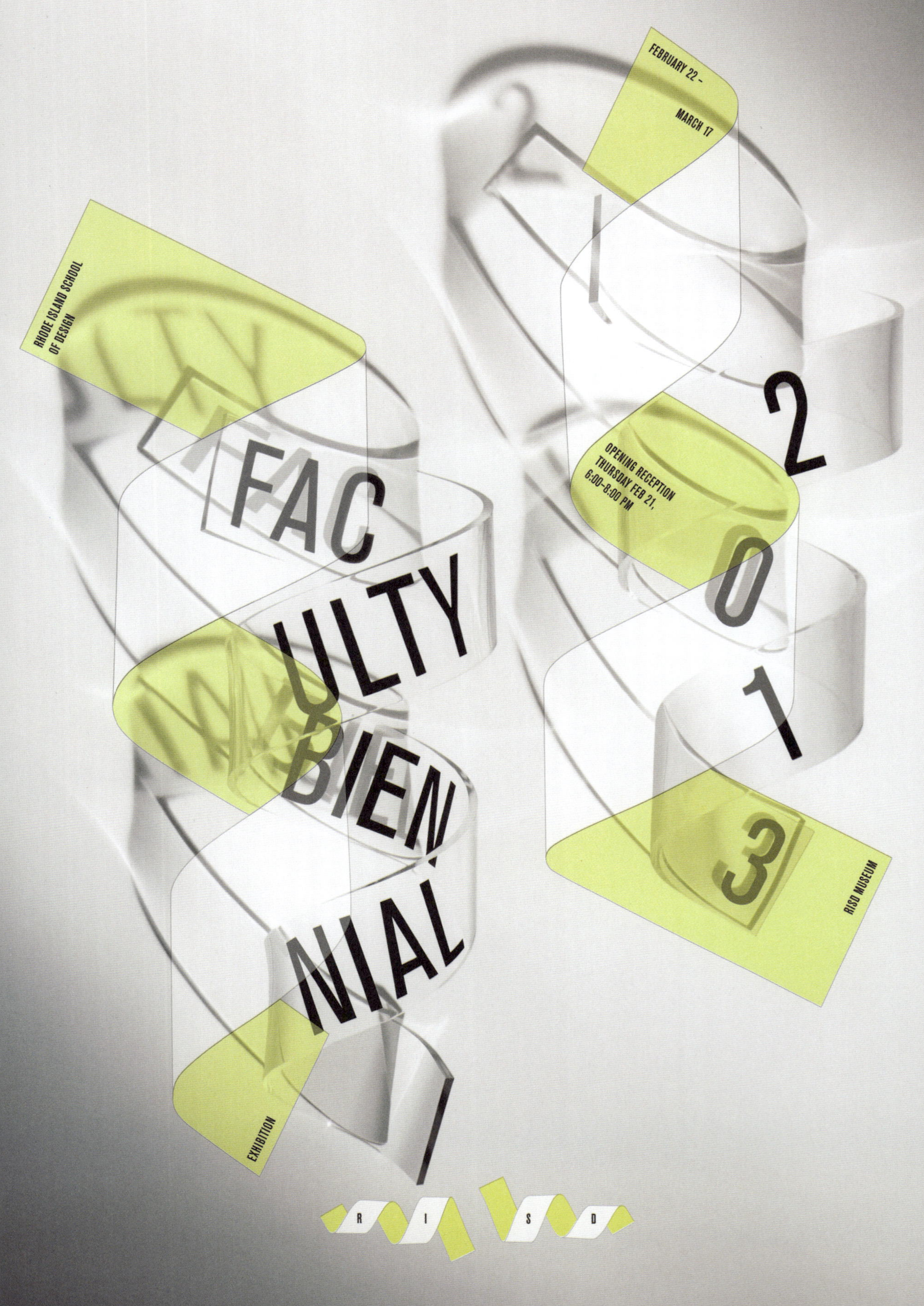

Faculty Biennial Exhibition Poster, Rhode Island School of Design, 2013, Fuji OnSet S-20 print, 50 1/2 × 35 1/2 in.

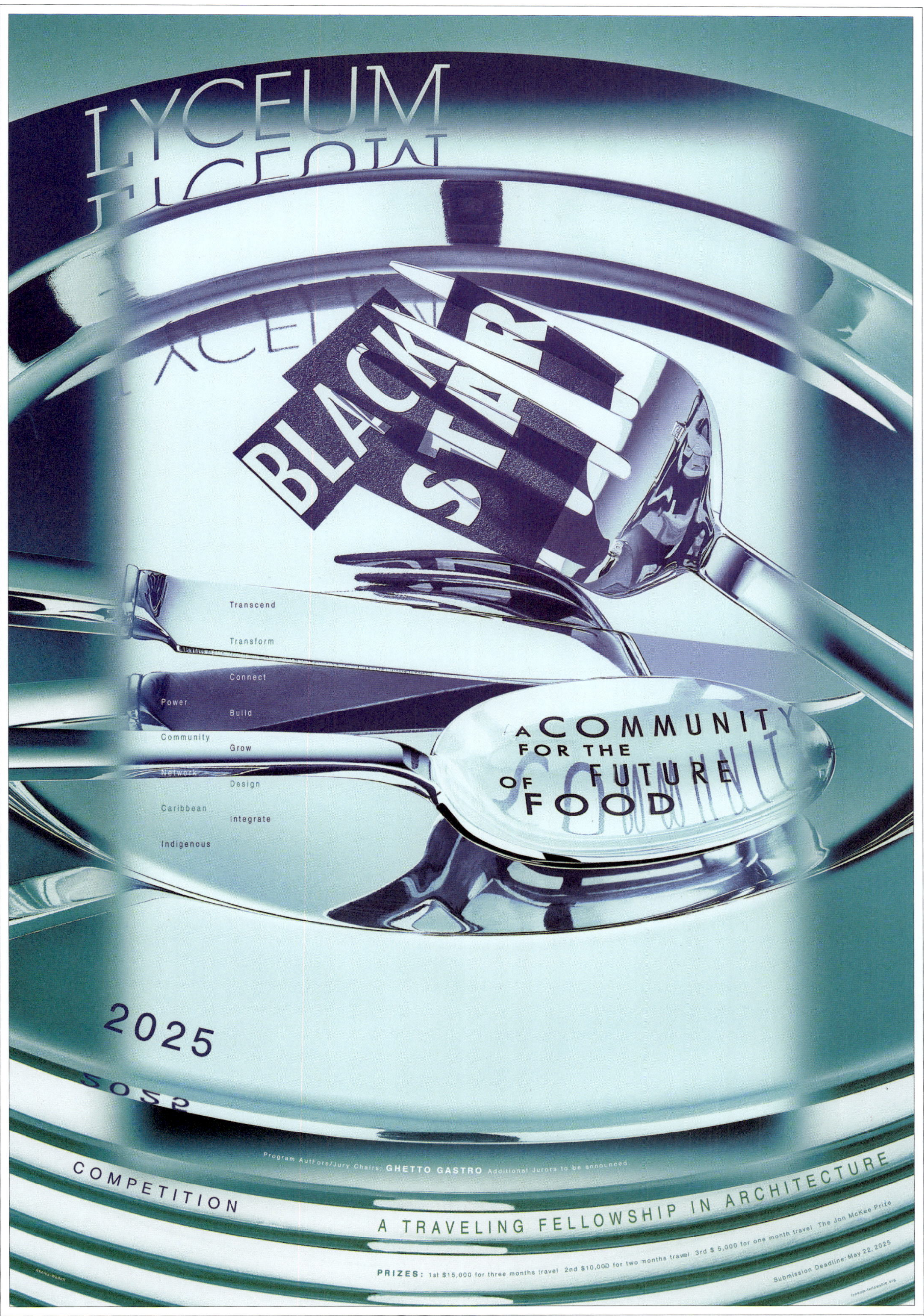

Lyceum Fellowship, Student Architecture Competition Poster, 2025, Fuji OnSet S-20 print, 50 1/2 × 35 1/2 in.

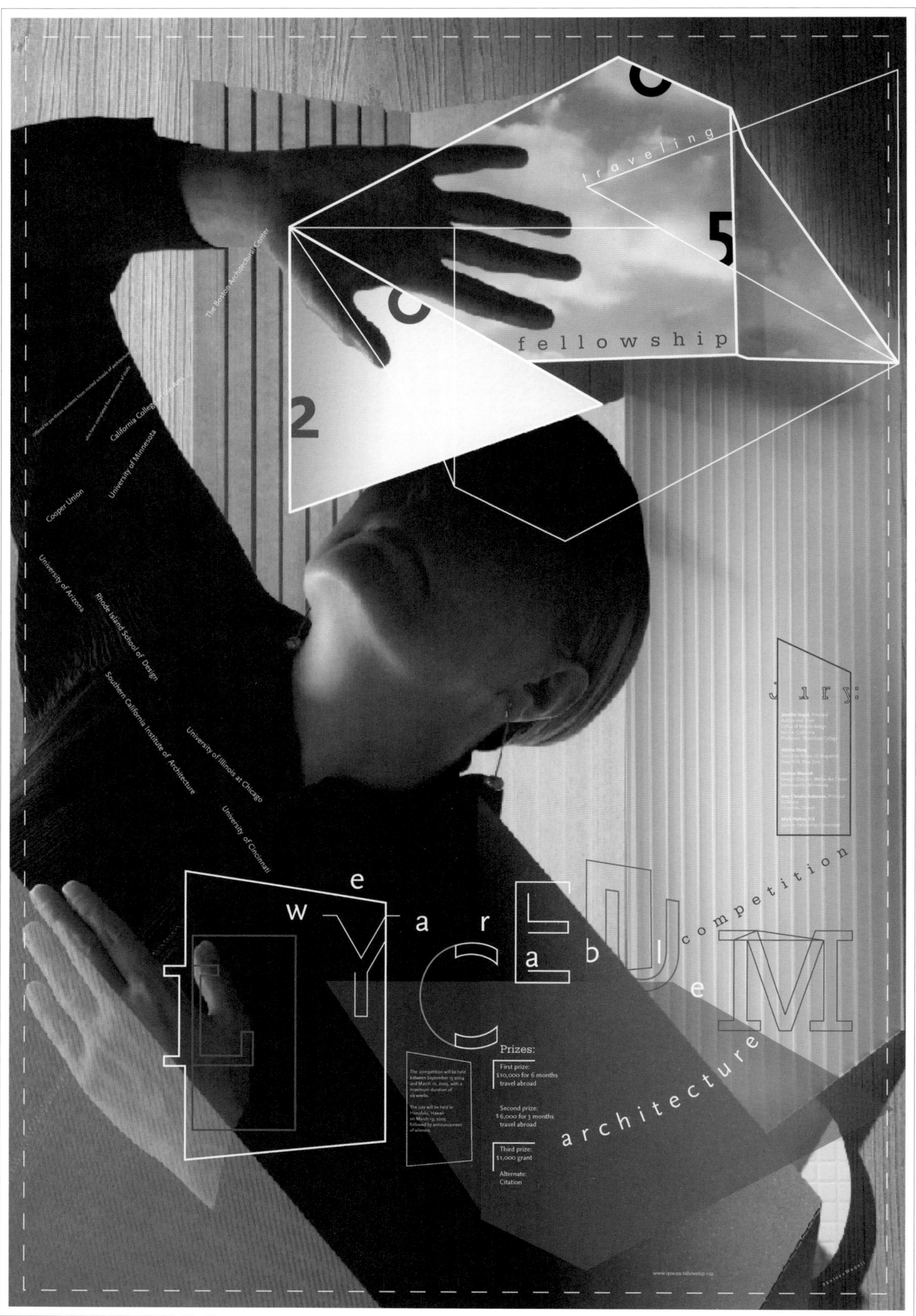

Lyceum Fellowship, Student Architecture Competition Poster, 2005, silkscreen, 50 1/2 × 35 1/2 in.

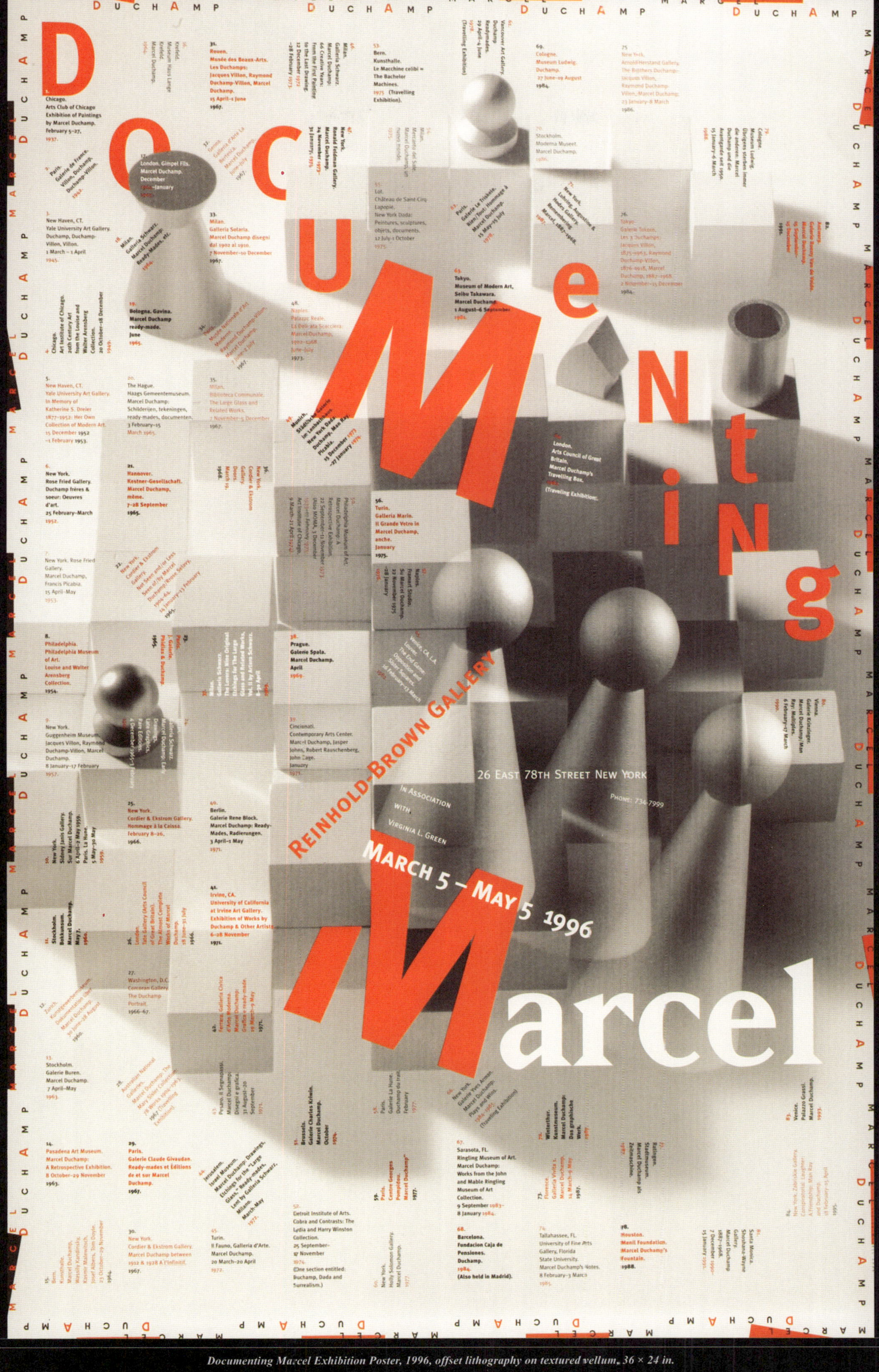

Documenting Marcel Exhibition Poster, 1996, offset lithography on textured vellum, 36 × 24 in.

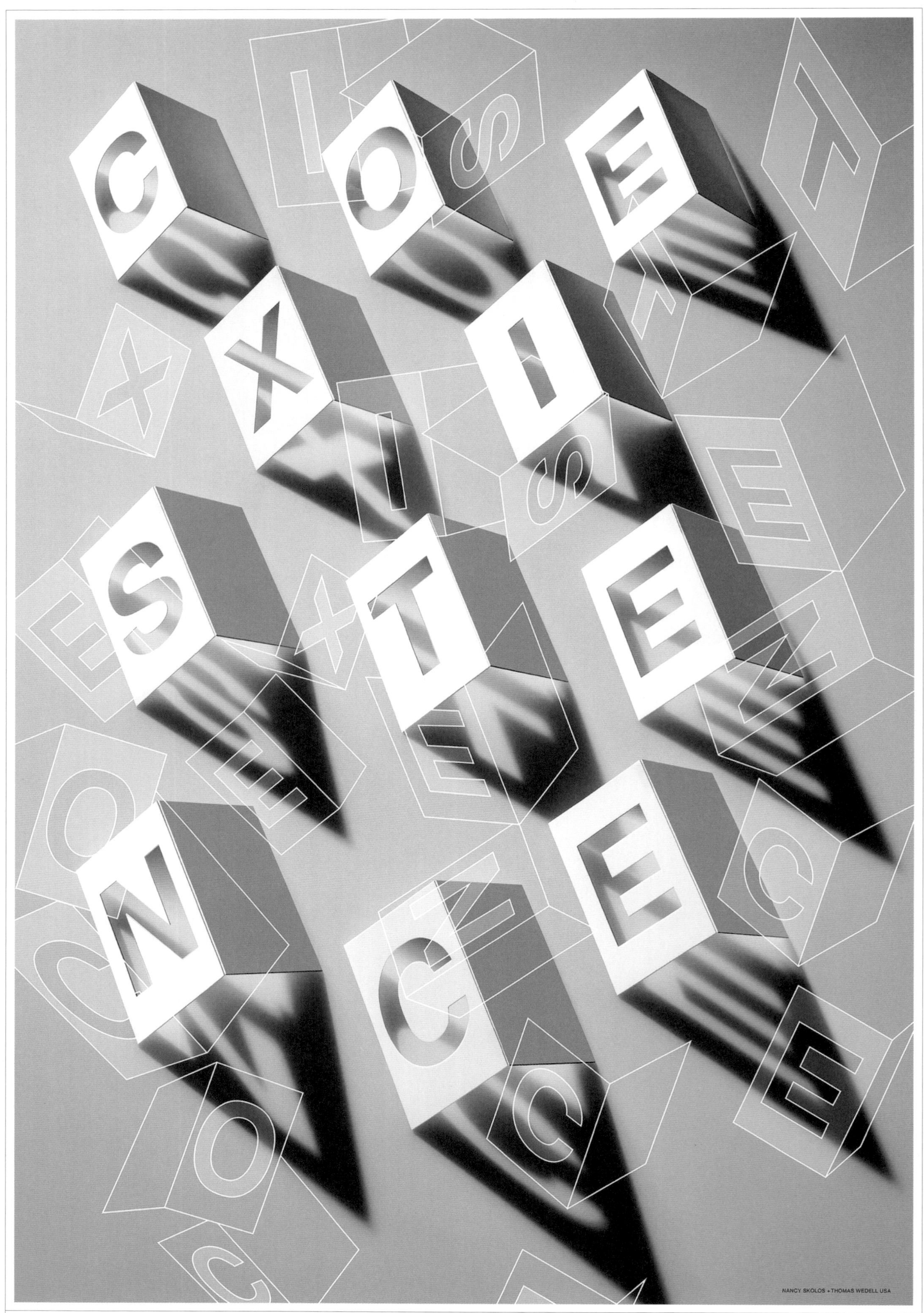

Coexistence Poster, Special Project for the Alliance Graphique Internationale (AGI) Conference, 2015, Fuji OnSet S-20 print, 50 1/2 × 35 1/2 in.

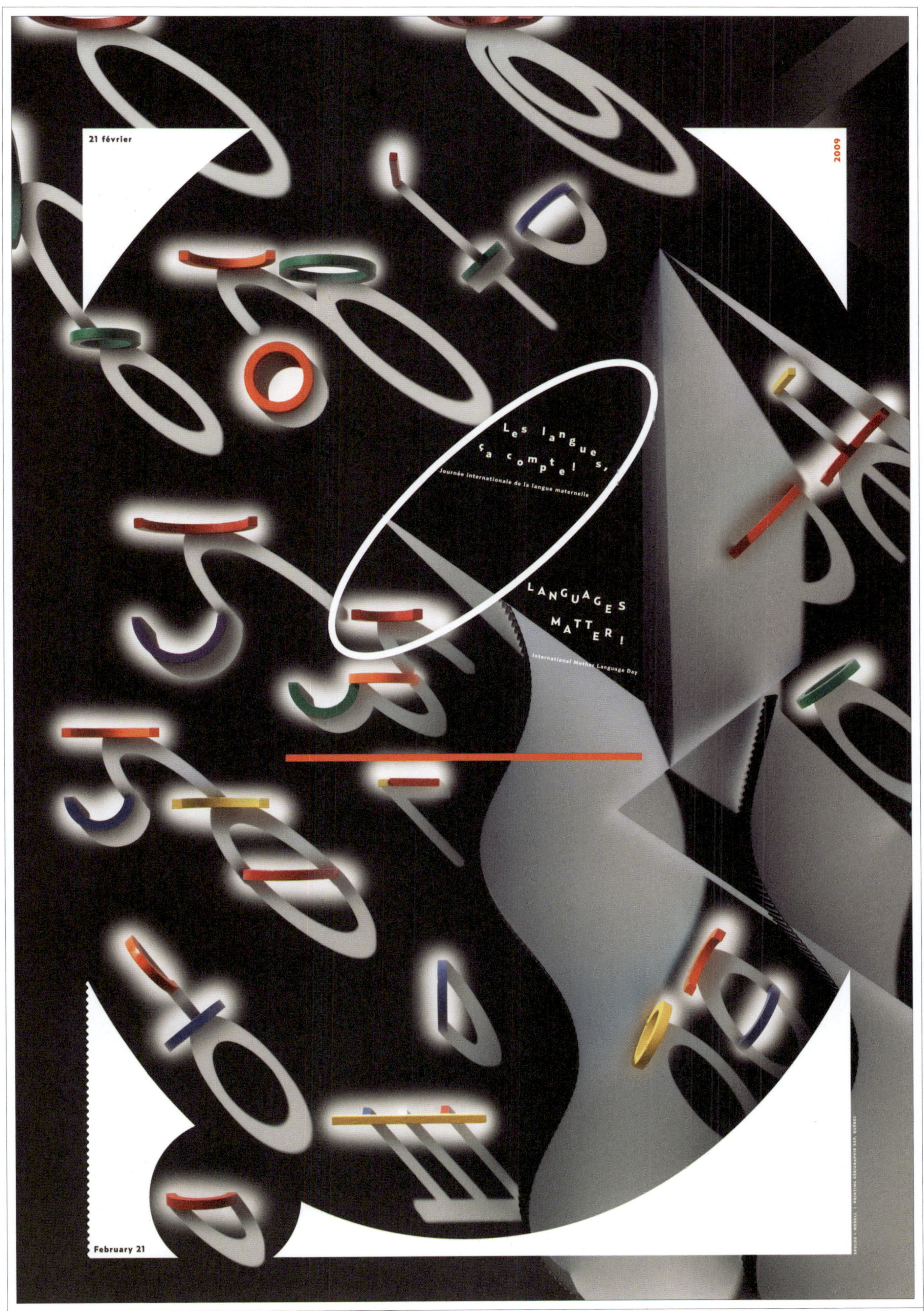

UNESCO, Languages Matter! Poster, celebrating International Mother Language Day, 2009, Fuji OnSet S-20 print, 50 1/2 × 35 1/2 in.

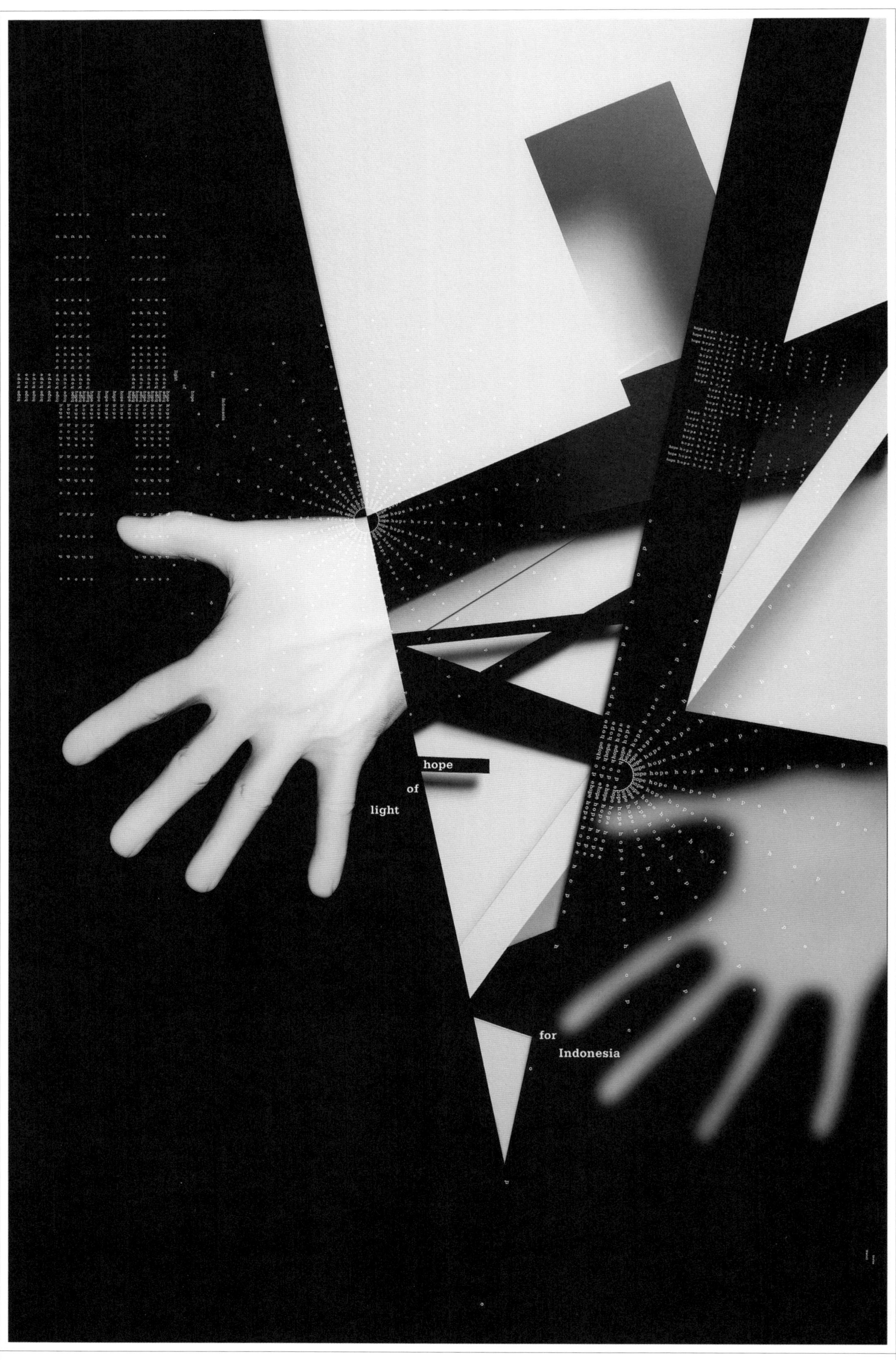

Light of Hope for Indonesia Poster, 2005, silkscreen, 50 1/2 × 35 1/2 in.

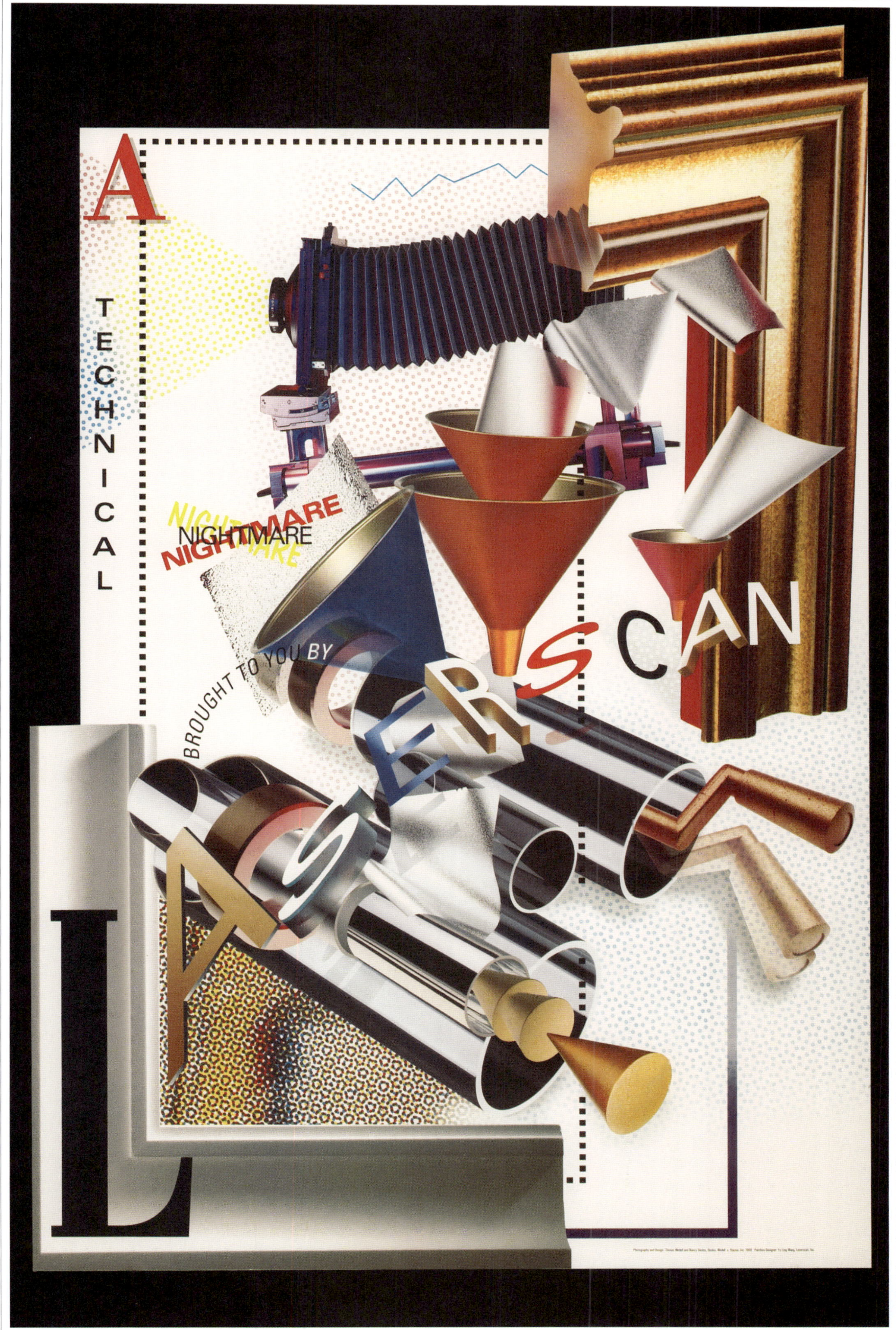

LaserScan Poster, 1989, offset lithograph with die cut, 36 × 21 1/2 in.

THEIR DAZZLING WORK ALWAYS LANDS WITH BOTH IMAGINATION AND PRECISION. IT COMMUNICATES EVEN BEFORE IT IS UNDERSTOOD. IT ALWAYS INVITES YOU IN. THESE DAYS, THAT'S A MIRACLE.

Brian Collins, *Co-founder, Creative Director, & Designer, COLLINS*

BEYOND THEIR CREATIVE GENIUS, TOBEN IS AN EXCEPTIONAL COLLABORATOR—THOUGHTFUL, RESPONSIVE, AND DEEPLY COMMITTED.

Tanya Babić, *Director, Versus*

WE APPROACHED TOBEN TO HELP WITH A COMPLETE BRAND REFRESH. TOBEN HAS EXPERTLY NAVIGATED A COMPLEX TERRAIN OF STAKEHOLDERS AND CREATED A CLEAR AND EXCITING NEW BRAND VISION AND EXPRESSION THAT RESONATES STRONGLY.

Rachel Maher, *Chief Operating Officer, McGrath Estate Agents*

TOBEN ELEVATED OUR BRAND AND SHARPENED OUR PRESENCE IN THE MARKET. THEY DELIVERED A VISUAL IDENTITY THAT FEELS CONFIDENT, DISTINCTIVE, AND COMPLETELY ALIGNED WITH WHO WE ARE AND WHERE WE'RE GOING.

Jessica Womersley, *Head of Marketing & Branding, Central Element*

TOBEN DELIVERED A POWERFUL, IMPACTFUL INTERPRETATION OF KOMPLYAI'S SAFER AI BELIEFS, PROVING THAT AI CUTTING-EDGE COMPLIANCE DOESN'T NEED TO BE BORING.

Kristen Migliorini, *Founder & CEO, KomplyAi*

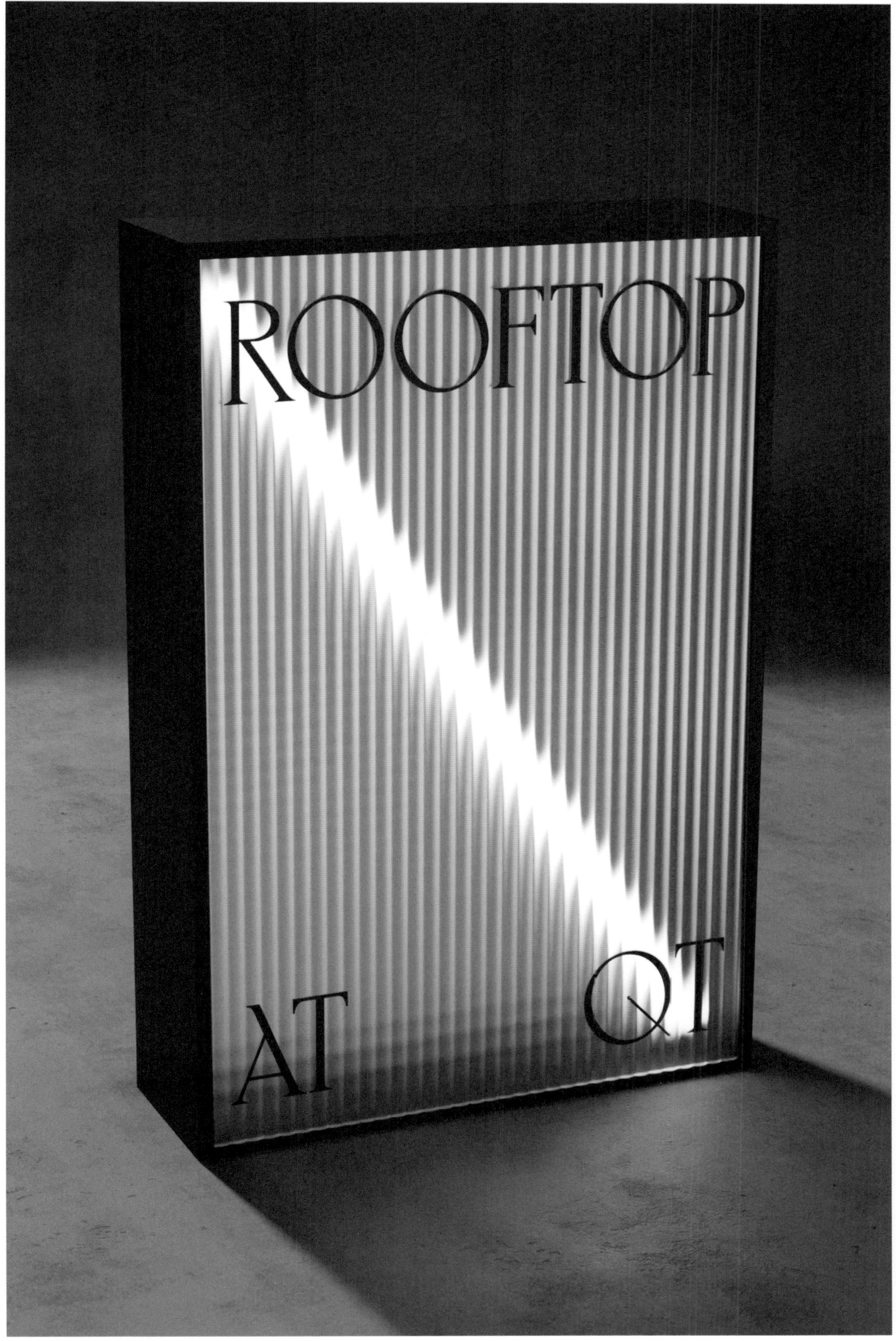

Rooftop at QT - Signage

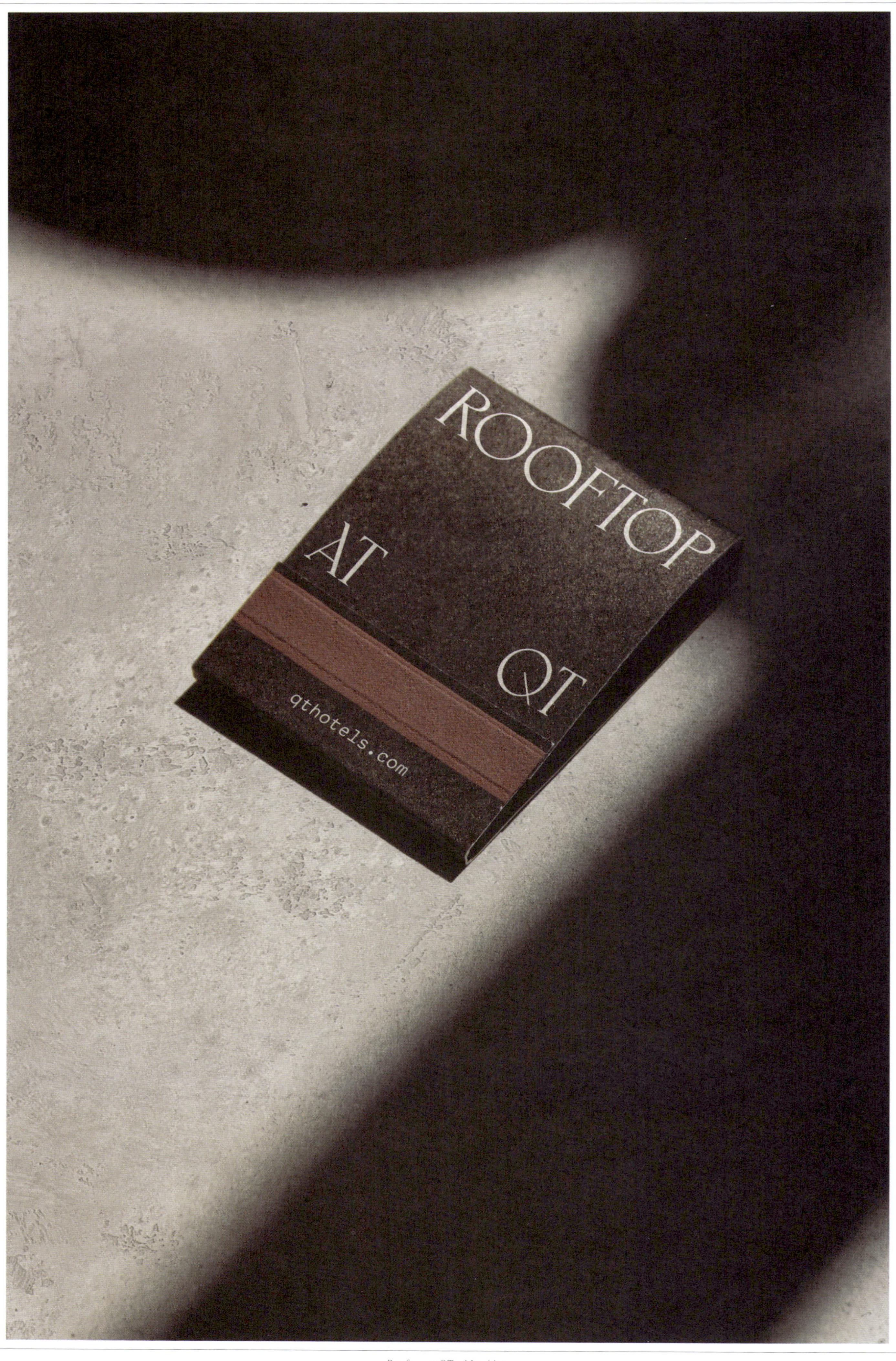

Rooftop at QT - Matchbox

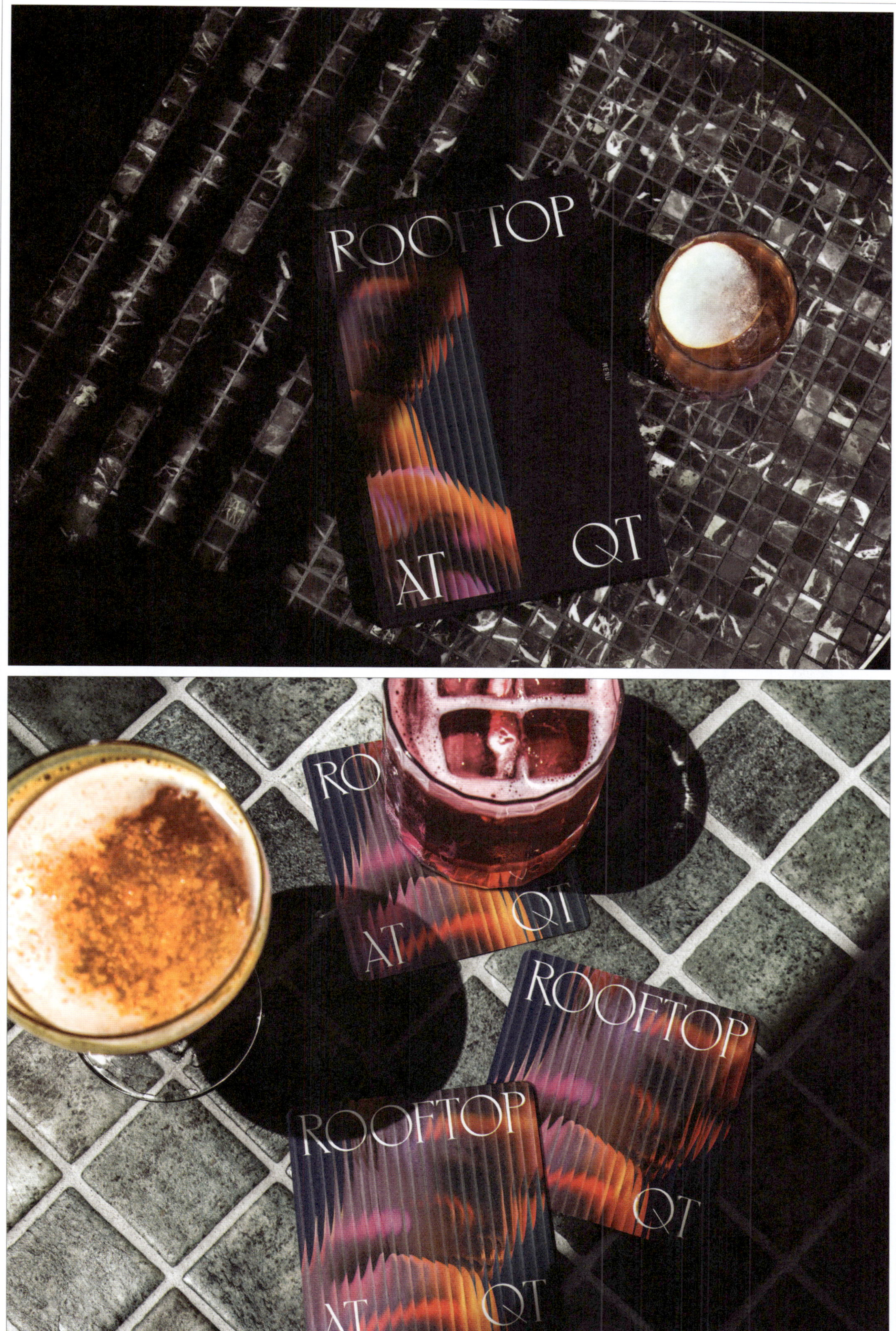

(Top) Rooftop at QT - Menu / (Bottom) Rooftop at QT - Coaster

Introduction by Nicholas Graham *Interior Designer & Founder, Nic Graham & Assoc.*

We have been working with our friends at Toben for many years. Their ability to comprehend our often complex and weird brief for environmental design-based graphics is always well received with a generous and collaborative approach. They always bring fresh new ideas and interpretations to our initial brief and provide options and flexibility, working collaboratively to achieve the end result. Edgy, fashion-forward, and thought-provoking, their graphics add a wonderful layer to our work and have become synonymous with our studio's practice in hotel design.

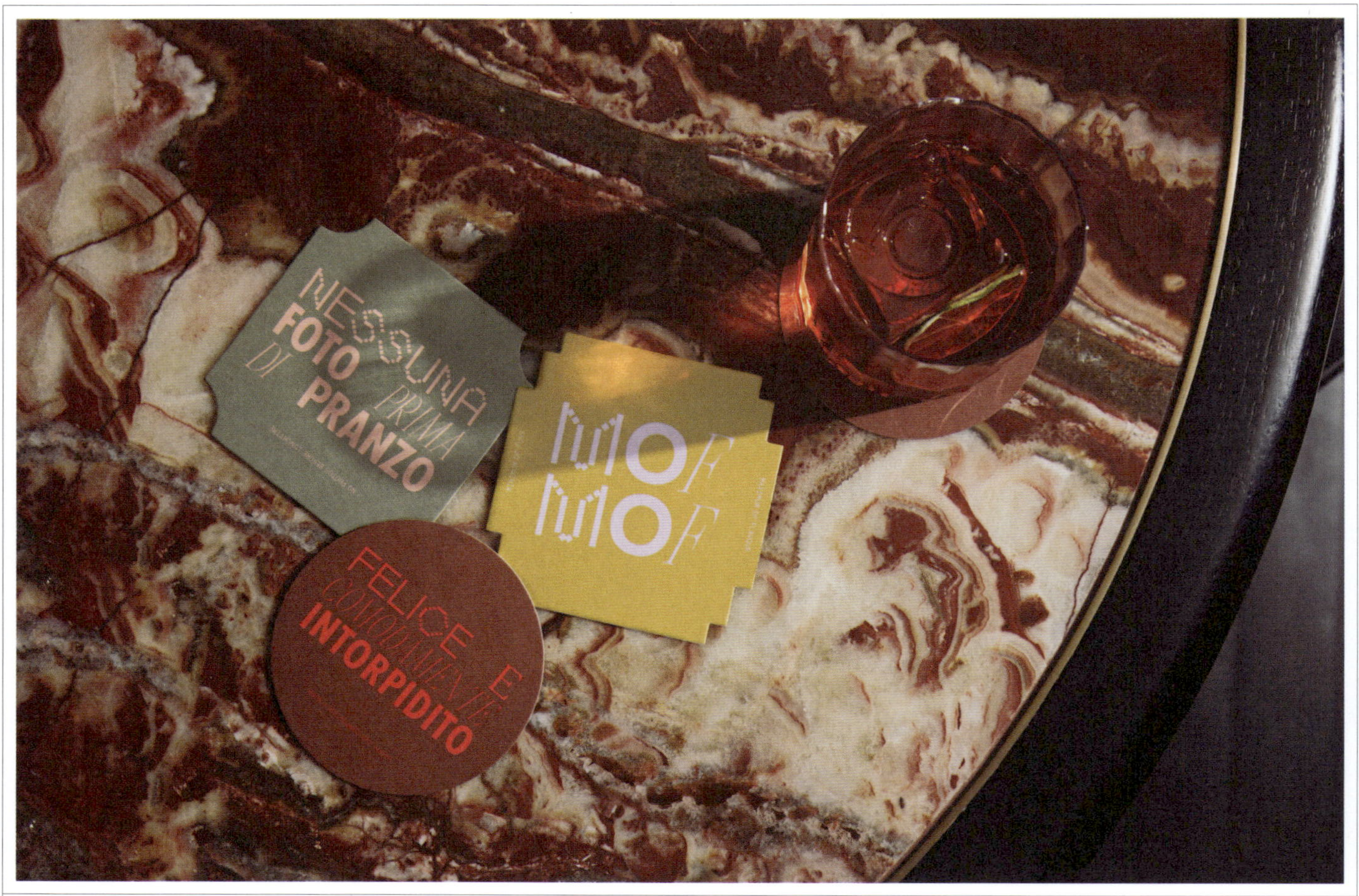

Gowings Bar and Grill - Coaster / (Opposite page) Gowings Bar and Grill - Bar Menu

I USED TO LIVE BY THE MANTRA, "WORK HARD." THESE DAYS, I'M FOCUSING MORE ON WORKING SMARTER.

Thorsten Kulp, *Chief Creative Director & Co-founder, Toben*

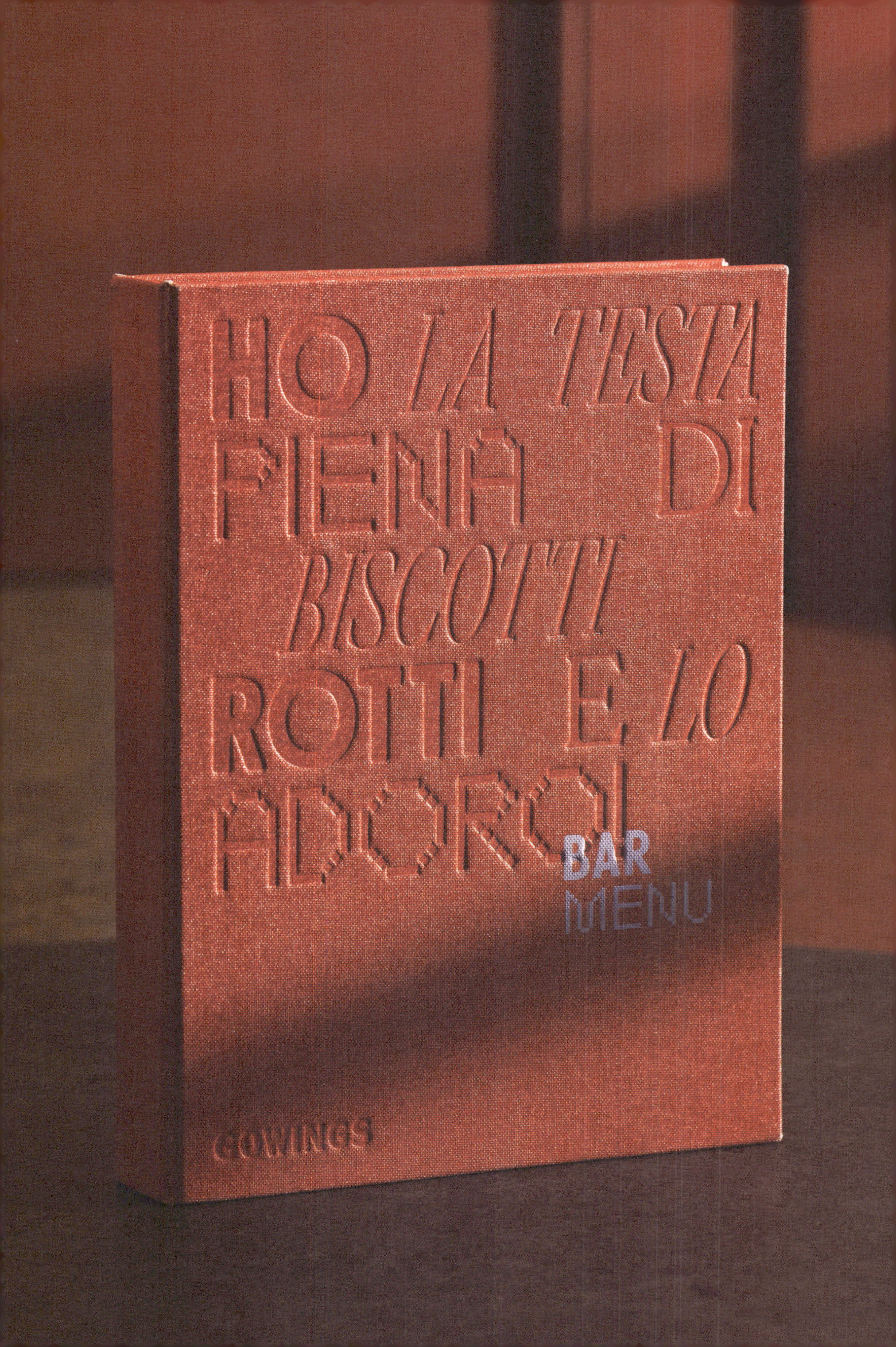

HO LA TESTA
PIENA DI
BISCOTTI
ROTTI E LO
ADORO!

BAR
MENU

GOWINGS

What inspired or motivated you to have a career in design?
Thorsten Kulp, Chief Creative Director & Co-founder: I sort of stumbled into design, inspired by metropolitan culture and the vague sense that I had some creative talent. Katja and I eventually moved from Germany to Australia for our studies. We fell in love with the place, met and worked with some very inspiring people, and ultimately started our own studio.
Katja Hartung, Director, Creative Director, & Co-founder: I've always been a bit of a hybrid thinker. I grew up in a family that was half artistic and half business-oriented. Initially, it was the applied arts that drew me in—a way to join a creative field that might pay the rent one day.

What is your work philosophy?
K.H.: I grew up with the belief that if you do something, you should do it well. That mindset still holds true for me, but I have found it can be draining if you don't define what "well" actually means. Over time, I've added a few new principles: enjoy the process, take care of myself, and adopt a growth mindset. A big part of that is working with people who are smarter than I am. It can be daunting, but it has led to incredible learning and fulfillment over the years.
T.K.: I used to live by the mantra, "Work hard." These days, I'm focusing more on working smarter.

Who is or was your greatest mentor?
T.K.: Personally, throughout our creative journey, including the pre-Toben years, we never really had creative mentors in the traditional sense. I always worked in small agencies that embraced a collaborative environment with as flat a hierarchy as possible. This meant that everyone I closely collaborated with had a significant influence on me.
K.H.: In my early years, I always looked for a mentor, as I admired many of my senior designers and colleagues, but I never actually reached out, which I now see as a missed opportunity. As studio directors, though, we've made a conscious effort to invest in our learning by working with some fantastic mentors, particularly on management and business matters.

What is it about design that you are most passionate about?
T.K. & K.H.: There are probably two parts to what drives us and Toben, both relating to the power of branding. The first is about clearly defining brands and bringing them to life so they can be intuitively understood. Seeing clients understand their special power and embrace their brand is very rewarding.

The second is our passion for creating meaningful connections between people and brands—to shape positive experiences. When the experience becomes the brand, you have the chance to truly connect with someone. That's why we approach every project holistically and work across multiple disciplines to make that connection possible.

What is the most difficult challenge you've had to overcome to reach your current position?
T.K. & K.H.: We've always had a strong creative vision for Toben, but there are so many more sides to a creative business. Leaning into the business side was a major challenge, especially since we had no formal training in this area. It took us a few years to work out some markers that allowed us to plan more effectively and confidently.

Marketing and new business development is another area full of questions and plenty of trial and error. We've been fortunate to grow largely through client referrals, but we still feel this is a challenge we're actively working to overcome.

Who have some of your greatest past influences been?
T.K. & K.H.: Our surroundings have probably been our biggest influence. We both grew up in Germany, so German design has naturally shaped us simply by being immersed in it. Designers like Dieter Rams, known for the iconic Braun clock, and Erik Spiekermann, who designed countless typographic brand guides such as the one for Deutsche Bahn (railways) and Deutsche Post, left a lasting impression. Their minimalistic and considered design approach is deeply ingrained in both of us.

At the same time, we've spent 25 years living and working in Sydney. The vibrant colors and boldness of many Australian artists and designers definitely rubbed off on us—from legendary artists like Brett Whiteley, Reg Mombassa, and Adam Cullen to contemporaries such as Ben Quilty, Jonathan Zawada, and Anthony Lister, as well as the countless creatives we've collaborated with and peers we've admired over the years.

Who among your contemporaries today do you most admire?
T.K. & K.H.: This is a very tough question to answer because there are so many amazing design studios and designers out there. One studio we've been following for a long time is Made Thought. They first caught our attention with their amazing branding for Established & Sons, and since then, they've remained one of the studios we truly admire. Others include Gretel, COLLINS, AUGE Design, Wedge, SeaChange, Base, Spin, and too many others to list.

Who have been some of your favorite colleagues or clients?
T.K. & K.H.: Oh gosh, we've had the privilege of working with so many talented people over the years, and we've grown with every client. However, some projects have marked distinct milestones for us, including the Museum of Contemporary Art Sydney, Art Series Hotels, ECP Asset Management, and QT Hotels & Resorts. All of these clients treated us with the utmost respect and trust, even when we lacked specialized experience, and they were not only the most intelligent but also the nicest people to work with. Our latest milestone would be the brand refresh for McGrath Estate Agents. We've had so many talented creatives at Toben that we're incredibly grateful for. Our current team—including Amanda Lawler and Geoff Courtman—is truly amazing.

There are too many collaborators and partners to list, but we've gained some dear creative friends over the years, including Nic Graham, Versus, Greg Turner, Chris Thomson, and Brendan Foster.

What are the top things you need from a client in order to make successful work for them?
T.K. & K.H.: We believe trust is probably the biggest determining factor in a project's outcome. Without our clients' trust, we wouldn't be able to dig deep, ask tough questions, propose bold solutions, and make confident decisions together. We invest a fair amount of time building a strong foundation through insights and strategy at the start, immersing ourselves in their business and industry to earn the trust that we truly understand their needs—not just the design side of things.

What part of your work do you find the most demanding?
T.K. & K.H.: As directors and creative/art directors, juggling many hats is currently the most demanding part for both of us. Carving out time to focus on what's important—not just what's urgent—and creating uninterrupted deep thinking and creative time is a real challenge.

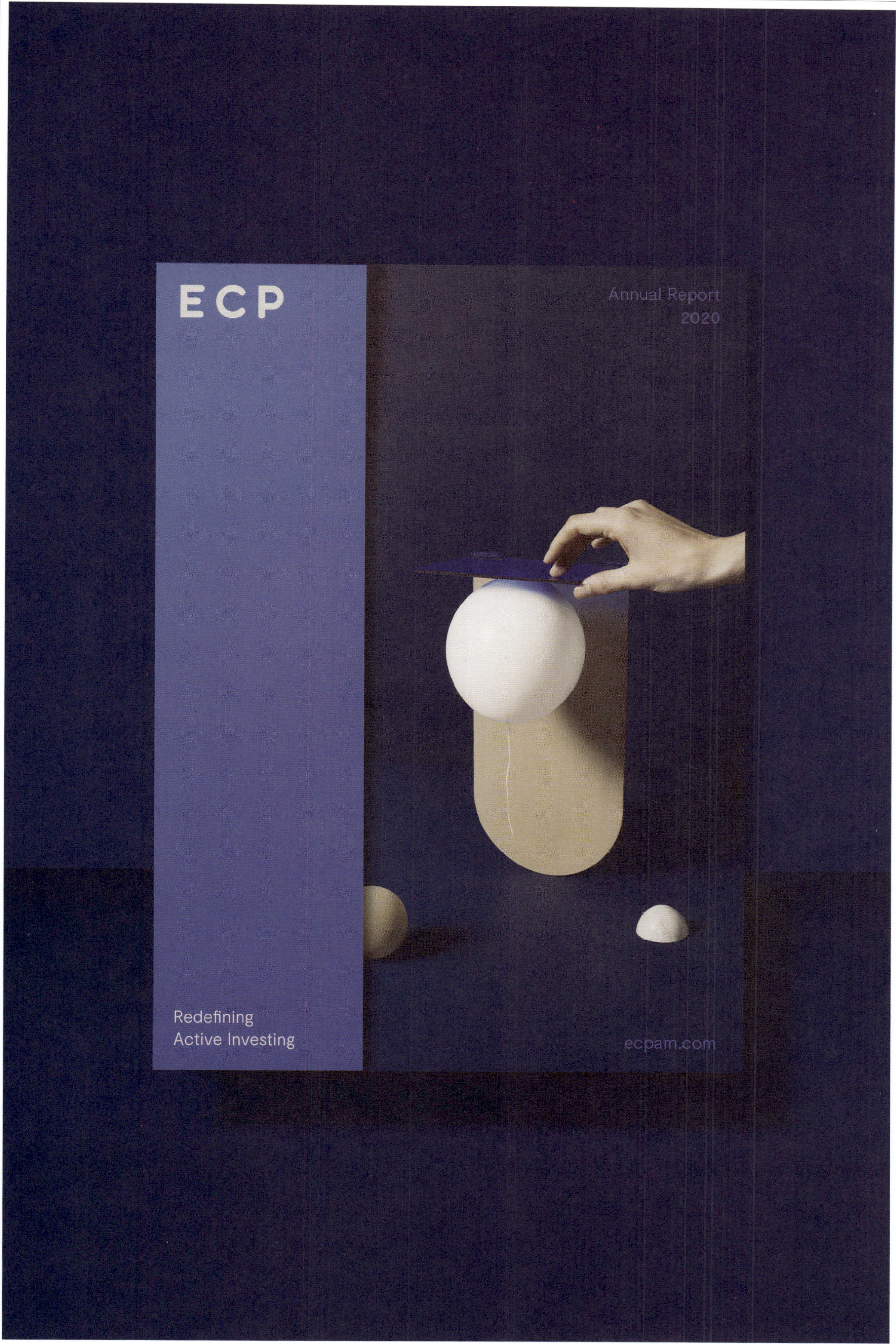

ECP Asset Management - Annual Report

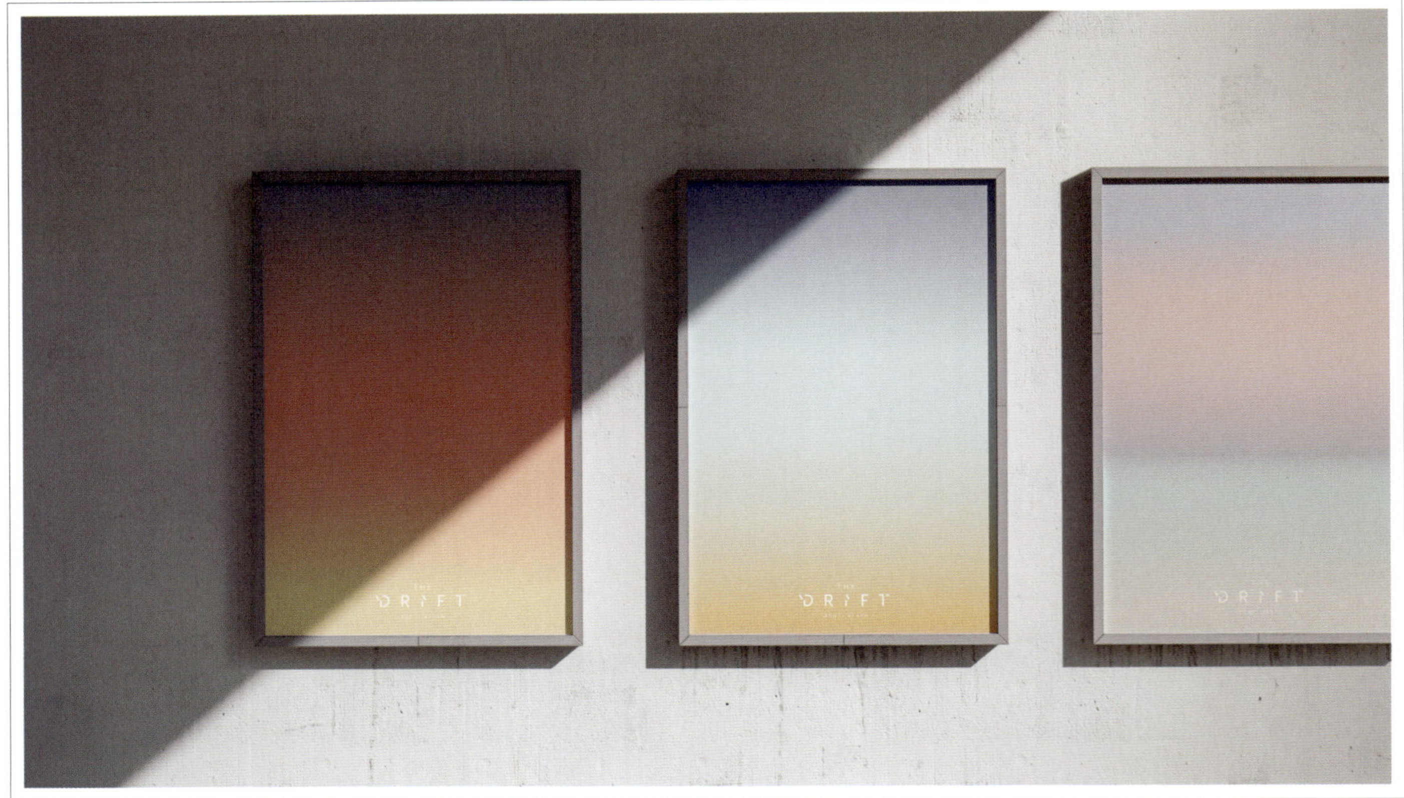

The Drift - Poster Wall

What advice do you have for students starting out today?
K.H.: I'd say focus on personal development just as much as on professional growth. This industry can be demanding, so it's important to stay grounded and treat the career as a marathon, not a sprint. I've seen many talented designers leave the industry. Look after yourself.

What do you value most in life?
T.K.: Freedom. The freedom to speak my mind, the freedom to be who I am, and the freedom of being able to do what I do.
K.H.: Yep, I second that. Freedom has been one of the great perks of working in the creative industry.

What would you change if you had to do it all over again?
T.K. & K.H.: That is hard to say. If we had to do it all over again and wanted to take some shortcuts, we'd look for an investor, build a skill-complementary team, and be a bit more calculated in some of our decisions. That said, we don't believe there are any shortcuts. It's all been part of the journey, and every experience has fed into the next, making us a bit richer along the way.

How do you define success?
T.K. & K.H.: On a project level, a few key highlights for us include creating a meaningful impact for our clients, watching the brands we've built flourish, seeing teams reignite their energy, and witnessing audiences connect with and gain value from those brand experiences. Those are real proud moments for us. If we have achieved this by pushing creative boundaries or in a way that has challenged and helped us grow, then that's even more special.

How do you balance your work with your personal life if there is a distinction between the two for you?
T.K. & K.H.: We're partners in business and in life. Before we had kids, there wasn't much balance, and the lines between work and personal life were very fluid. Since becoming parents, we've made a conscious effort to keep these two areas separate to keep everyone sane. Surprisingly, this approach has been quite productive. So far, so good.

What interests do you have outside of work?
T.K. & K.H.: We have two kids, which makes for a pretty rich life. The little spare time we have left is spent traveling, experiencing art, drinking good coffee, climbing, and enjoying nature.

In what ways do you see your field changing over the years?
T.K. & K.H.: In branding, there has been a significant shift from brand identity to brand experience and from "selling" to "engaging" based on purpose and shared values. Brands have become much more meaningful, client-centric, and empathetic over the years. We've now reached a point where brands recognize their role in addressing social and environmental issues as well. Hopefully, the transparency of all channels and the pressure from the next generation will continue this, allowing branding to help transform businesses into meaningful enterprises.

You offer a full range of services from brand development to print, digital, campaign, packaging, and spatial design. What type of project is your favorite to work on?
T.K. & K.H.: The most accurate answer would be when we get to combine it all. We see all of those services as an extension of a brand idea. Developing that idea and then having the space to explore it across all those mediums is our best-case scenario—truly bringing the brand to life.

What makes Toben stand out from other design firms, both locally and internationally?
T.K. & K.H.: We think it's the equal focus on brand substance and idea as well as visual and intuitive appeal. Or, at least, this is the space that we love to play in. Some people know us best for our hospitality work, where we blend brand identity and brand experience. This is an area we truly enjoy and have gained quite a bit of experience in by now.

Toben www.toben.com.au

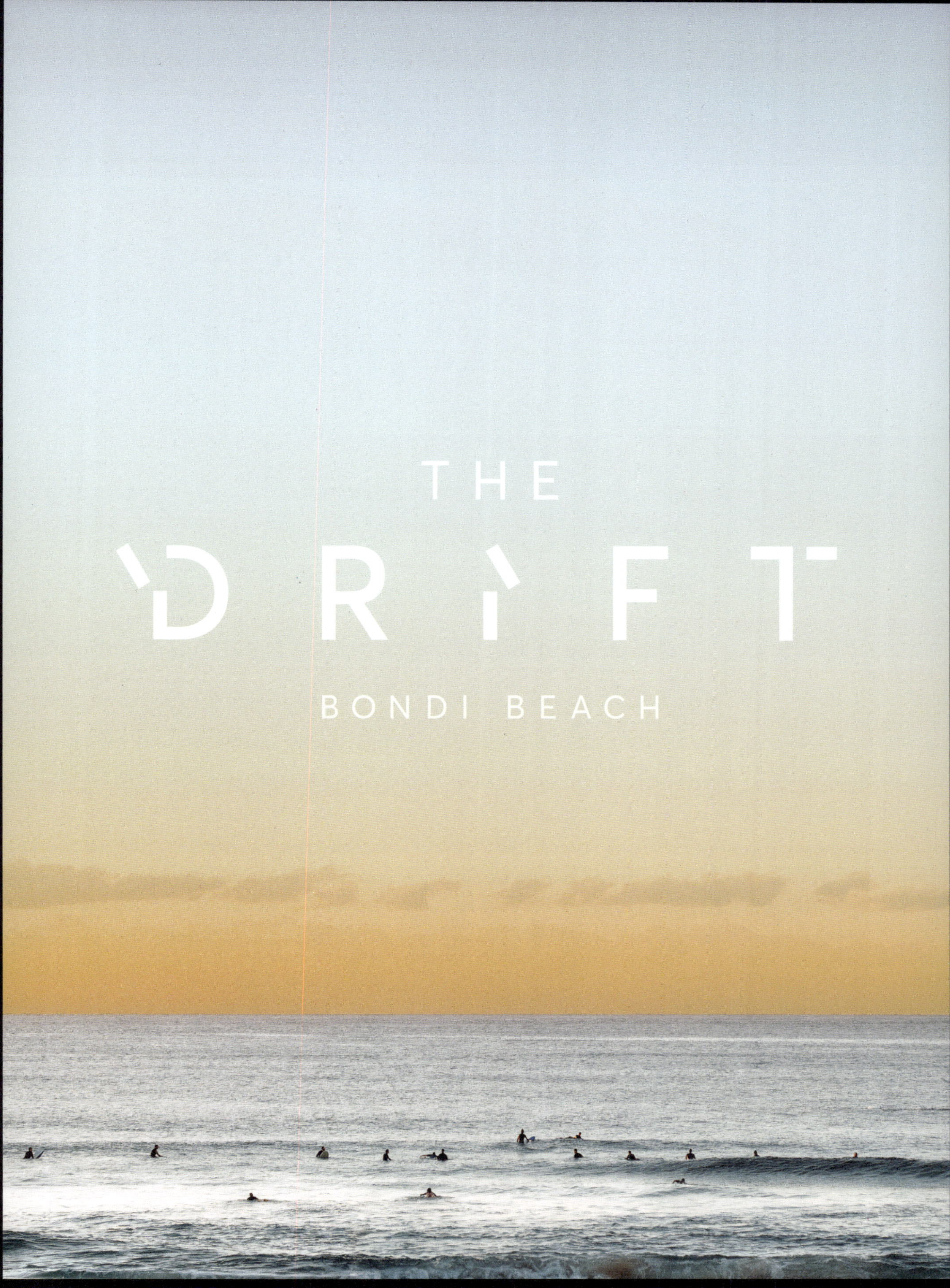

THE

DRIFT

BONDI BEACH

The Drift - Logo

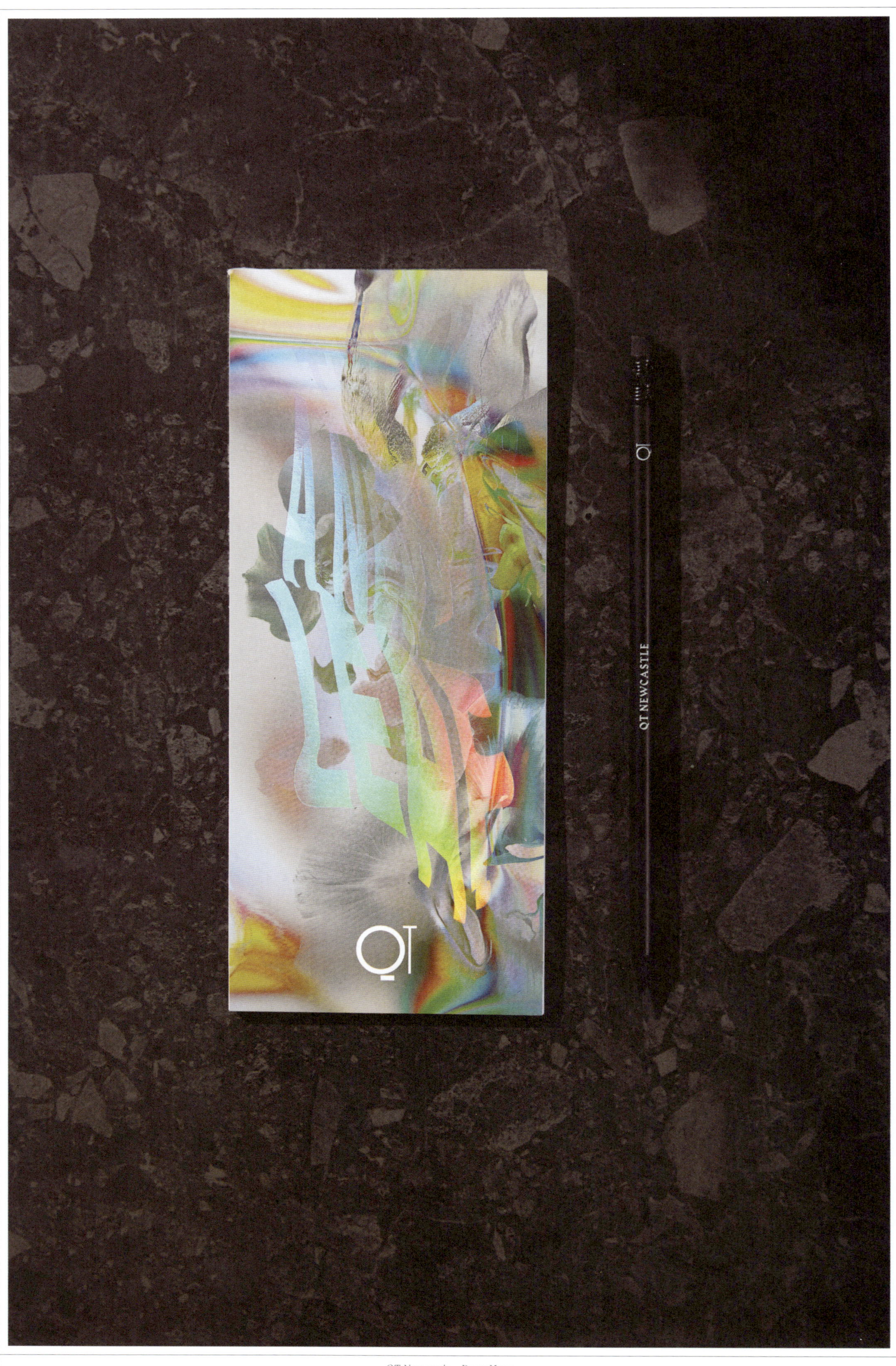

QT Newcastle - Door Hang

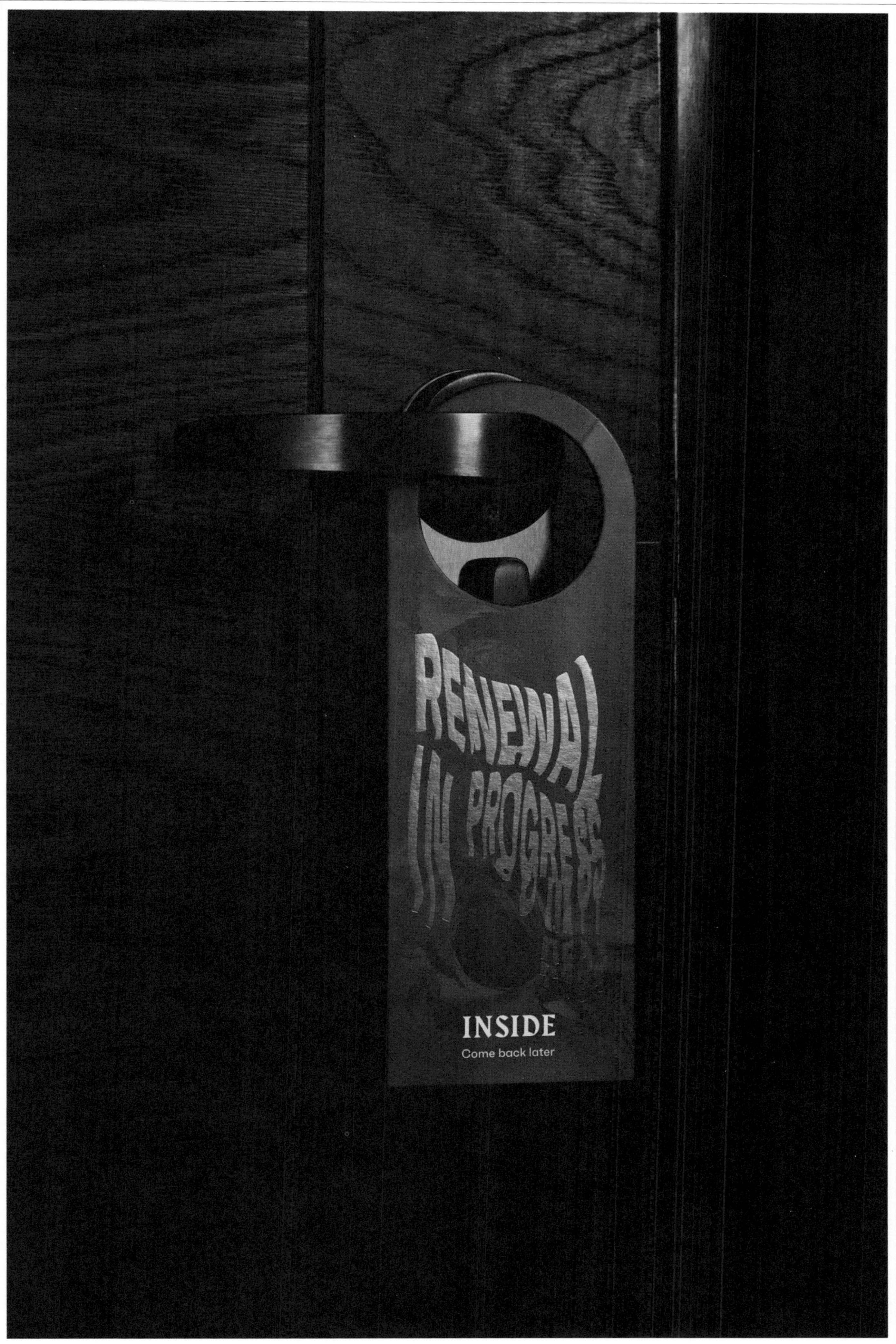

QT Newcastle - In-room Notepad

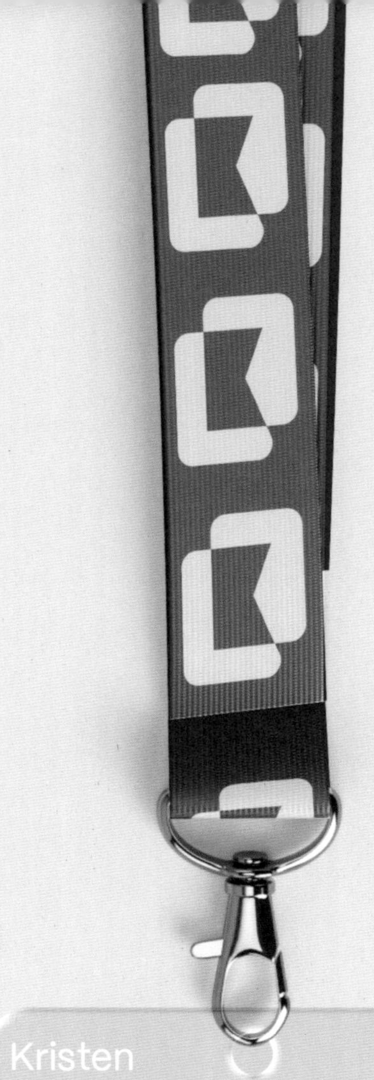

Kristen
Migliorini
Founder & CEO
ID: 25508
KomplyAi®

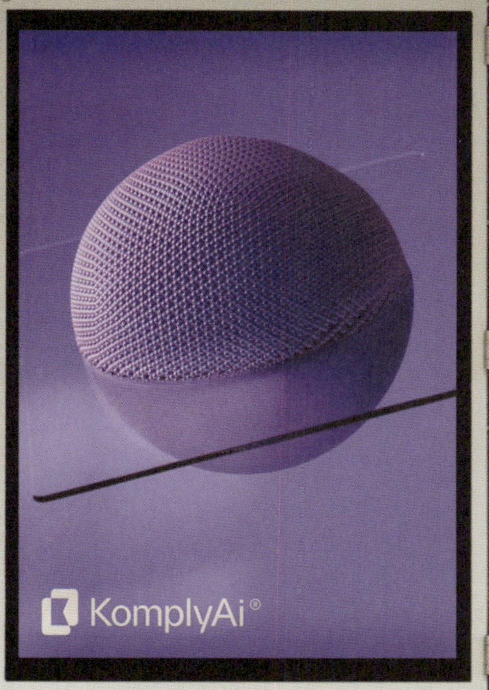

(Opposite page) KomplyAi - Lanyard / (Top) KomplyAi - Advertising / (Bottom) KomplyAi - Mission Statement

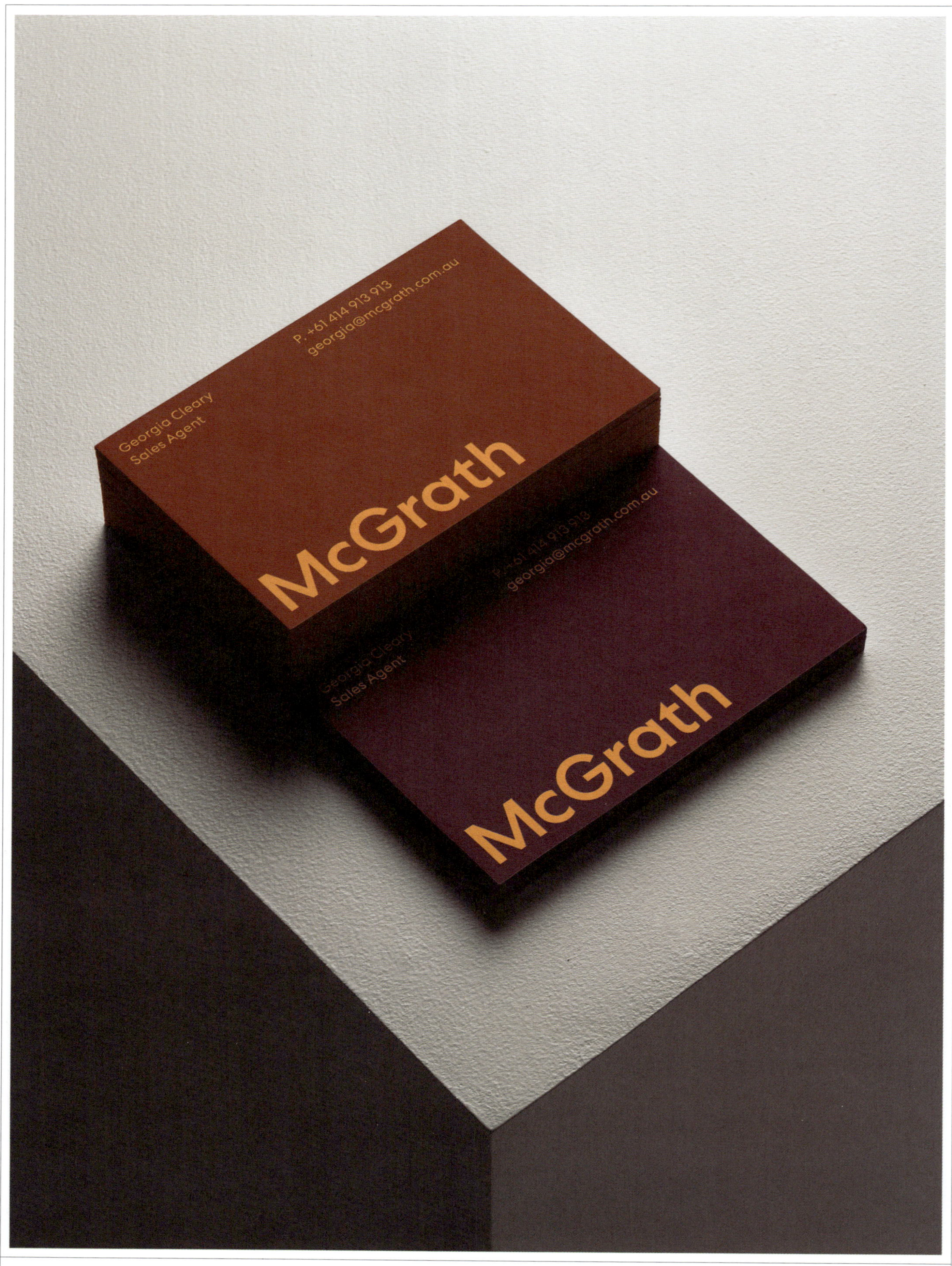

McGrath - Business Cards / (Opposite page) McGrath - Keybox

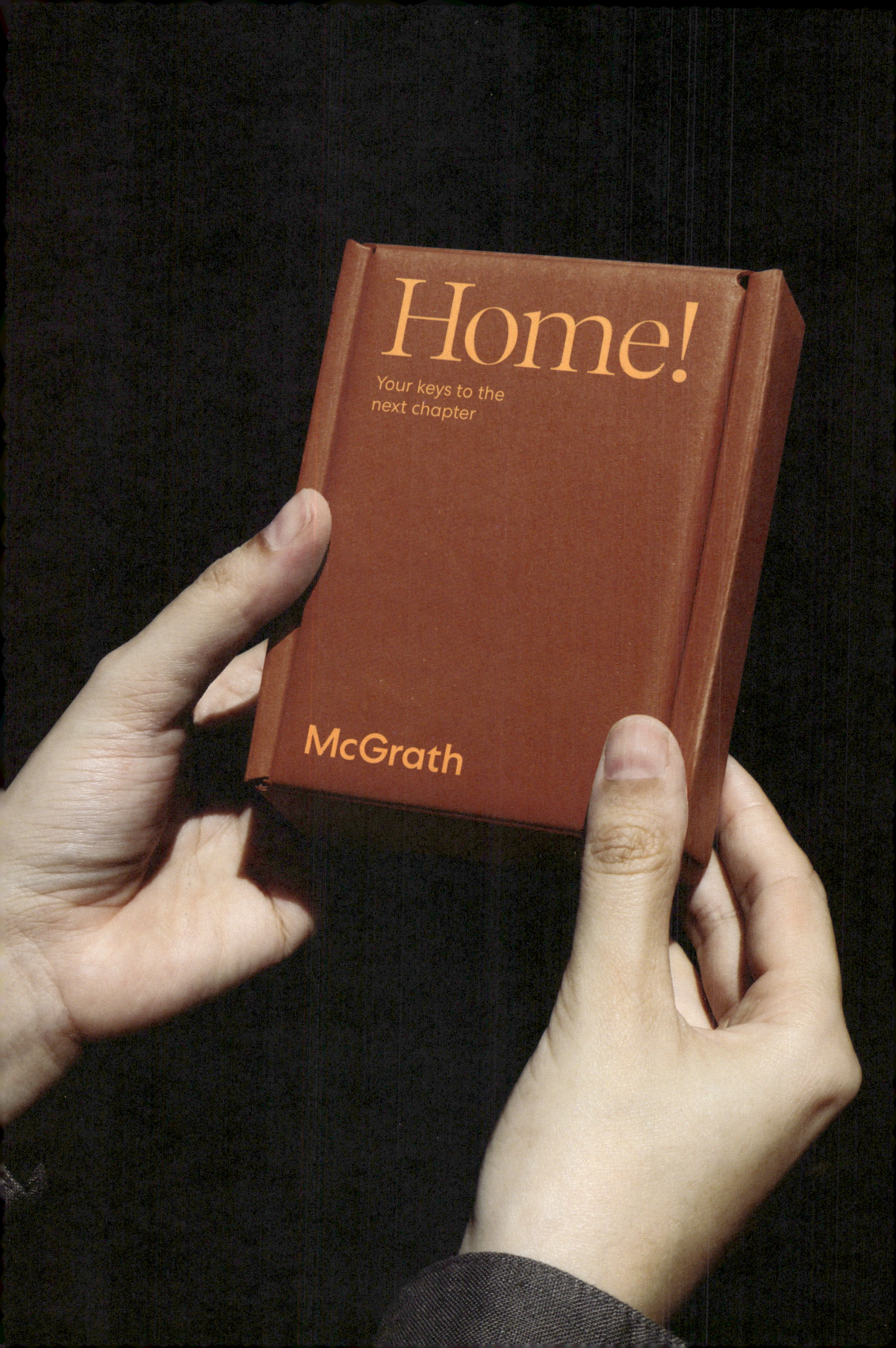

Home!
Your keys to the next chapter
McGrath

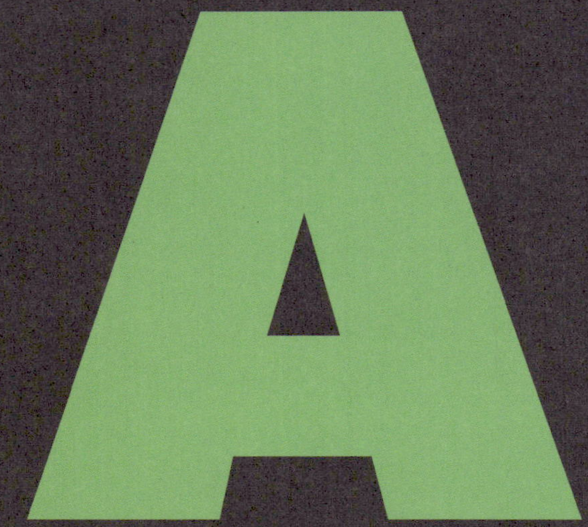

ADVERTISING

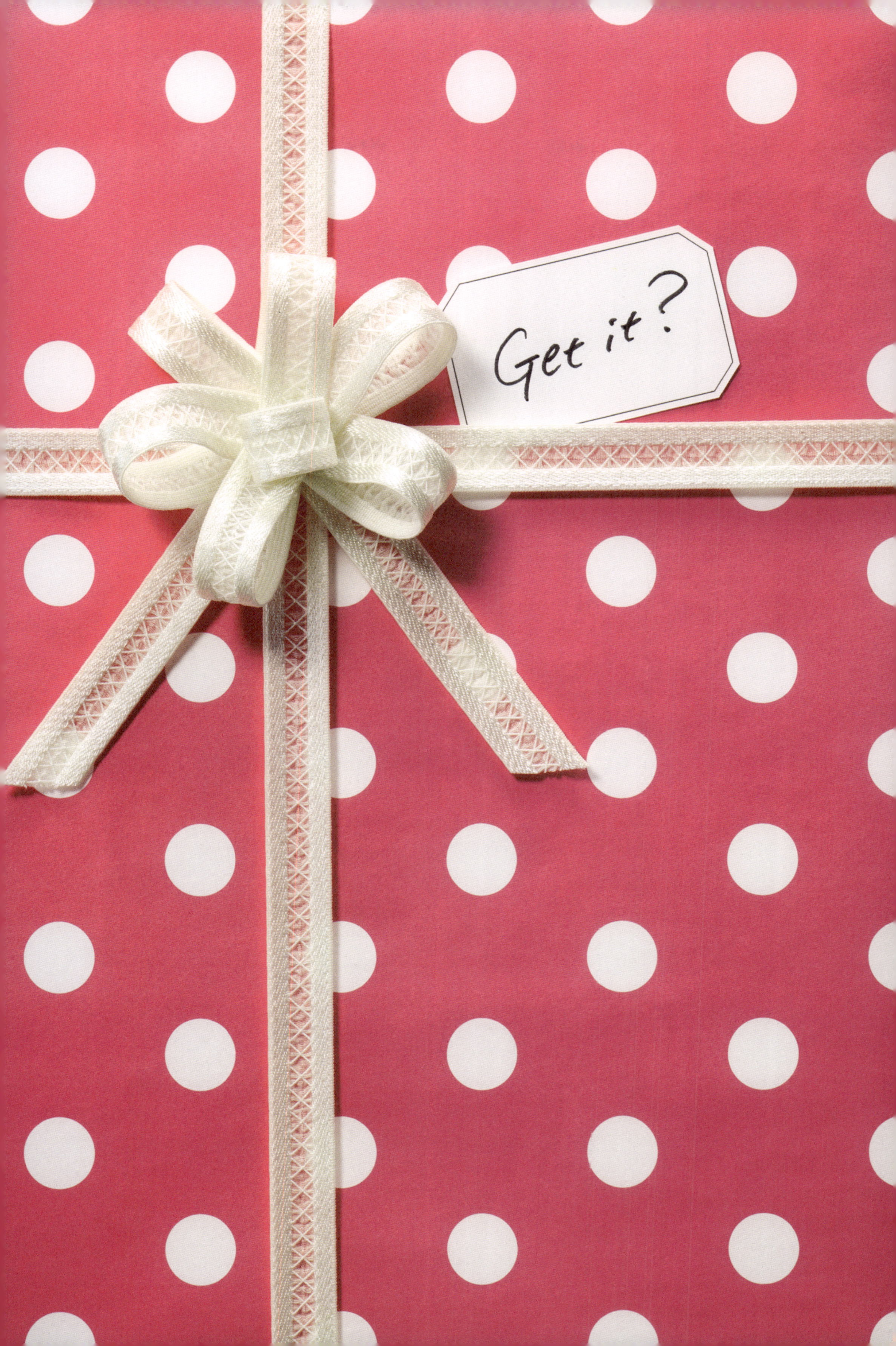
Get it?

THEY BRING CLARITY AND CREATIVITY TO EVEN THE MOST COMPLEX SOCIAL THEMES. THEIR THOUGHTFUL APPROACH AND SHARP EXECUTION MAKE THEM A VALUED CREATIVE PARTNER WE LOOK FORWARD TO WORKING WITH AGAIN.

Kiyohiro Yamada, *Communication Department, LayerX Inc.*

I'VE HAD THE PLEASURE OF WORKING WITH MR. NAKAMURA A FEW TIMES, AND I'M STRUCK BY THE METICULOUSNESS AND DELICACY THAT REFLECT A UNIQUELY JAPANESE SENSIBILITY.

Hirohito Okayasu, *Photographer, MASH Co. LTD*

HIROYUKI NAKAMURA'S WORK RADIATES THE SAME WARMTH AND KINDNESS THAT HE HIMSELF EMBODIES. HE IS AN ART DIRECTOR WHO BRINGS BOTH HEART AND DETERMINATION TO EVERY PROJECT.

Tetsuro Ikejima, *Photographer, MASH Co. LTD*

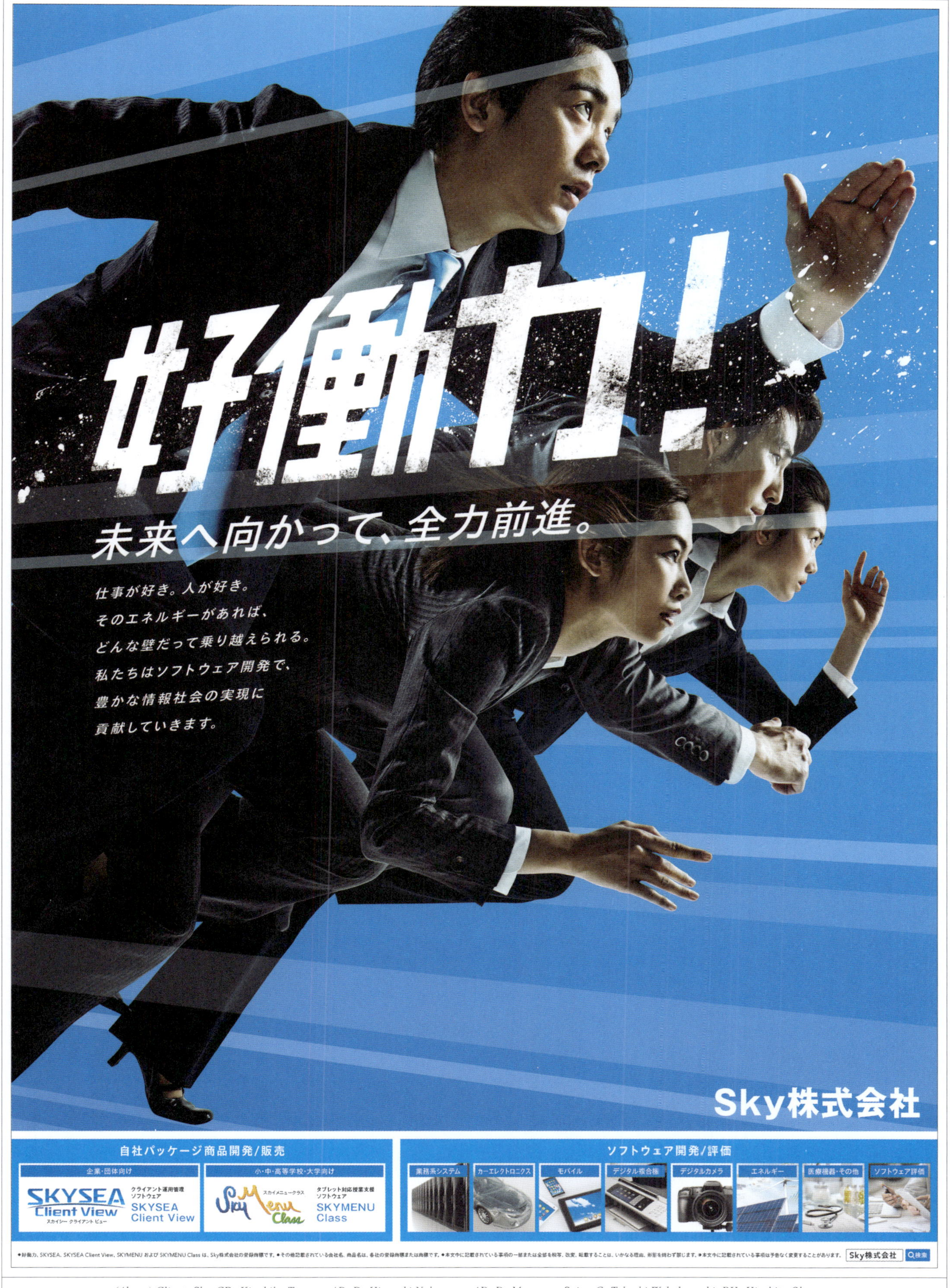

(Above) Client: Sky. CD: Kiyohiko Tozawa. AD, D: Hiroyuki Nakamura. AD, D: Masayasu Saito. C: Takeshi Wakabayashi. PH: Hirohito Okayasu.
(Page 45) Client: Japan Advertising Agencies Association. CD: Hidetaka Sugiyama. AD, D: Hiroyuki Nakamura. C: Naoto Miyazaki. PH: Tetsuro Ikejima.

Introduction by **Kiyohiko Tozawa** *Freelance Creative Director & Copywriter*

Hiroyuki Nakamura has demonstrated his unique talent in both illustration and typography, as evidenced by his multiple awards at the Bologna Children's Book Fair. While it may seem challenging to incorporate a fantastical sensibility into B2B advertising, he has overcome this hurdle with his innovative thinking. For example, the blue lines in the background of the Sky poster and the silhouette of a sewing machine laid out within the typography of "100" in the JANOME newspaper ad both reflect this approach. Having the opportunity to work with him on several projects has been a true privilege for me.

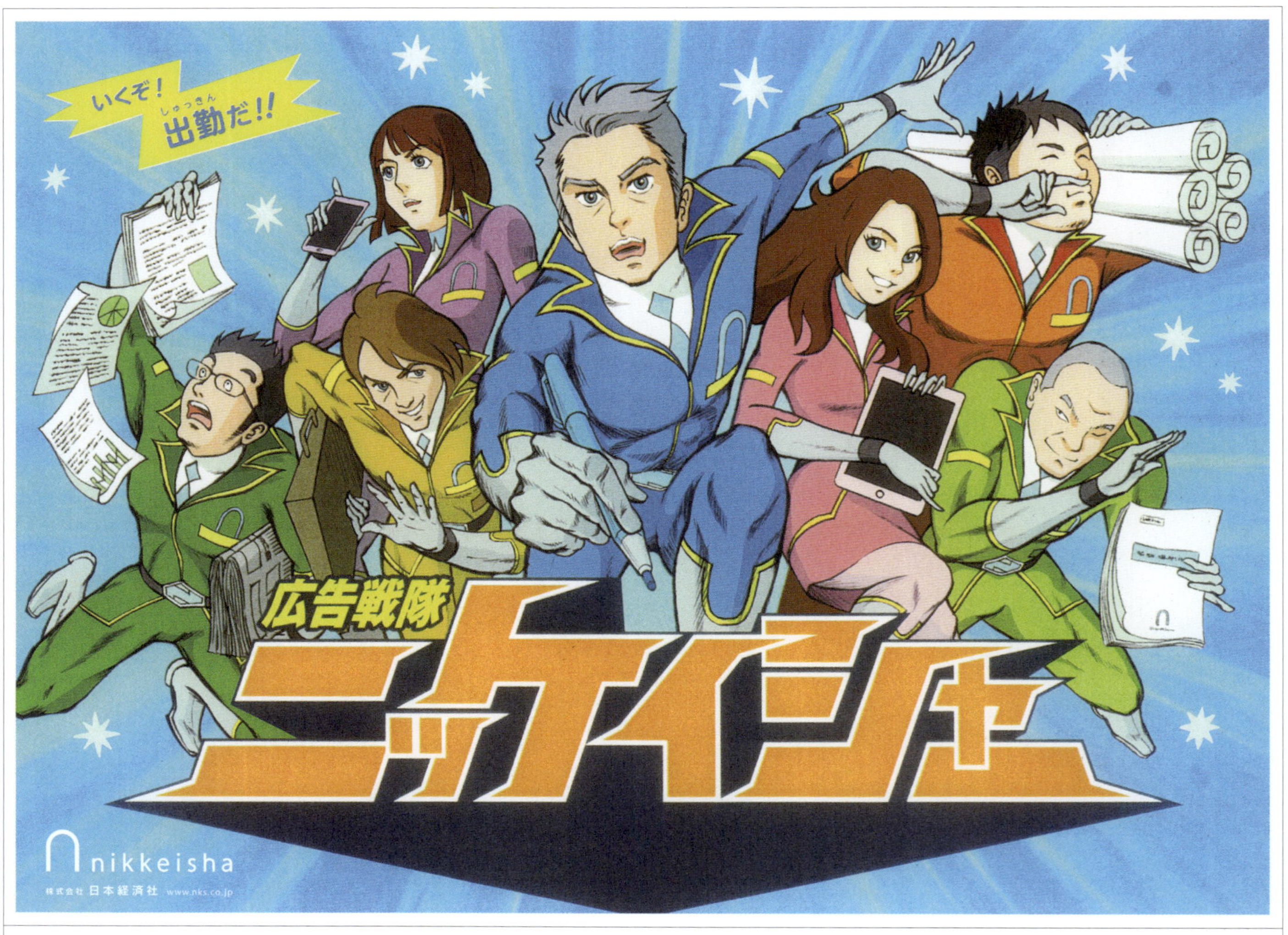

Client: Nikkeisha, Inc. CD: Hidetaka Sugiyama. AD, D: Hiroyuki Nakamura. C: Naoto Miyazaki. I: Nobco Uemura.

I APPROACH EVERY TASK AS UNCOMPROMISINGLY AS POSSIBLE.

Hiroyuki Nakamura, *Creative/Art Director, Nikkeisha, Inc.*

ども！シロクマです。なんや最近異常気象や思わへん？うちとこもだんだん暖ったかなってる気いすんねん。そのくせ天然ガスやら石炭やらエネルギー原料が高うなって、かなんなあ。環境のこと考えたら、これからはグリーンエネルギーなんとちゃう？それをグローバルな体制できっちりやるんが **Abalance** ゆう会社や！「あ…ばらんす？」ちゃうよ。「えーばらんす」や！国際的にも高ーい評価*を受けた太陽光パネルやら、グリーンエネルギーに関するサービスを自社グループでフルサポートしとるんやで。エネルギーはバランスが大事。そやから、太陽光発電で日本トップクラスの会社と一緒にもっともっとグリーンエネルギーの割合を増やしていきましょ、ちゅうことや。それが「良(え)えバランス」せやから **Abalance** やねん、なんてな(笑) 名前だけでも覚えていってな。ほな、また！

*太陽光発電パネルを生産するAbalanceグループの「Vietnam Sunergy Joint Stock Company」は、サプライチェーンを主体とするESG、サスティナビリティの世界的な評価機関であるEcoVadis（エコバディス）の評価にて2020年度に続いてブロンズメダルを受賞しました。さらに、Bloomberg NEF, Tier1 Module Maker List (November 22, 2022) にランクインしております。

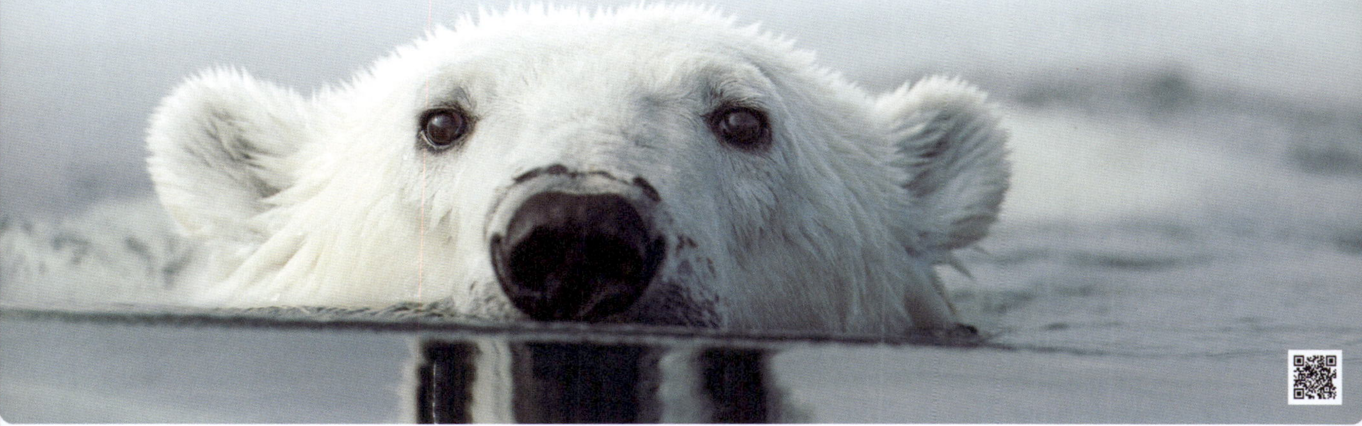

グリーンエネルギーを、もっと日本へ。もっと世界へ。

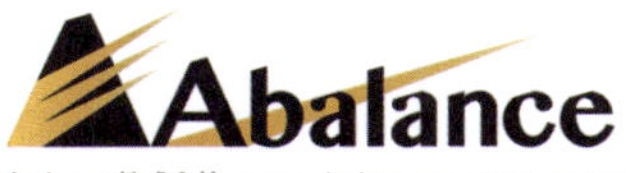

Abalance株式会社 www.abalance.jp 証券コード 3856

グループ会社： WWB株式会社 FUJI SOLAR株式会社 Vietnam Sunergy Joint Stock Company 株式会社バローズ PV Repower株式会社 バーディフュエルセルズ合同会社 Abit株式会社 株式会社デジサイン 株式会社FORTHINK 日本光触媒センター株式会社

持分法適用関連会社： 明治機械株式会社（東証スタンダード上場：証券コード 6334）

Client: Abalance Corporation. CD, AD, D, C: Hiroyuki Nakamura. D: Hikari Maesaka. D: Yuya Obata. C: Takeshi Wakabayashi.

What has inspired or motivated you in your career?
Hiroyuki Nakamura, Creative/Art Director: Being selected for several design awards has made me feel that my creative journey is on the right track.
Genki Asano, Designer: I'm motivated by the stimulation I receive from my colleagues, who are passionate about advertising and creativity.
Yuya Obata, Designer: My teacher in college. She spent a lot of time and effort teaching me the basics of design and how to build a career. I want to become a designer that she would be proud to call her student.
Takeshi Wakabayashi, Copywriter: My first boss after I was hired as a copywriter. No matter how much copy I wrote, he made me rewrite everything. My greatest motivation was to write copy that would please him—no matter how many years it took.

What is your work philosophy?
Hikari Maesaka, Designer: Take the plunge—do it and say it. Stop assuming, "I don't think I can do it."
H.N.: As a professional, I approach every task as uncompromisingly as possible.
G.A.: Since advertising is a team effort, I strive to understand my role in each project and fulfill it to the best of my ability.
Y.O.: Create work I can confidently show to family and friends and say, "This is mine."
T.W.: My work philosophy is to develop creative work that exceeds the client's expectations.

Who is or was your greatest mentor?
H.N.: I had two mentors at the advertising production company where I first began my career. They taught me everything—from the fundamentals of graphic design to the importance of attention to detail.
G.A.: My first mentor. He taught me the basics of both design and professional work. When I'm struggling, I still go to him for objective and insightful advice.
H.M.: My current supervisor.
Y.O.: My first professional mentor, who taught me about design in detail, right down to the smallest elements.
T.W.: A senior copywriter I met when I was 23. He encouraged me by saying, "You'll make it big." That's what kept me going.

What is it about advertising that you are most passionate about?
H.N.: Improving the quality and completeness of the work as much as possible.
G.A.: While creating ads, I also see myself as a consumer and evaluate whether the ad works from that perspective.
H.M.: Generating ideas.
T.W.: I am passionate about creating messages that inspire people to take positive emotional action.

What is the most difficult challenge you've had to overcome to reach your current position?
H.N.: Making the career change from a designer at a production company to an art director at an advertising agency.
T.W.: Facing prejudice due to color blindness. Most agencies wouldn't even accept my application. I was turned away at the door.

Who have been some of your greatest past influences?
H.N.: Fujiko Fujio, the Japanese manga artist. His work taught me the power of wild ideas and shifting perspectives.
G.A.: Takuma Takasaki, a Japanese creative director.
H.M.: Photographer Mika Ninagawa, art director Yuni Yoshida, and female creators in general.
Y.O.: When I studied Milton Glaser's "I Love NY" campaign, I understood the impact of design in advertising. I knew I wanted to create work like that.
T.W.: David Bowie. I admire his ability to move freely between creative worlds.

Who among your contemporaries today do you most admire?
H.N.: Kazunari Hattori, a Japanese art director.
G.A.: Kimiko Sekido, a Japanese art director.
H.M.: My classmates who have become artists.
Y.O.: Shohei Ohtani, the baseball player. Though he's a bit older than I am, I respect both his personality and his dedication.
T.W.: Joe Strummer, the frontman of *The Clash*. Every word he left behind inspires me.

What would be your dream assignment?
H.M.: Collaborating with my classmates, who are now artists.
Y.O.: Because many teachers have helped me, I would love to become a teacher someday and pass that on.

Who have been some of your favorite colleagues or clients to work with?
H.N.: Team members who offer diverse opinions and salespeople who understand creativity. I also appreciate clients who welcome bold proposals.
G.A.: My favorite colleagues and clients are those who are passionate and share common goals.
H.M.: People who genuinely enjoy their work and relaxed, cool senior colleagues.
Y.O.: Fellow designers from my generation—those I can compete with and admire at the same time.
T.W.: Designers who think logically and salespeople who dive enthusiastically into creative ideas.

What are the top things you need from a client to make successful work for them?
H.N.: A shared commitment to pursuing strong ideas, visual beauty, and high-quality execution.
G.A.: A unique approach to solving problems.
H.M.: A deep understanding of the client's issues and an openness to proposals that exceed expectations.
T.W.: New perspectives and compelling creative copy that stems from them.

What do you consider your greatest professional achievement so far in your career?
H.N.: Winning a Platinum Award from Graphis and being selected for the TDC Competition.
G.A.: Helping develop a project that achieved strong results and which evolved into a long-term campaign.
T.W.: My greatest professional achievement is turning a client that had never advertised into a frequent award-winner within a few years, helping increase their corporate value.

What gives you the greatest satisfaction in your work?
H.N.: When the visuals and copy align perfectly, and the photographer's work turns out beautifully.
G.A.: What gives me the greatest satisfaction is when our work is recognized and the project continues long-term.
H.M.: When my ideas are liked and brought to life, especially when clients and consumers remember them.
Y.O.: When consumers appreciate the work.
T.W.: I am satisfied when clients are truly pleased and the work earns social recognition.

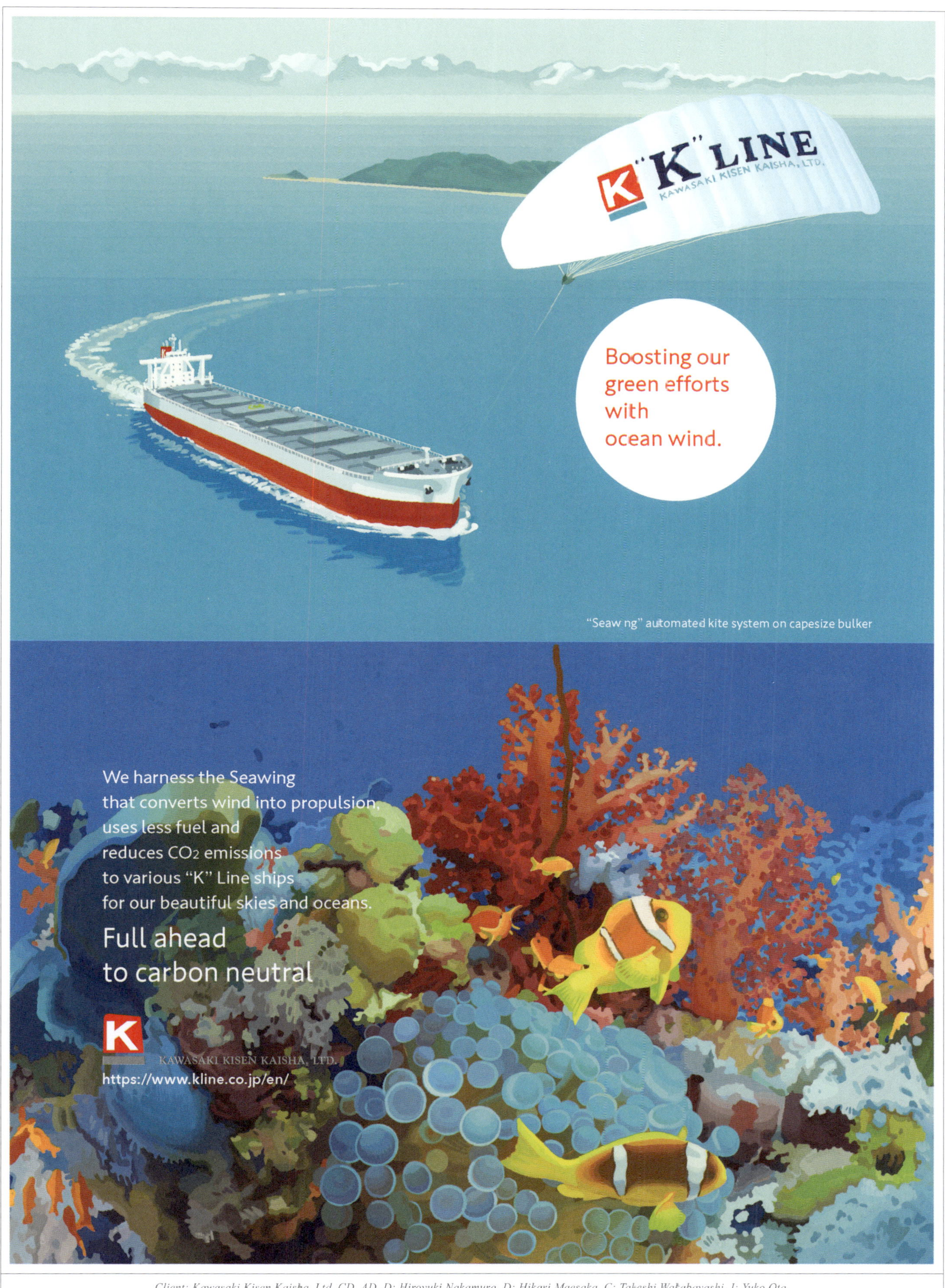

Client: Kawasaki Kisen Kaisha, Ltd. CD, AD, D: Hiroyuki Nakamura. D: Hikari Maesaka C: Takeshi Wakabayashi. I: Yuko Ota.

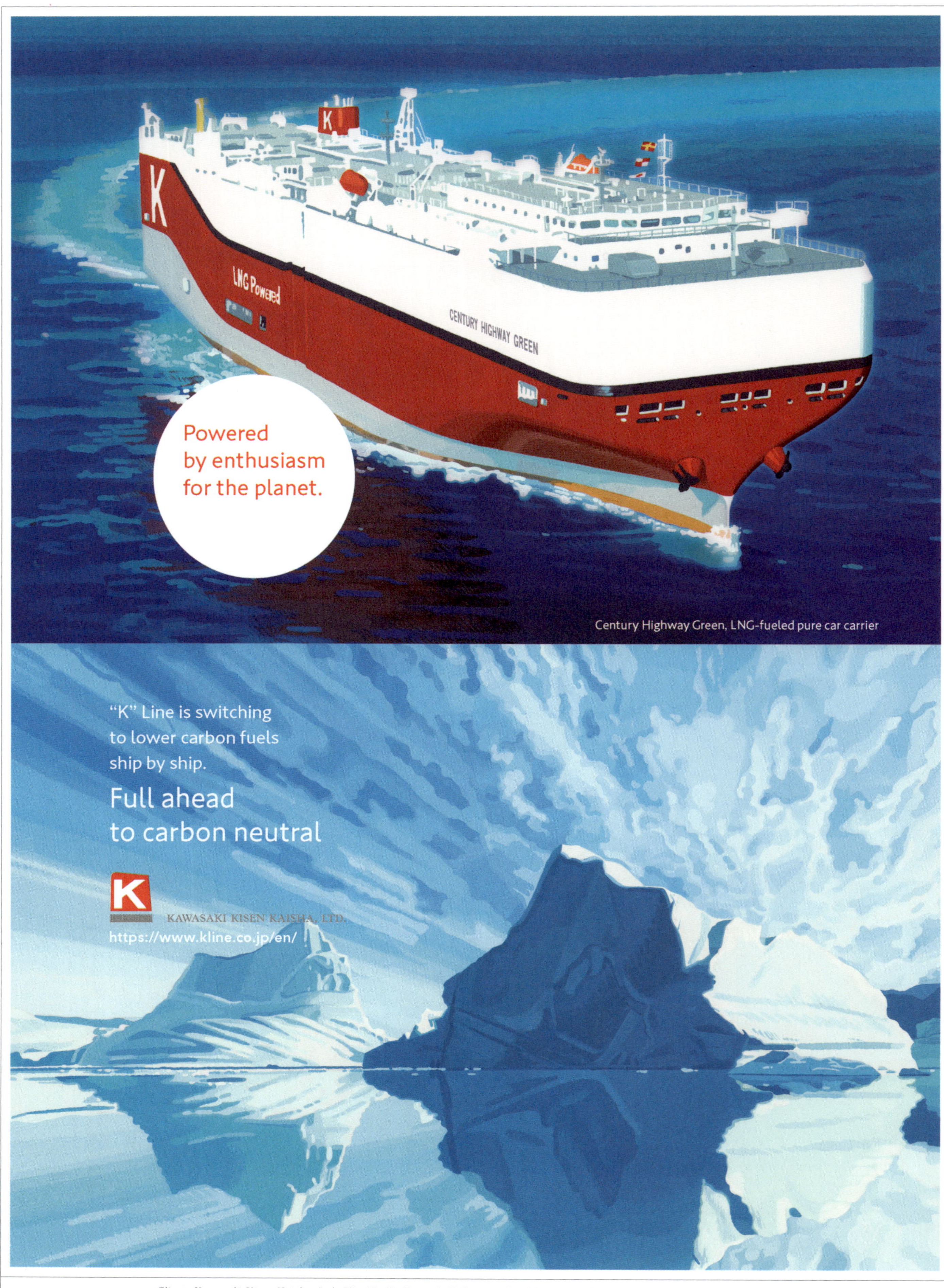

Client: Kawasaki Kisen Kaisha, Ltd. CD, AD, D: Hiroyuki Nakamura. D: Hikari Maesaka. C: Takeshi Wakabayashi. I: Yuko Ota.

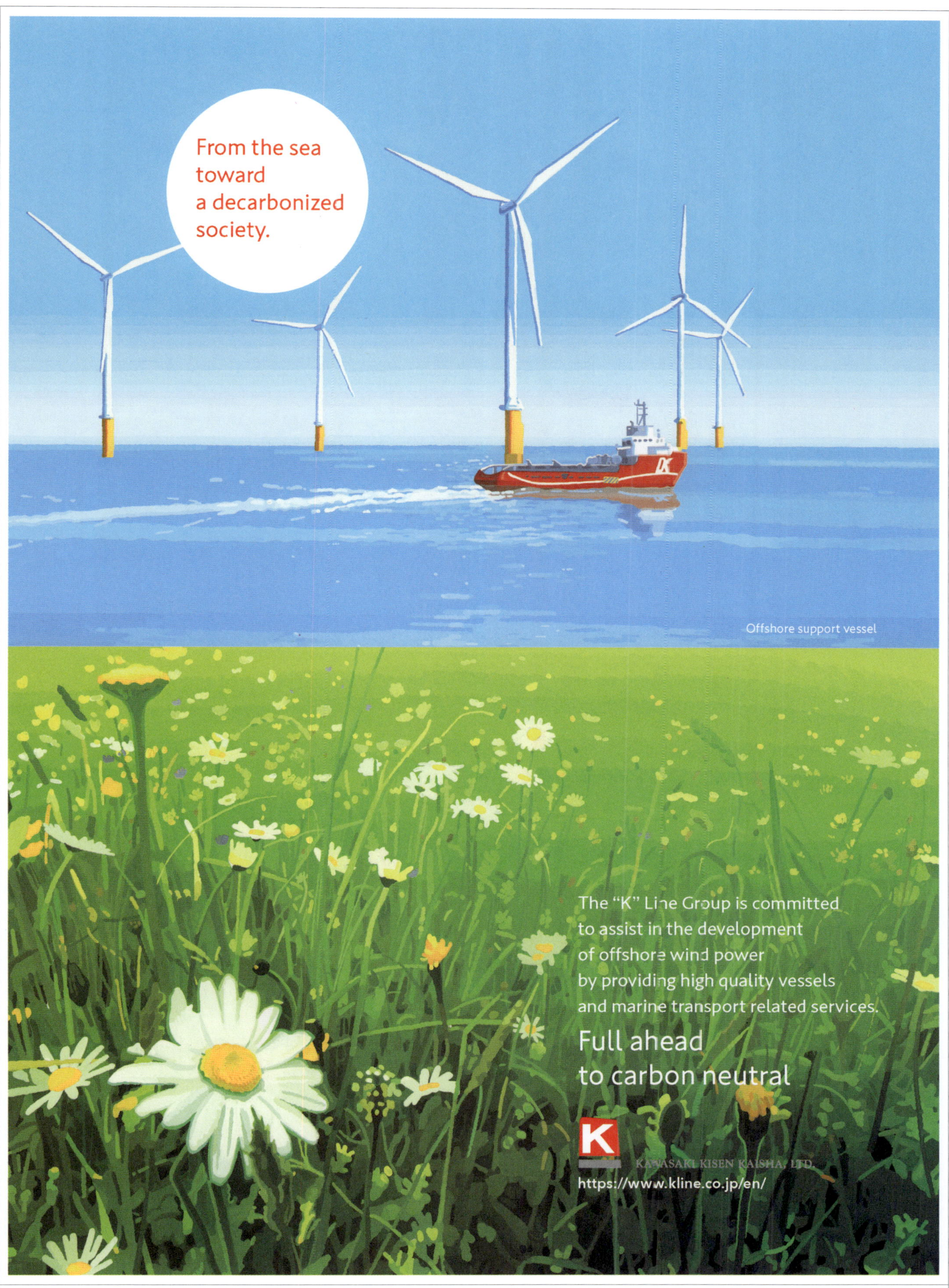

Client: Kawasaki Kisen Kaisha, Ltd. CD, AD, D: Hiroyuki Nakamura. D: Hikari Maesaka. C: Takesai Wakabayashi. I: Yuko Ota.

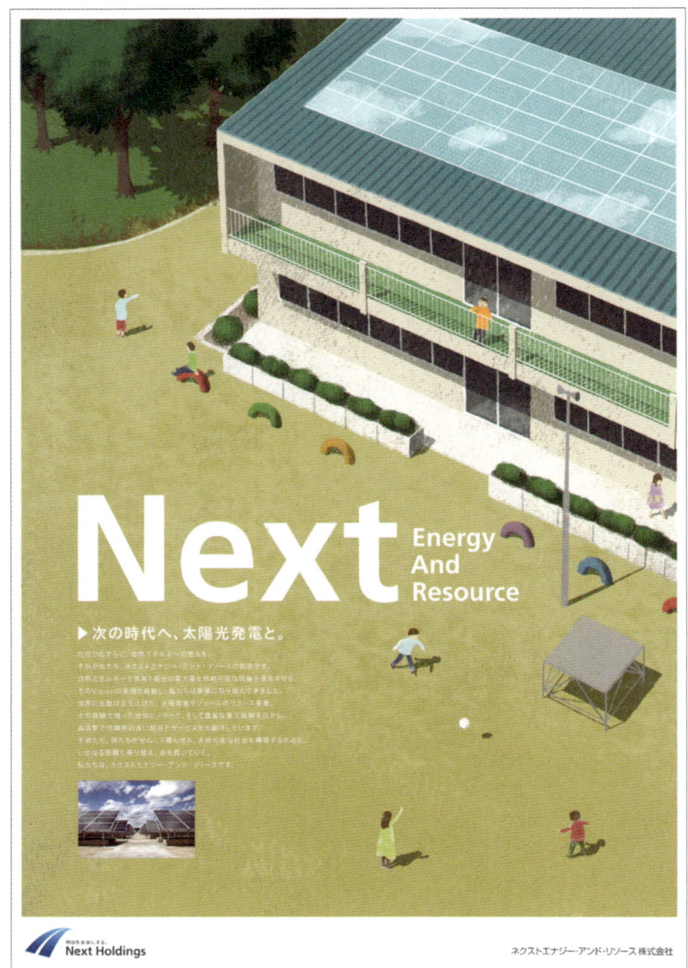

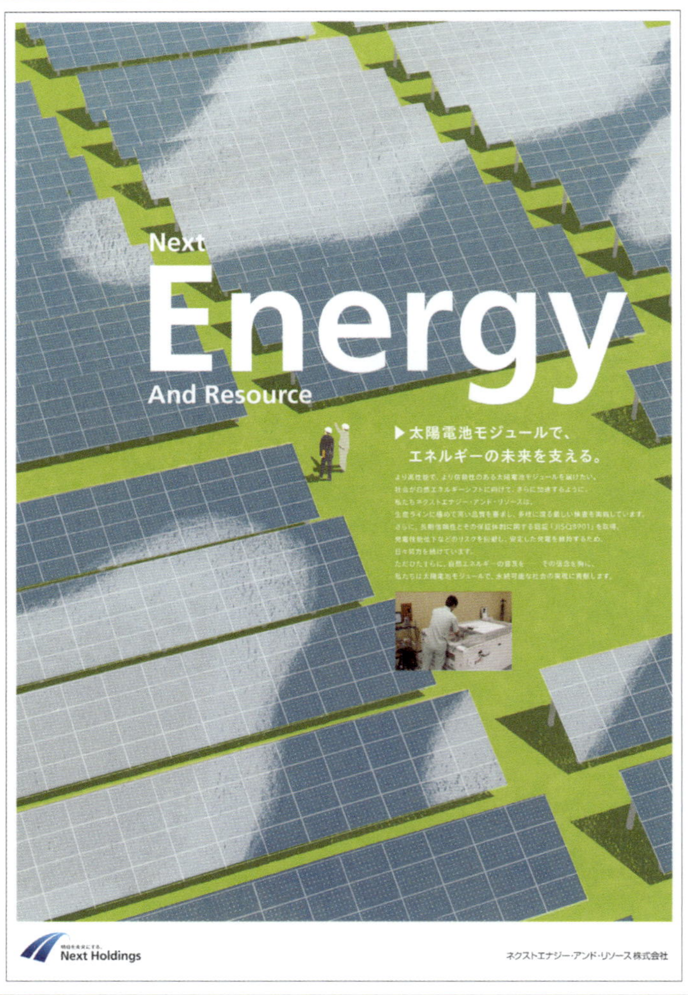

Client: Next Energy & Resources Co., Ltd. CD: Kiyohiko Tozawa. AD: Hidetaka Sugiyama. AD, D, I: Hiroyuki Nakamura. C: Naoto Miyazaki.

What part of your work do you find the most demanding?
H.N.: When a proposal that was already approved is canceled due to internal client politics.
G.A.: Winning competitive pitches.
H.M.: Generating ideas when the target isn't clearly defined.
Y.O.: Creating work that's good for the creators, the client, and the consumer.
T.W.: The most demanding part is the creative process—until I land on an idea that truly satisfies me.

What professional goals do you still have?
H.N.: To create advertising and design that can be understood even across language barriers.
G.A.: My professional goal is to craft ads that leave a lasting impression and spark conversations.
H.M.: To become a fully fledged professional by 30.
Y.O.: As someone still gaining experience in advertising, I want to proactively explore diverse work and collaborate with many different people.
T.W.: For me professionally, I want to win awards and increase visibility to reduce prejudice against aspiring copywriters with color blindness like myself.

What advice would you give to students starting out today?
H.N.: See as much as you can—art, movies, comics—and travel abroad to experience different cultures.
G.A.: Actively develop your strengths and work on your weaknesses without giving up.
T.W.: Take care of your health—especially your mental health.

What interests do you have outside of work?
G.A.: Comics and illustrations.
H.M.: Dancing.
Y.O.: Hip-hop, cars, dogs, fishing—just about anything.

What would you change if you had to do it all over again?
G.A.: I'd make my own decisions more often, even about minor things. I wish I had developed better judgment earlier, especially in situations that required quick choices.

Where do you find inspiration?
H.N.: Picture books, comics, and art.
G.A.: Various forms of expression—comics, films, and art.
H.M.: In conversations.
Y.O.: Movies, music videos, comics—any medium, really.
T.W.: Jogging—it clears my mind more than anything else.

How do you define success?
G.A.: Success is the ability to sustain a project long-term—not just short-term wins.
T.W.: The degree to which I feel satisfied and fulfilled—on my own terms, not by others' standards.

How do you balance your work and personal life if there is a distinction for you?
G.A.: I try to look at advertising not just through a creator's lens but also from the consumer's point of view.
H.M.: I immerse myself in hobbies that help me disconnect.
Y.O.: It's a 50/50 split. Since my work and personal life are intertwined, I try to enjoy both without separating them too much.
T.W.: Work 80%, personal life 20%. That feels like a healthy balance to me.

Nikkeisha, Inc. www.nks.co.jp

Next
Energy
And

Resource

▶太陽電池の再利用事業で培った、
リソースがあります。

太陽光発電の全量買取期間は、20年*。
その間、太陽電池は少なからず劣化し、トラブルも起こり得ます。
十分な売電収益を得るためには、適切な管理が欠かせません。
私たちネクストエナジー・アンド・リソースは
世界に先駆け、太陽電池リユース事業に着手。
3万枚を超える使用済み太陽電池を検査・評価し、
再利用したこの事業で培った技術とノウハウを活かし、
最適なモニタリングとメンテナンス、保安管理を
行うサービス「PVSAFETY」をお届けします。
太陽光発電を知り尽くした、私たちだけのリソースがあります。
ただひたすらに、自然エネルギーの普及を―― その信念を胸に、
私たちはPVSAFETYで、永続可能な社会の実現に貢献します。

*10kW以上の場合

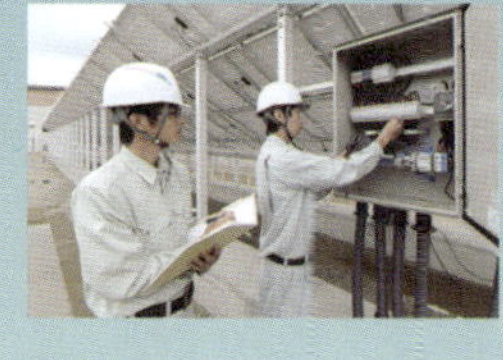

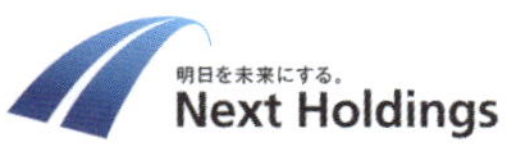

ネクストエナジー・アンド・リソース株式会社

Client: Next Energy & Resources Co., Ltd. CD: Kiyohiko Tozawa. AD: Hidetaka Sugiyama. AD, D, I: Hiroyuki Nakamura. C: Naoto Miyazaki.

日本の不動産をもっと良くしたい。

かっこいい家を借りたい。
かっこいい家を買いたい。
かっこいい家を建てたい。
住まいをお探しの方々のそんな想いにお応えします。
賃貸をお考えのお客さまには、
賃貸仲介はもちろん、
デザイナーによる独自の賃貸住宅をご提案。
購入や新築をお考えのお客さまには、
コンサルティングから始まる
トータルコーディネートを通じて、
あなたに合った土地、
あなたに合った家づくりをご提案いたします。
不動産、建築のあらゆるお悩みを
解決するために。
あなたの“ああしたいこうしたい”を
ぜひお聞かせください。

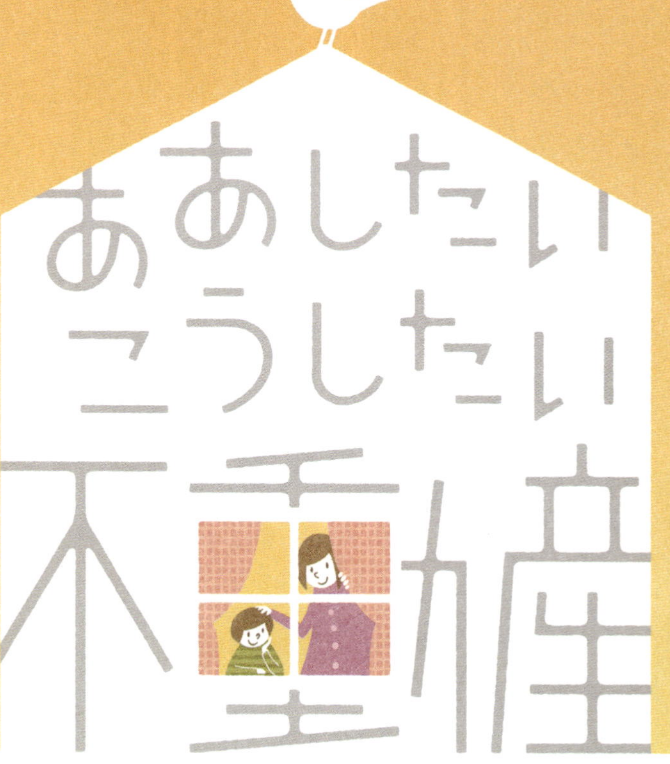

RE-NOBLE
CONSULTING

株式会社リノーブル 東京都世田谷区弦巻4-24-12 インエクスビル1F tel 03 5799 7063 株式会社インエクス建築工房 東京都世田谷区弦巻4-24-12 インエクスビルB1F tel 03 6383 0160

Client: RE-NOBLE CONSULTING. AD, D, I: Hiroyuki Nakamura.

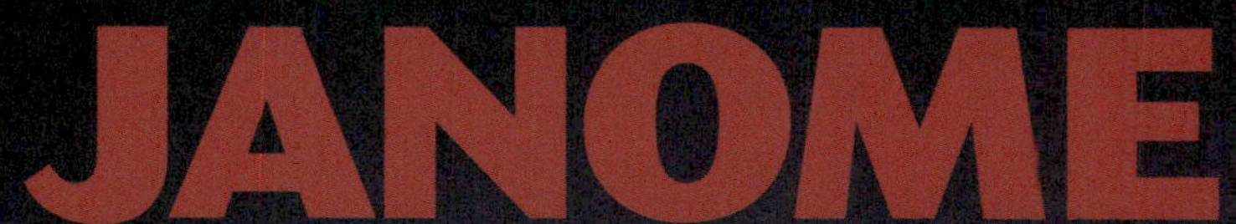

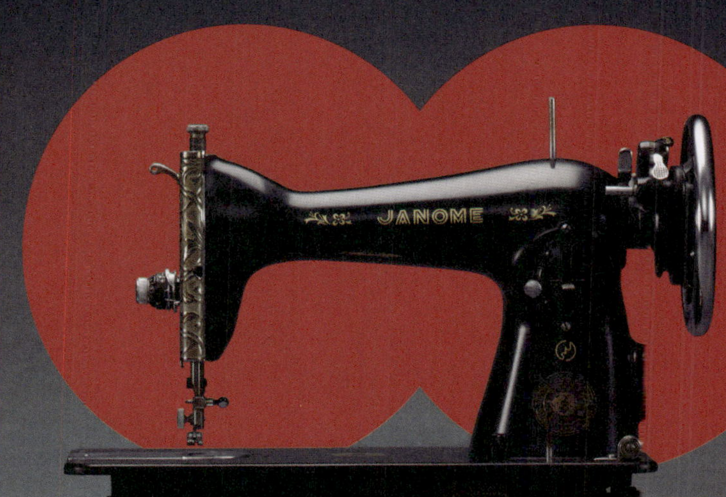

YEARS
since 1921

1921年、蛇の目ミシン工業は、日本初の国産ミシンメーカーとして創業。
手廻しミシンでひと針目をスタートした私たちは、
日々、お客さまによろこんでいただくための製品づくりに向き合ってきました。
手廻しだったミシンは、電動へ、コンピューター制御へ。
今日では誰もが手軽に使える家庭用ミシンを、世界中にお届けしています。
大きく変わりゆく時代のなかを、ともに歩みつづけてくださったお客さまに感謝を。
そして創業100周年である節目に、私たちは新たなスタートを切りました。
2021年10月、蛇の目ミシン工業は「ジャノメ」へ。
“つくる”を楽しく、“つくるを支える”をもっと。
皆さんのものづくりに寄り添った商品やサービスを提供する総合企業として、
これからも挑戦をつづけます。

創業100周年を迎え、
「蛇の目ミシン工業」は「ジャノメ」へと社名変更しました。

www.janome.co.jp

Client: JANOME Corporation. CD, AD, D: Hiroyuki Nakamura. D: Hikari Maesaka. C: Shu Morihira. PH: Tetsuro Ikejima.

クリエイティブが日本の切り札。

J

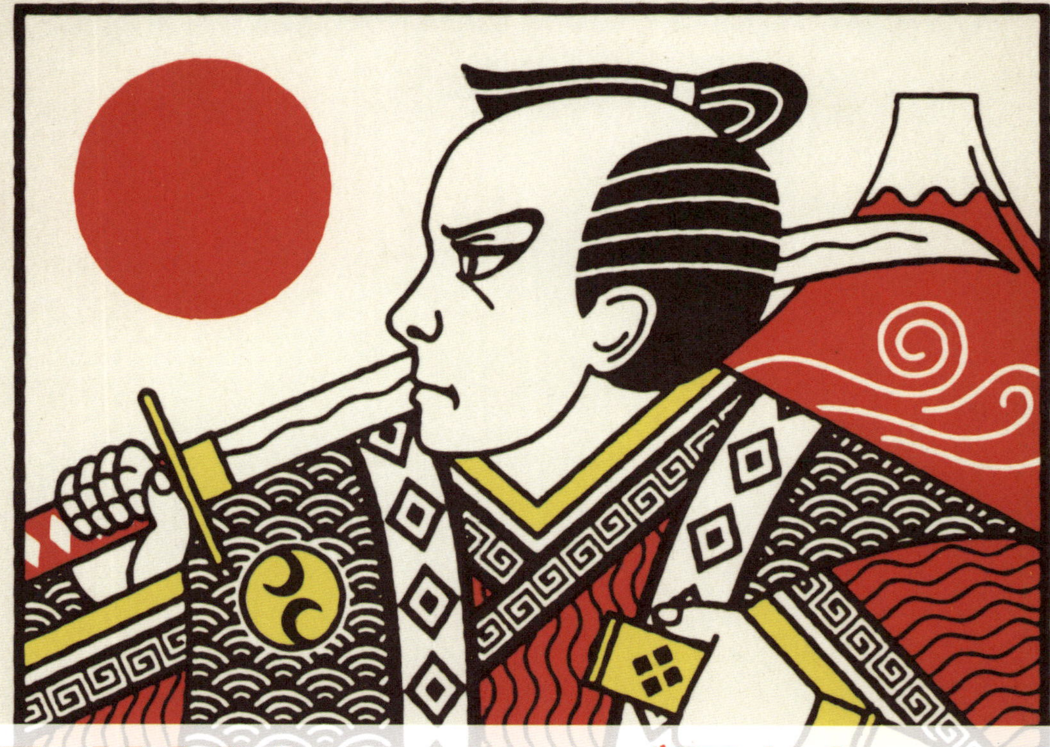

第68回 JAAAクリエイティブ研究会

「日本の未来と21世紀のクリエイティビティー」

スピーカー：レイ・イナモト（AKQA チーフクリエイティブオフィサー）　モデレーター：河尻亨一（元「広告批評」編集長）

日時：平成25年2月28日（木）13:00〜15:00（開場12:30）　場所：ヤクルトホール（港区東新橋1-1-19）

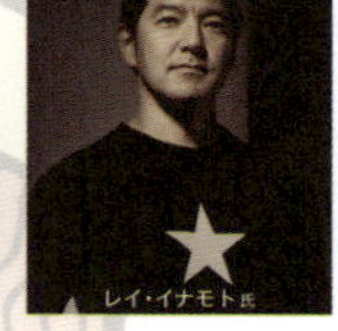

◆コーディネーター：戸澤清彦（日本経済社 シニアクリエイティブディレクター）　◆主催：日本広告業協会 クリエイティブ委員会　◆参加費：一般3,150円 会員2,100円 学生1,050円（定員500名になり次第締切）　◆お申し込み方法：［会員・一般］事務局宛に所定用紙でお申し込み後、お振込みいただき、事務局よりチケットを送付。［一般・学生］「チケットぴあ」での購入。0570-02-9999（10:00AM〜18:00PM）Pコード〈623−026〉　◆お問い合わせ先：日本広告業協会 〒104-0061 東京都中央区銀座7-4-17電通銀座ビル8F TEL:03-5568-0876 FAX:03-5568-0889

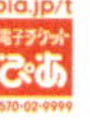

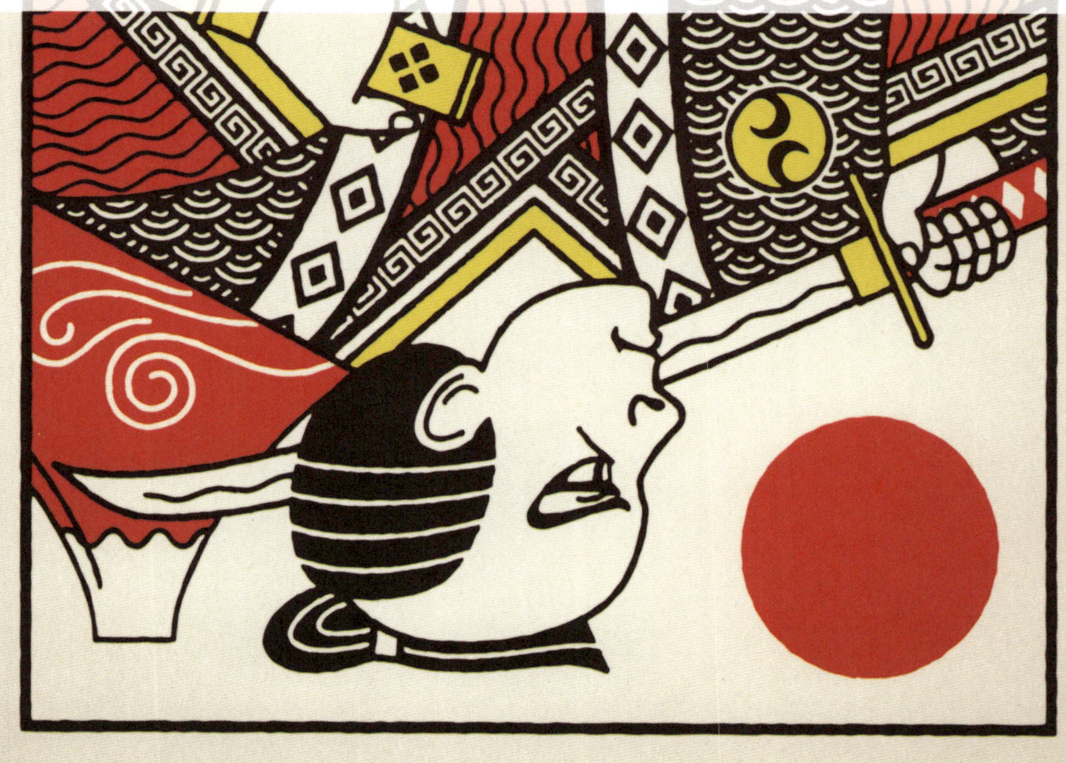

J

Client: Japan Advertising Agencies Association. CD: Kiyohiko Tozawa. AD, D, I: Hiroyuki Nakamura. C: Naoto Miyazaki.

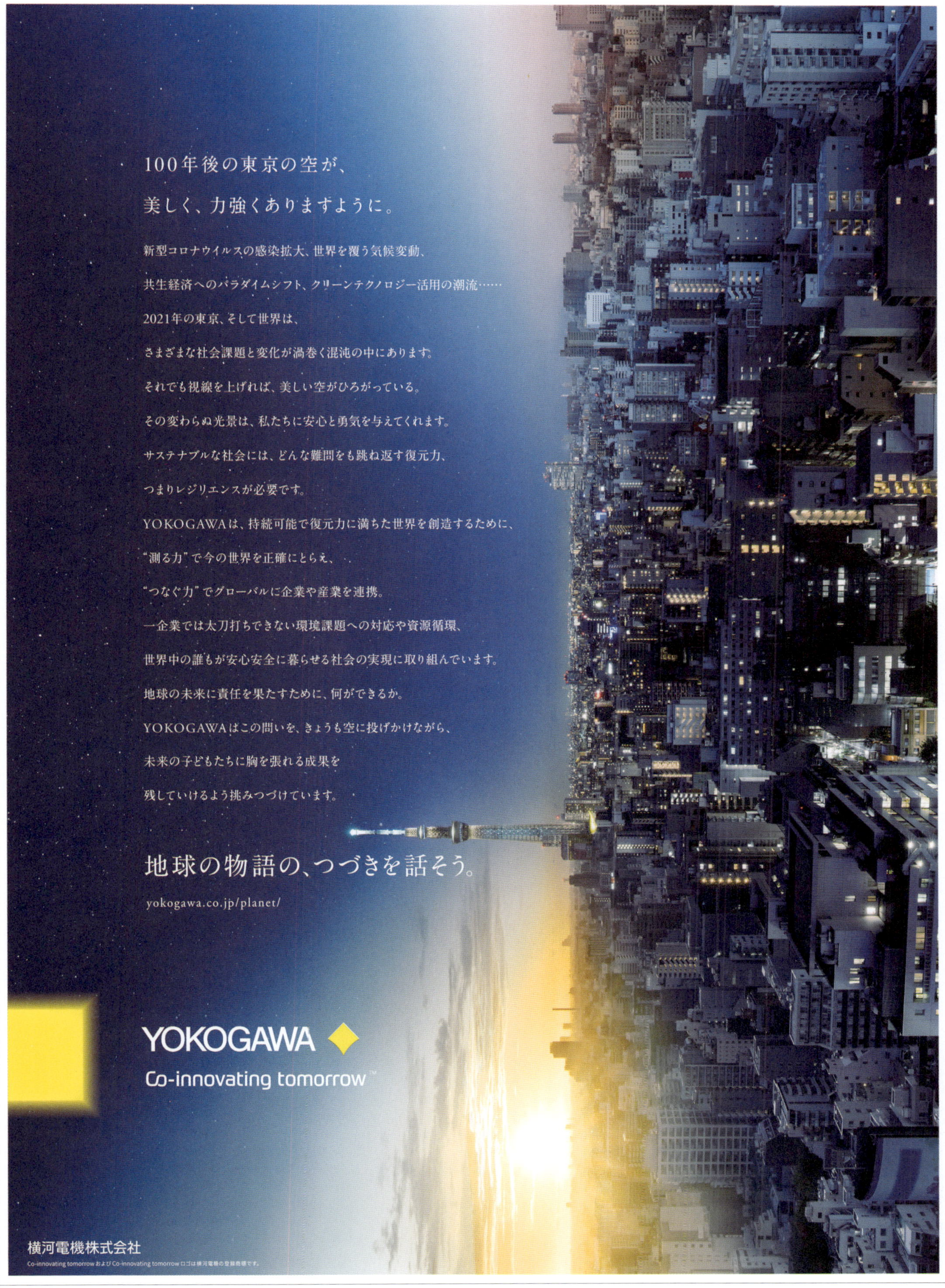

Client: Yokogawa Electric Corporation. CD, AD, D: Hiroyuki Nakamura. D: Hikari Maesaka. C: Takeshi Wakabayashi. PH: Kazuya Hokari.

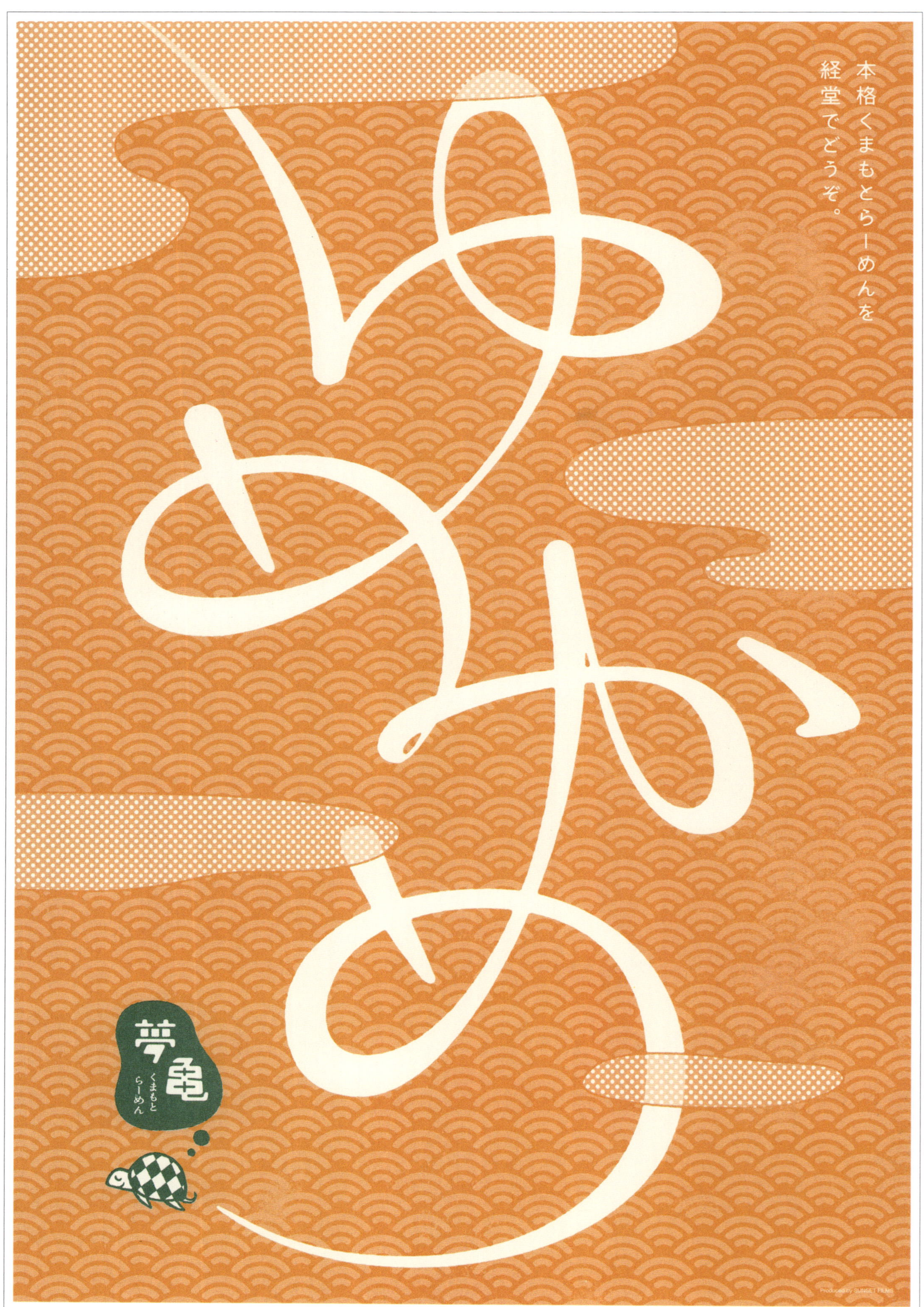

Client: Yumekame. AD, D, I: Hiroyuki Nakamura.

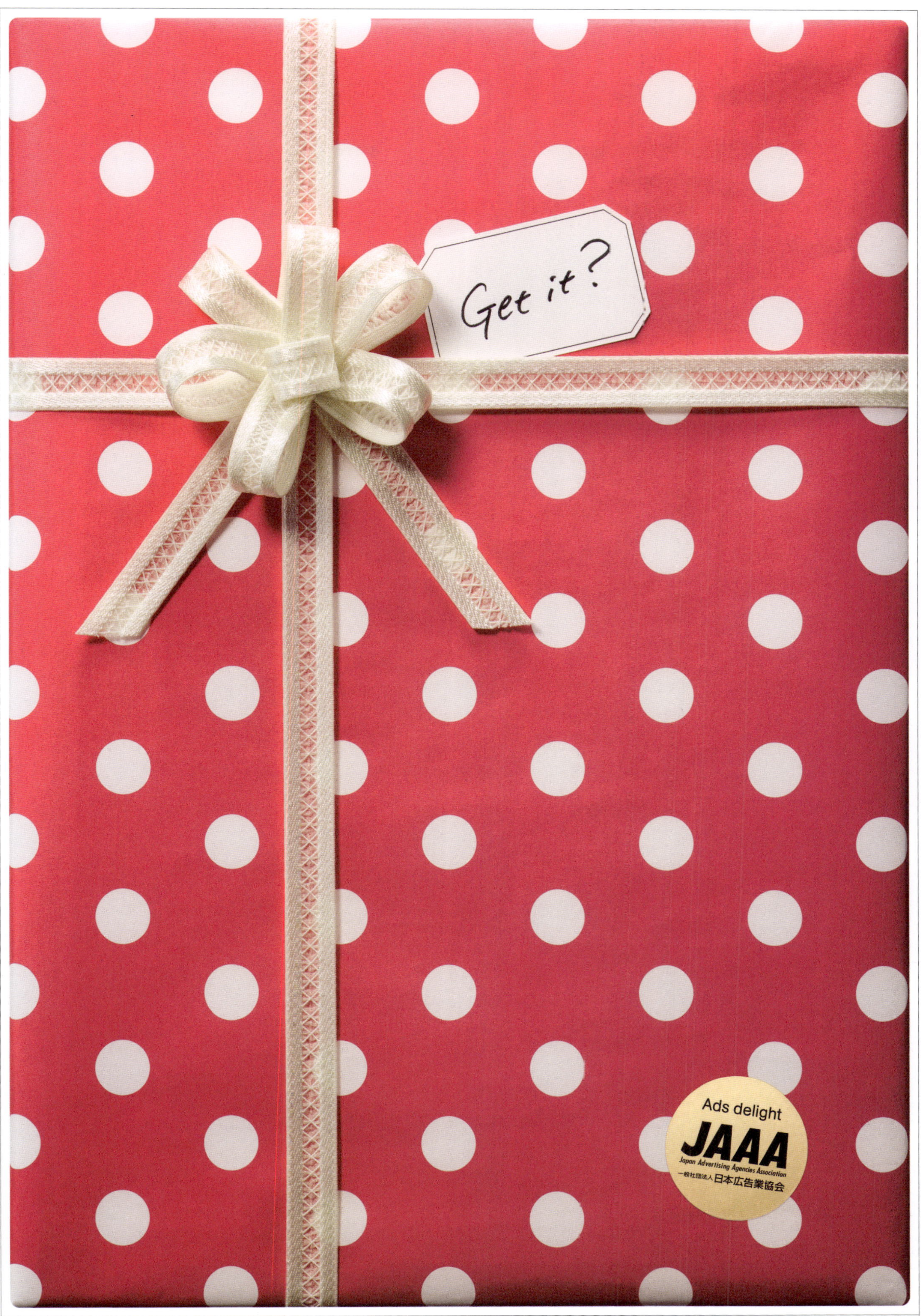

(Page 45 & Above) Client: Japan Advertising Agencies Association. CD: Hidetaka Sugiyama. AD, D: Hircyuki Nakamura. C: Naoto Miyazaki. PH: Tetsuro Ikejima.

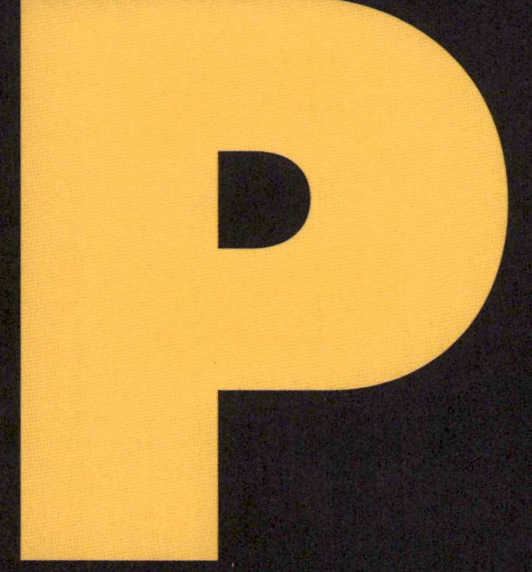

PHOTOGRAPHY

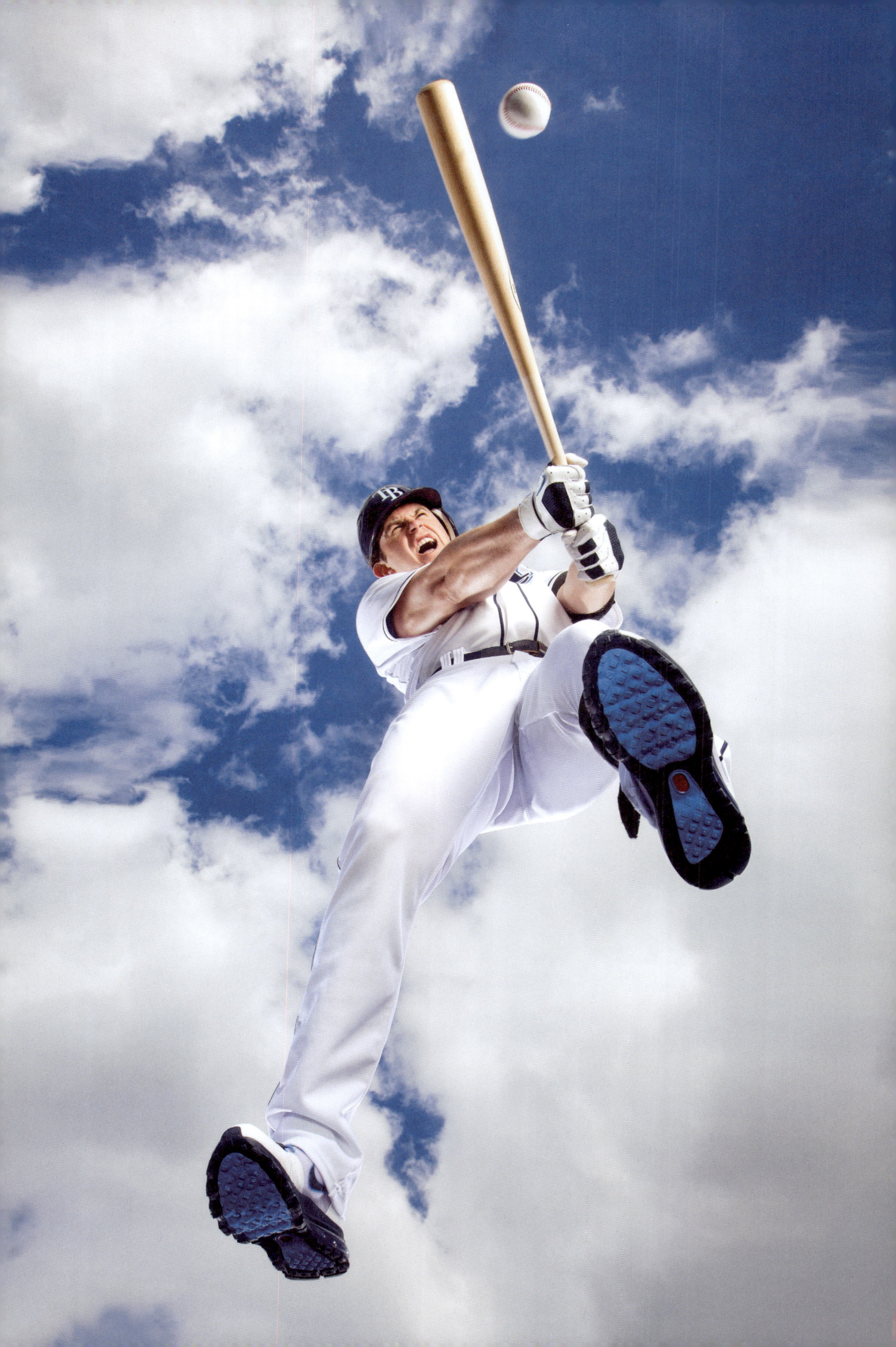

Robert Seale: Making the Mundane Interesting

THERE ARE FEW PHOTOGRAPHERS WORKING TODAY WHO CAN COMBINE THE TECHNICAL WITH THE AESTHETICAL AND PRODUCE IMAGES THAT TRANSCEND THE COMMERCIAL WORLD TO THAT OF FINE ART. ROBERT SEALE IS ONE OF THEM.

Arthur Meyerson, *Photographer, Arthur Meyerson Photography*

WHETHER ROBERT IS IN THE STUDIO OR IN SOME REMOTE LOCATION, HIS ATTENTION TO DETAIL AND LIGHTING IS EXQUISITE.

Sandro Miller, *Photographer, SANDRO, INC.*

ROBERT'S PORTRAITS ARE MODERN ICONOGRAPHS.

Doug Menuez, *Photographer & Director, Menuez Pictures, LLC*

ROBERT'S IMAGES REVEAL INTIMATE STORIES TOLD THROUGH THE LANDSCAPES THEY OCCUPY AND THE EMOTIONAL WEIGHT THEY CARRY.

Mark Seliger, *Photographer, Mark Seliger Photography*

WITH THE EYE OF A GREAT DESIGNER, ROBERT'S COMPOSITIONS DRAW YOU IN AND COMPEL YOU TO LOOK WELL PAST THE SURFACE.

RJ Muna, *Photographer, RJ Muna Pictures*

EQUALLY COMFORTABLE ON JOB SITES OR IN BOARDROOMS, ROBERT EXCELS AT CAPTURING PEOPLE IN THEIR ENVIRONMENTS.

John Luu, *Multimedia Advisor, ExxonMobil*

HE TRANSFORMS PORTRAITS INTO REFLECTIONS OF PERSONALITY AND ART—HIS WORK IS BOTH MASTERFUL AND DEEPLY INSPIRING.

Keith Ladzinski, *Photographer, National Geographic*

(Page 63) Tampa Bay Rays Evan Longoria portrait on Plexiglas in Pt. Charlotte, Florida on Tuesday, March 15, 2011. / (Opposite page) SLB offshore technology project, Houma, Louisiana.

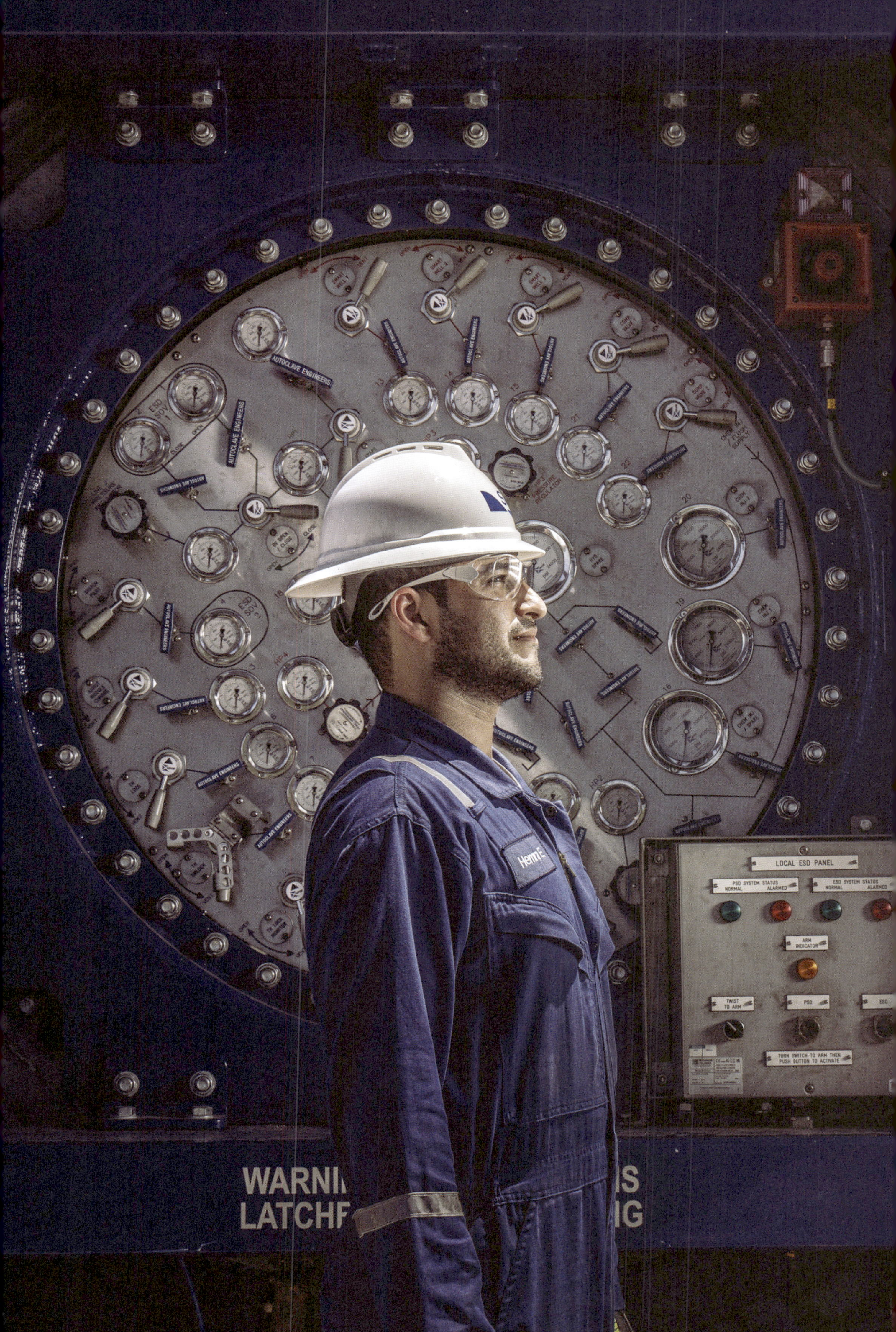
AUTOCLAVE ENGINEERS
LOCAL ESD PANEL
PSD SYSTEM STATUS
NORMAL ALARMED
ESD SYSTEM STATUS
NORMAL ALARMED
ARM INDICATOR
TWIST TO ARM
PSD
ESD
TURN SWITCH TO ARM THEN PUSH BUTTON TO ACTIVATE
WARNIN IS
LATCHF IG

Introduction by Quinn Stewart

Senior Graphic Design & Multimedia Specialist, Corporate Communications, W. R. Grace & Co.

I had the pleasure of working with Robert on several projects where our goal was to reflect on how our employees set our company apart. Robert's breadth of industry knowledge was helpful as he understood how to navigate a manufacturing environment. His eye for composition and technical precision was valuable in conveying our complex environments and the people within them accurately and with humanity. The work he helped us produce showcased our company in the professional light we were looking for, and Robert's experience ensured we did so with no interruption to our site's operations.

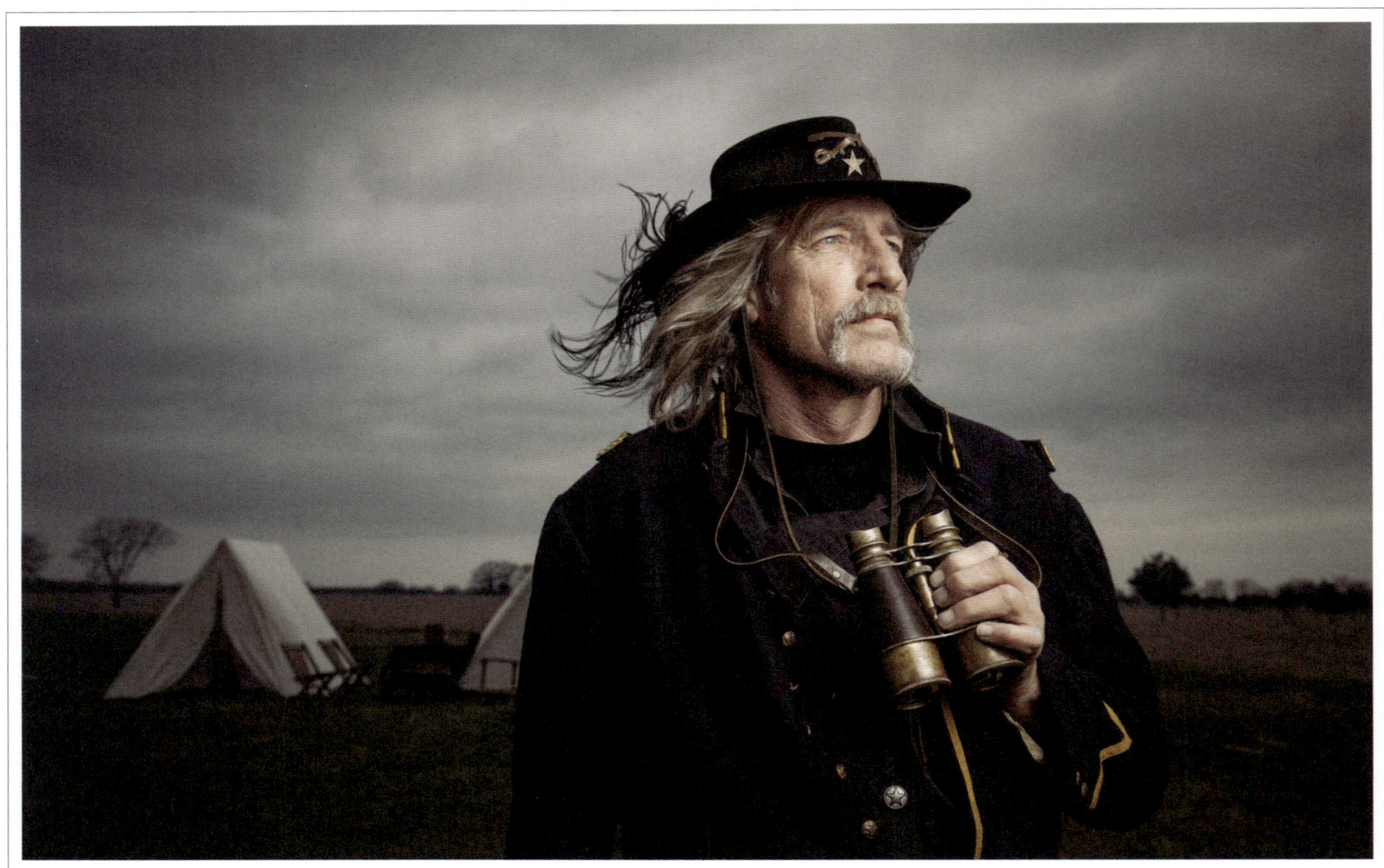

(Above) Howard R. Green, Major, Union Army "Redlegs" before the Civil War reenactment by the 3rd Texas Cavalry and other units recreating the Battle of El Camino Real at Mosser Longhorn Ranch in Midway, Texas on Saturday, February 9, 2013.
(Opposite page) Annual report image of two giant chemical plant modules, constructed in Asia and delivered by barge to the GCGV project in South Texas, USA.
(Page 69) Annual report image of a tanker undergoing sea trials in the Gulf of Mexico during commissioning.

Q&A: Robert Seale

What inspired you to pursue a career in photography, and how has that motivation evolved over time?

In school, I was good at art and drawing, and I had an aptitude for science and math. Because of that, my counselors and parents thought I should be an architect, and I initially headed in that direction. But after talking to a lot of people and visiting an architecture school, it became clear that there were only so many Philip Johnsons in the world designing cool skyscrapers. Most architects spent their lives indoors, in cubicles, deciding which way the bathroom doors should swing—LOL. When my architecture bubble burst, I turned to photography. I had previously worked at a one-hour photo lab and was on the yearbook staff as a photographer in high school. Those experiences really encouraged me to pursue that path.

What was your path to the photography business you run now?

I graduated college with a double major in journalism and art and immediately landed an internship at a large metro newspaper, which led to a staff photographer job at a paper for three or four years. I then went to work for the *Sporting News*, a national weekly sports magazine founded in 1886. I worked there as a staffer for 11 years, traveling all over the country, shooting Super Bowls, Final Fours, and NBA games. We also did a lot of portraits for covers and features, so I really dove into lighting and worked to refine my portrait skills.

Eventually, I left to start my own commercial business—partly because I aspired to be a contractor for *Sports Illustrated* but also because I wanted to take on diverse assignments in different industries. I thought my skills would translate well to athletic apparel companies, and I've had some success there. But honestly, I've done even better in the industrial space.

How would you describe your philosophy on taking photographs?

My philosophy has always been to take the mundane and make it interesting or different—to see things others might not notice. When I worked in newspapers, most photographers dreaded "wild art" assignments (newspaper-speak for stand-alone feature photos). They needed a story and a formal assignment

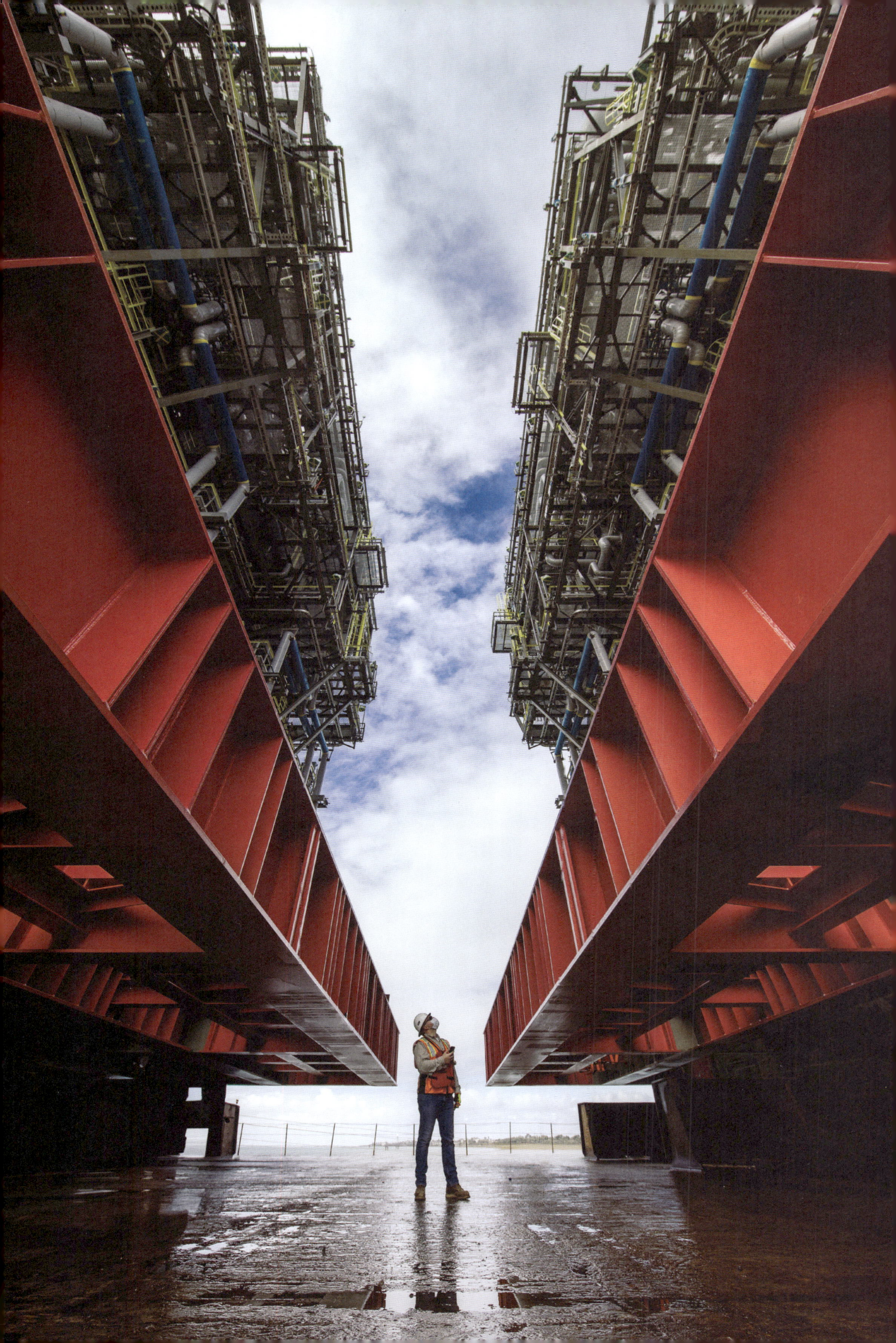

to thrive. I actually loved the freedom of trying to turn nothing into something and was successful at finding graphic feature photos where others saw chaos. Sometimes, that meant using long lenses to compress backgrounds, shooting from unexpected angles, or just camping out in a spot with great lines, architecture, or color and waiting for something to happen in that little sliver of the world.

Which contemporaries do you most admire, and who deserves a wider audience?
It varies by genre:

- Commercial: Doug Menuez—because he hasn't been pigeonholed into a single style or industry. People hire him for his unique vision. Joe McNally is another—he can shoot for a trucking company or a ballet company, and it'll always be beautifully lit and interesting.
- Outdoor: Keith Ladzinski is incredibly prolific and consistently creates stunning work. He's also one of the nicest, most humble people around.
- Photojournalism: I admire Kansas City AP photographer Charlie Riedel. Most AP photographers are just-the-facts types, but Charlie has a distinctive point of view that's as graphically sophisticated as Jay Maisel's best.

What other photographers or artists do you turn to for inspiration?
Gregory Heisler, Albert Watson, Richard Avedon, Arnold Newman, Annie Leibovitz, Pete Turner, Jay Maisel, Herb Ritts, Patrick Demarchelier, Arthur Meyerson, RJ Muna, Sandro Miller, Michael O'Brien, Walter Iooss, Frank Ockenfels III, Mark Seliger, and Dan Winters.

In what ways does your personal life influence your work behind the lens?
Though I seem calm on the outside, maybe there's something to having Larry David-level anxiety—it keeps me prepared for anything. I play tennis, I like to cook, and I play drums in an '80s cover band. If there's a personal/life influence, it's probably that combination of being organized, detail-oriented, and always ready with a healthy dose of worry.

Who has been your greatest mentor, and what impact have they had on your approach to photography?
I've had many mentors. Early on, my college photo professor, Dr. Michael Roach, was fantastic—he custom-tailored independent study classes for me since our school didn't have a traditional photo program. My university's student publications advisor, Pat Spence, was not only a wise mentor but also became a second mom to me. I worked with her for four years as the photo editor of the school newspaper and editor of the yearbook, and I maintained a close relationship with her until she passed away last year.

Then there were people who probably had no idea they were mentors—like Gregory Heisler and Walter Iooss—but they had just as much impact. I studied their work constantly and looked to them for guidance and inspiration, especially when I was working in sports magazines.

What piece of advice early on helped shape the way you shoot?
A few key moments come to mind:

- I once read an *American Photo* interview with William Albert Allard, where he scolded a student who complained about something distracting in the background of her photo. He basically said (paraphrasing), "Then why is it in the middle of your picture? You're responsible for every square inch of that space!" That stuck with me.
- A photo editor at the *Dallas Morning News* once told me, "The knees are the most important piece of photo equipment." In other words, don't shoot everything from six feet off the ground—bend your knees, lie down, climb a ladder, and find a new angle.
- *Miami Herald* shooter Jeffery Salter once told me to "saw the hot shoe off my camera." His point was that light is almost always more interesting when it doesn't come directly from the top of your camera. That sparked my deeper exploration of lighting.

What guidance and advice would you offer to students and emerging photographers today?
Study art history and photo history so you can reference the masters who came before you. Look at everything you can find and try to reverse-engineer how it was done. Study cinematography and film, and learn to shoot video. Also, invest time in learning marketing, business, advertising, PR, social media, graphic design, web design, and audio. It's tough to be just a photographer these days—having additional skills will serve you well.

What do you love most about photography, and how does that passion inform your work?
If I have a superpower, it's finding something aesthetically pleasing in situations where no one else sees anything. I love the challenge of starting with nothing—sometimes an ugly or chaotic scene—and problem-solving my way to a clean, compelling result. I enjoy wrangling chaos into something artful.

Can you describe your photography style in one word? What sets it apart from others?
I can't describe it in just one word, but I strive for images that are heroic, graphic, well-designed, and always artfully lit.

What's your go-to camera and why—and how has your equipment evolved over the course of your career?
These days, I primarily use the Canon R5. In my early *Sporting News* days, we used manual focus cameras and shot portraits on Hasselblads. I've been using Canon digital systems since the early 2000s and have stuck with them as the gear has evolved.

You're known for creating multiple creative concepts from a single location with limited time. How do you pull that off?
That skill traces back to my days at the *Sporting News*. We needed a lot of images for each story—cover, opening spread, inside photo, table of contents—often from a single, short shoot with a pro athlete. Since athletes don't have much time, I developed the ability to scout a location quickly and find one spot where I could set up multiple lighting options. Then, I'd rotate the athlete, change the light setups, or shift a few feet to get several unique looks without moving too much or losing their attention.

Every time you stop to adjust a light, switch a lens, or change a location, you risk losing the subject's focus. So, I would have everything set, tested, and choreographed in advance. Even with just two or three minutes, I could usually get several setups from one area. That experience has been invaluable for shoots with celebrities and CEOs.

With your venture into video work, how do you balance and blend the disciplines of still photography and filmmaking?
We often create a B-roll that mimics the stills we're shooting. I'm rarely in a position to hire a full video crew of 30 people. Usually, we add a few key team members when doing video: another DP (whom I'll direct), maybe a drone operator, or an audio tech. In many cases, I shoot the video content myself, switching between stills and motion—which is tricky with different cameras, lights, and rigs. Sometimes, I wish I had eight arms.

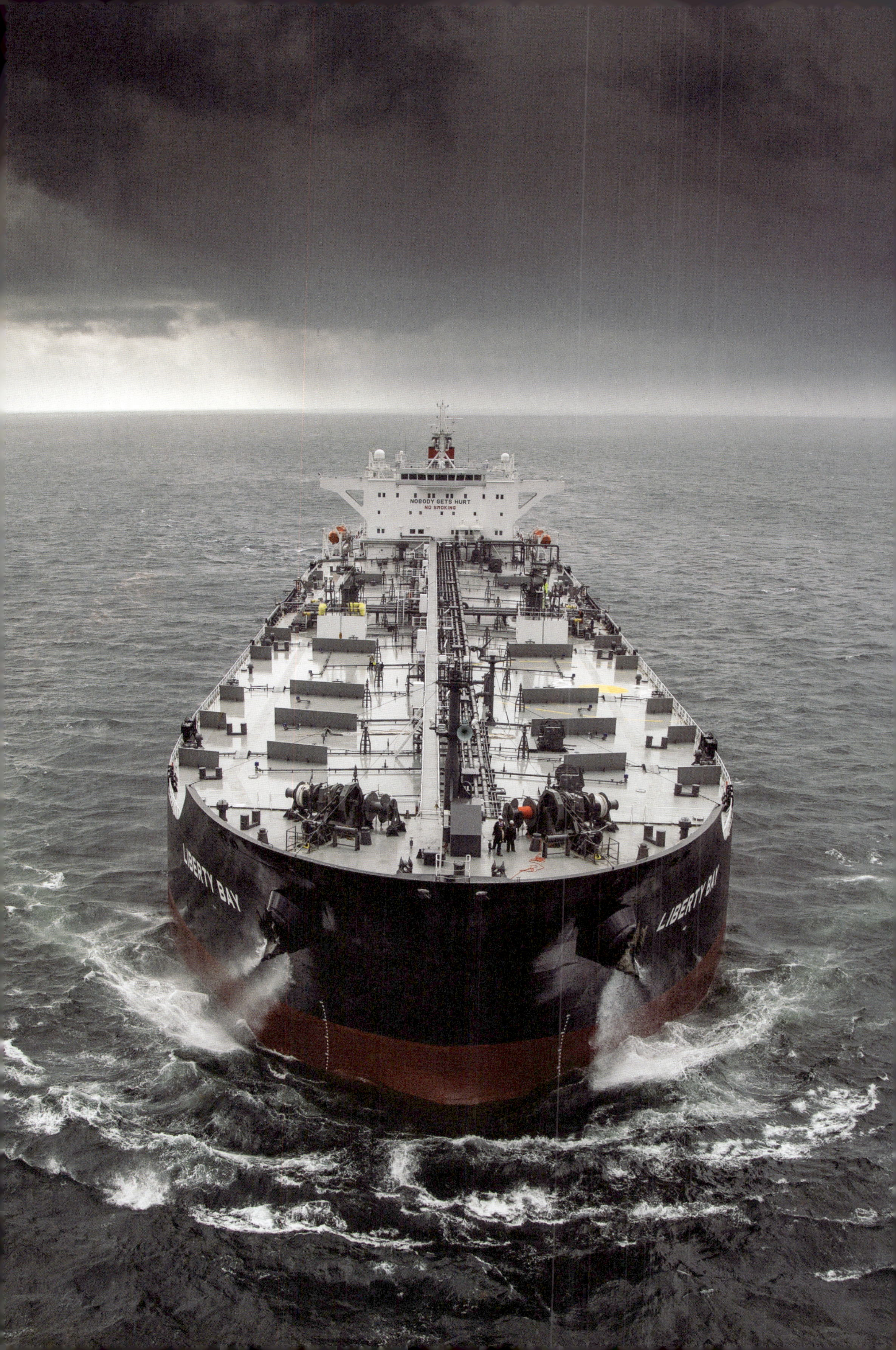
NOBODY GETS HURT
NO SMOKING
LIBERTY BAY
LIBERTY BAY

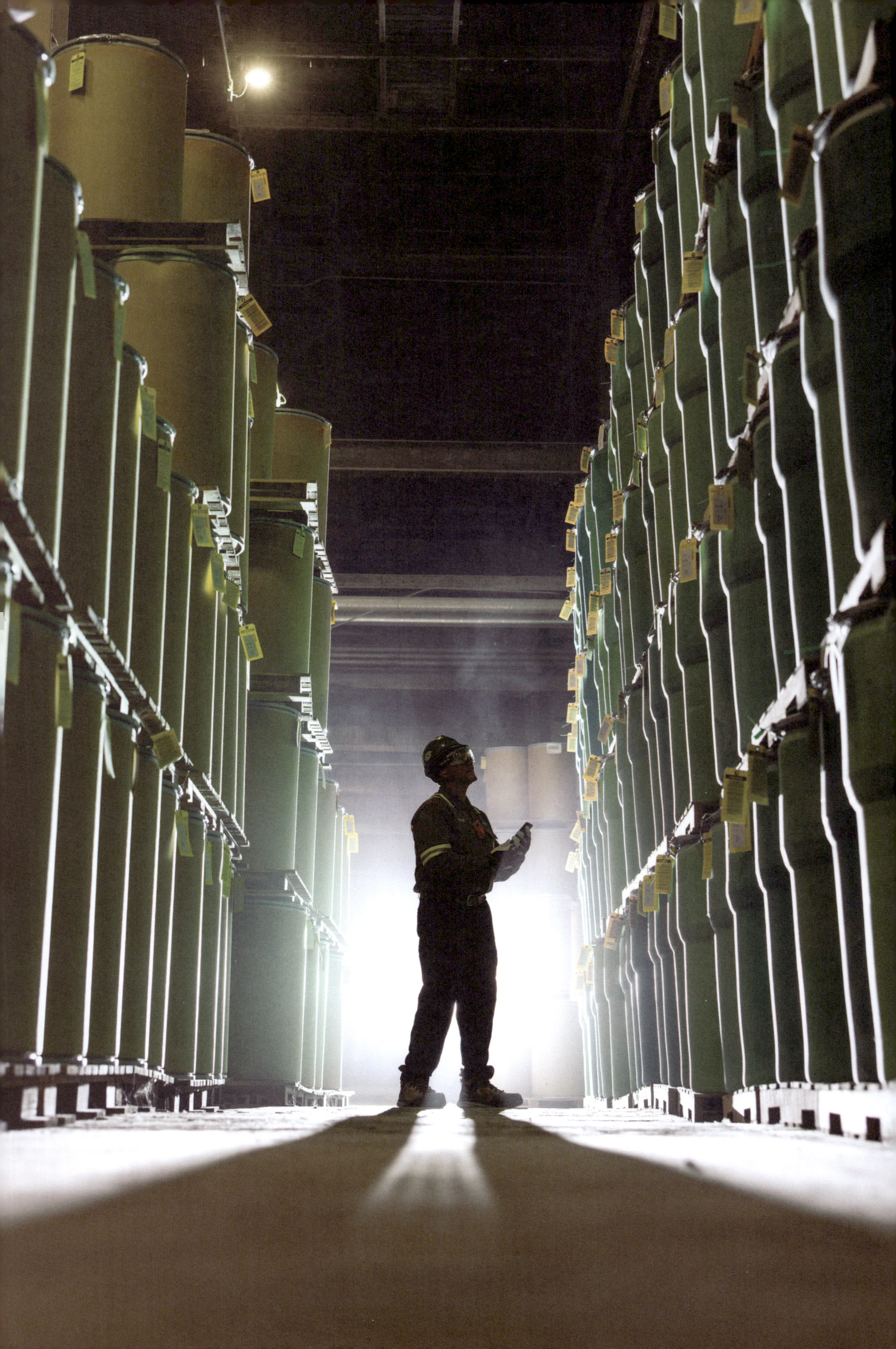

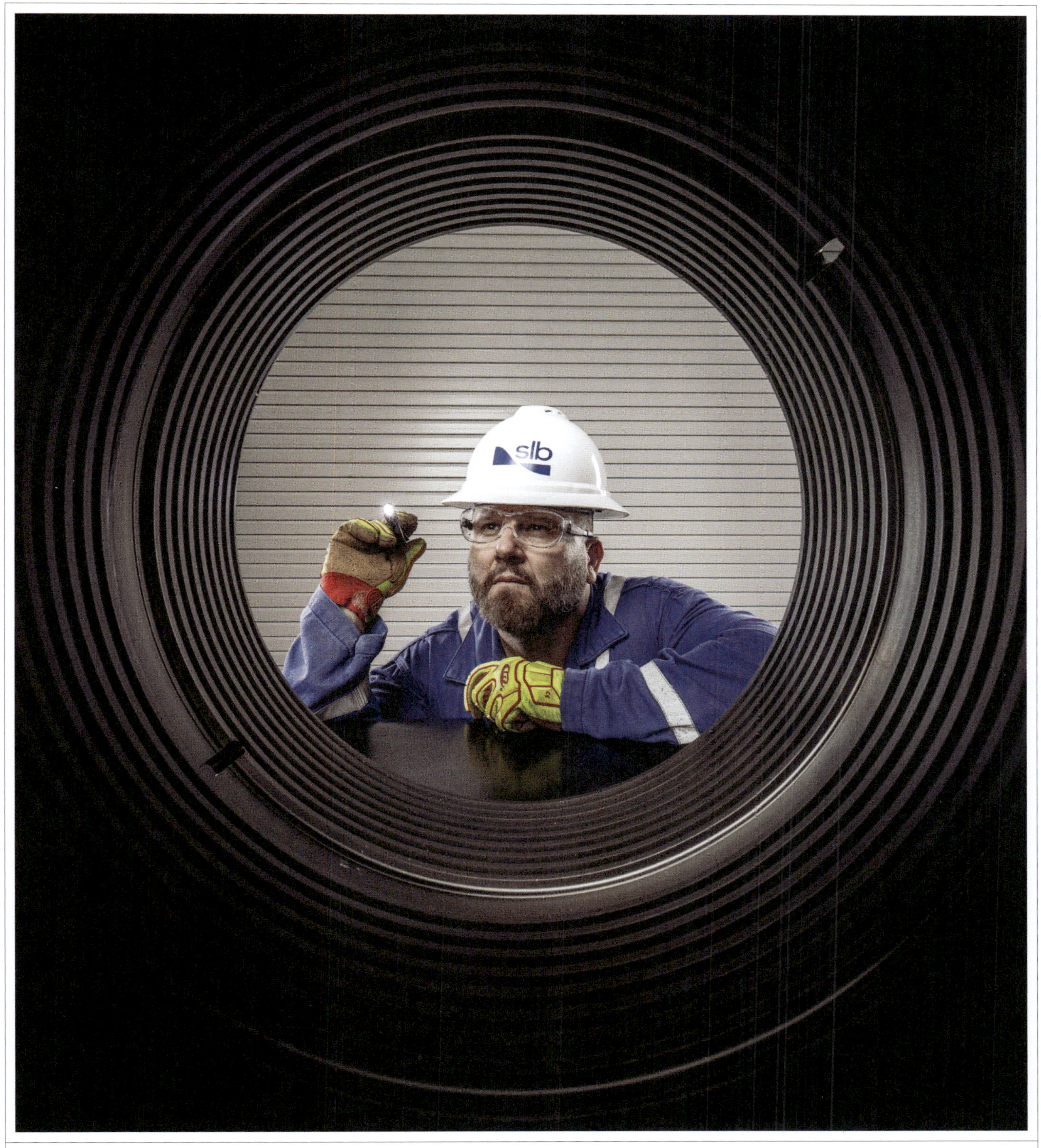

(Above) SLB offshore technology project, Houma, Louisiana. / (Opposige page) W. R. Grace facility in Curtis Bay, Maryland.

Your portfolio spans industrial subjects and corporate culture. How did you begin shooting for oil and gas companies, and what draws you to that work?

I grew up near Houston, where oil and gas companies were always a big part of the economy. During college summers, I wore a hard hat and steel-toed boots and worked in that industry, so I was already familiar with the environment. After college, I started as a photojournalist at newspapers and eventually moved into sports magazines. When I left my staff job at the *Sporting News*, I assembled a portfolio—mainly portraits of athletes—and reached out to top designers in Houston, including Jerry Herring of Herring Design. He took a chance on me and gave me some annual report assignments, which in Houston often involve the energy industry.

At the same time, I began shooting for business magazines in New York (*Barron's, Forbes*, etc.), and a few of those assignments led to contacts at oil companies. Eventually, I was asked to contribute to their annual reports.

Annual reports and corporate imagery can be challenging—how do you infuse these images with life and interest?

I think my background in photojournalism—especially the "feature-hunting" side—helps tremendously. In any industrial setting, I can usually find a strong graphic element or well-designed environment for the subject to interact with. Instead of posing people stiffly, I ask them to show me what they do: how they work, move, or operate their equipment. Then, I try to capture that naturally.

It's not pure documentary—we'll often repeat actions or re-light scenes—but that approach feels authentic and puts people at ease. I also like shooting people in pairs so they can walk and talk together. It makes them forget they're being photographed, and the resulting images feel much more genuine.

You've collaborated with major names—from ExxonMobil and Pepsi to Under Armour and Sports Illustrated. How do you approach projects for such institutions, and what have you learned from those experiences?

These fall into three very different categories: corporate, advertising, and editorial.

- Corporate (like ExxonMobil) often involves just me and a small team working on location to build an image library.
- Advertising (like Pepsi or Under Armour) tends to include larger crews, tighter shot lists, limited licensing, and clients watching live via a digital tech station.
- Editorial (like *Sports Illustrated*) might involve just me or one assistant, with a mix of reportage, portraits, and action—usually with a small footprint and lots of creative freedom.

Each type requires a different mindset and level of production, and learning to navigate those differences has been essential.

Reflecting on your career, which client relationships have most resonated with your photographic point of view?

Definitely my editorial work for sports magazines like the *Sporting News* and *Sports Illustrated.* I worked closely with directors of photography and photo editors who really let me use my full skill set. They trusted me. Typically, they'd give me an assignment, and I'd fly out, spend time with the subject, and bring back the story. There was minimal micromanaging—they knew I'd deliver.

A classic assignment might include game coverage (sometimes multiple games), documentary-style images of an athlete at home or in training, and a couple of setup portraits. Over time, as print space became more limited, we did fewer setups—but early on, we did full coverage like that for most features.

On the corporate side, I've also had great long-term relationships where clients would give me a basic brief and send me around the world to photograph offshore rigs, ships, new facilities, etc. That kind of trust and creative freedom is incredibly rewarding.

What has been your most memorable project to date, and what makes it stand out?

There have been several. During my newspaper career, I was sent to South Africa to shoot a swimsuit issue for the fashion section. At the *Sporting News*, I once flew around the country photographing nine famous baseball players in vintage 1930s uniforms with antique gloves for a black-and-white portrait essay on "throwback players."

For a corporate annual report, I traveled to northern Alberta to photograph massive mining trucks at an oil sands facility, with the aurora borealis in the background. I climbed the side of giant Q-Max tankers in Qatar via rope ladder in the dark to catch the sunrise from the bridge as they entered port.

I also worked on brochures for a major healthcare system in Texas, where I shot everything from cancer researchers and portraits of top doctors to real surgeries—including a kidney transplant and open-skull brain surgery while the patient was awake. I've been very lucky to experience so many incredible and unusual assignments.

Can you share a current project that excites you and why it holds special appeal?

I've always had a love for aviation, and for several years now, I've been photographing legendary pilots. A standout experience was spending time with the Doolittle Raiders, including flying in a B-25 bomber with Col. Dick Cole (age 95 at the time), who was Jimmy Doolittle's co-pilot on the famous Tokyo raid. Once we were airborne, the pilot gave up his seat, and Cole flew the plane for a while. That experience led to more portraits of notable aviators, aces, and even astronauts.

How do you keep your photography and filmmaking relevant in an ever-evolving creative landscape?

This ties back to my earlier point about studying art history and understanding your visual predecessors. To stay relevant, I think it's crucial to look at a lot of work—not just in photography but in design, cinematography, and pop culture—and be aware of current visual trends. That doesn't mean blindly following them, but it does mean understanding what's resonating with audiences and art directors right now.

I've seen trends come and go—the red/blue gel craze of the late '80s, the ring flash era in the '90s, and the harsh beauty dish look of the early 2000s. Many of those styles were lighting-driven. Even if I'm going to follow my own creative instincts (and ideally aim for something more timeless), it's still important to know what's "in" and avoid looking out of step, especially with client work.

With AI on the rise, where do you see the future of photography heading—and what's your take on its role in the creative process?

I'm deeply concerned about how AI tools are being trained on our work without permission. If this were writing or music, we'd call it plagiarism. From a national security standpoint, the threat of fake AI-generated photojournalism is terrifying. We're entering an era where manipulated imagery could easily be used to spread misinformation or even provoke conflict.

That said, I do think there's a role for AI in ethical post-production—removing a powerline, fixing a background, and solving retouching problems. I hope there'll always be high-level clients who value authenticity and will want to commission real photography that's honest, crafted, and human.

What do you hope viewers take away from your photographs?

Whether it's a portrait of a famous athlete or an image of an engineer working inside a refinery, I want the viewer to come away with the sense that the subject is heroic, positive, and important. I strive to create work that is well-crafted, clean, confidently lit, and designed with a strong visual point of view. I want the image to feel elevated—almost cinematic—but always rooted in authenticity.

Looking ahead, are there any companies or projects you'd love to shoot for in the future?

Absolutely! Here are a few dream opportunities that align with my interests and style:

- Aviation/Aerospace: Boeing, RTX (Raytheon), Lockheed Martin, Honeywell, Ad Astra, SpaceX.
- Industrial Giants: Caterpillar, General Electric.
- US Air Force Campaign: A heroic portrait series featuring pilots and personnel for a recruiting campaign.
- Olympic Preview Issue: A set of dynamic, well-lit environmental portraits of top Olympic athletes across various sports.
- Texas Music Essay: A portrait series on legendary Texas musicians photographed in their hometowns or a meaningful location—artists like Lyle Lovett, Willie Nelson, Billy Gibbons, Gary Clark Jr., Scarface, Ray Benson, Steve Miller, George Strait, Beyoncé, Jimmie Vaughan, Flaco Jiménez, and others.

Robert Seale Photography www.robertseale.com

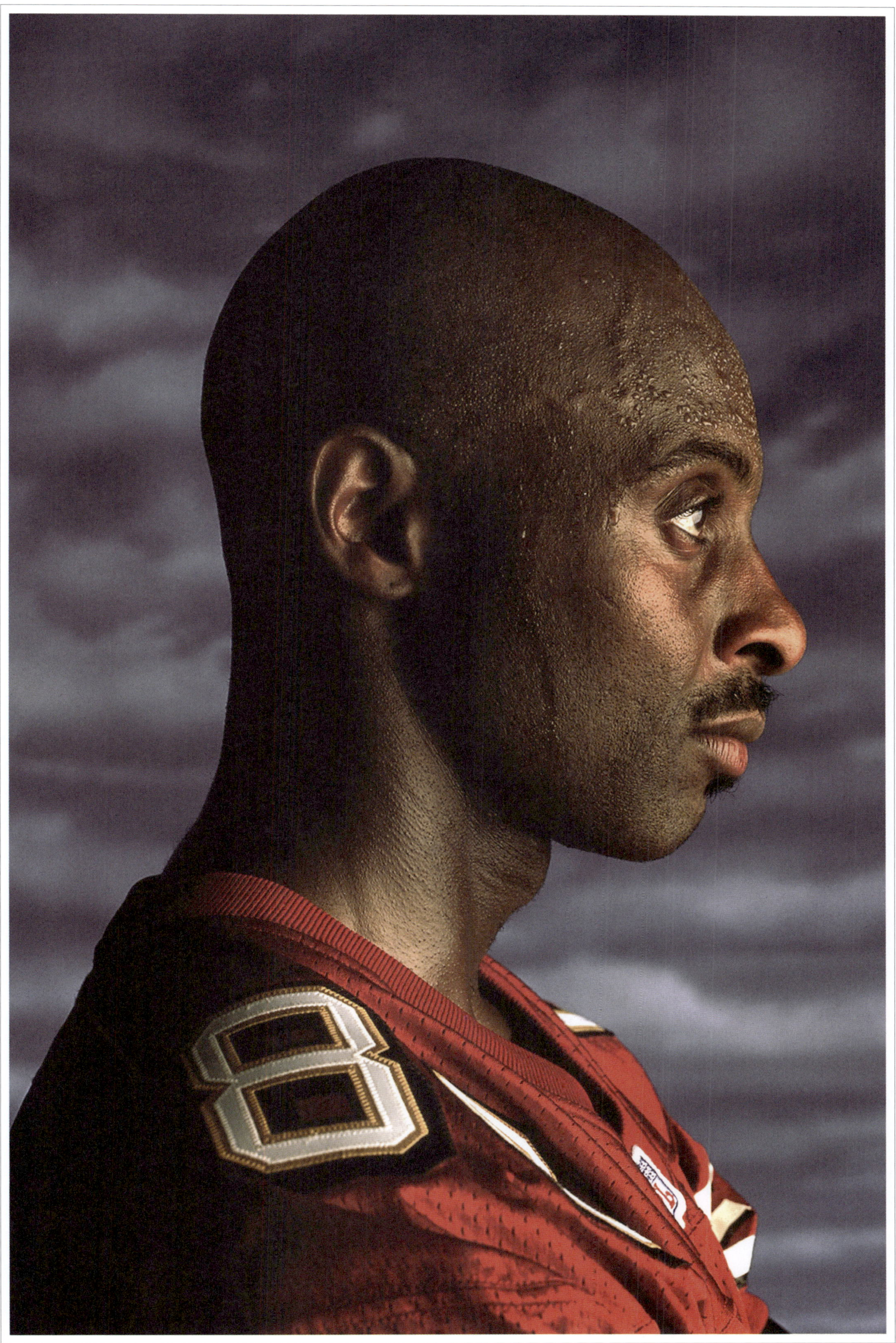

Portrait of football player Jerry Rice, San Francisco 49ers Hall of Fame receiver, in Stockton, California.

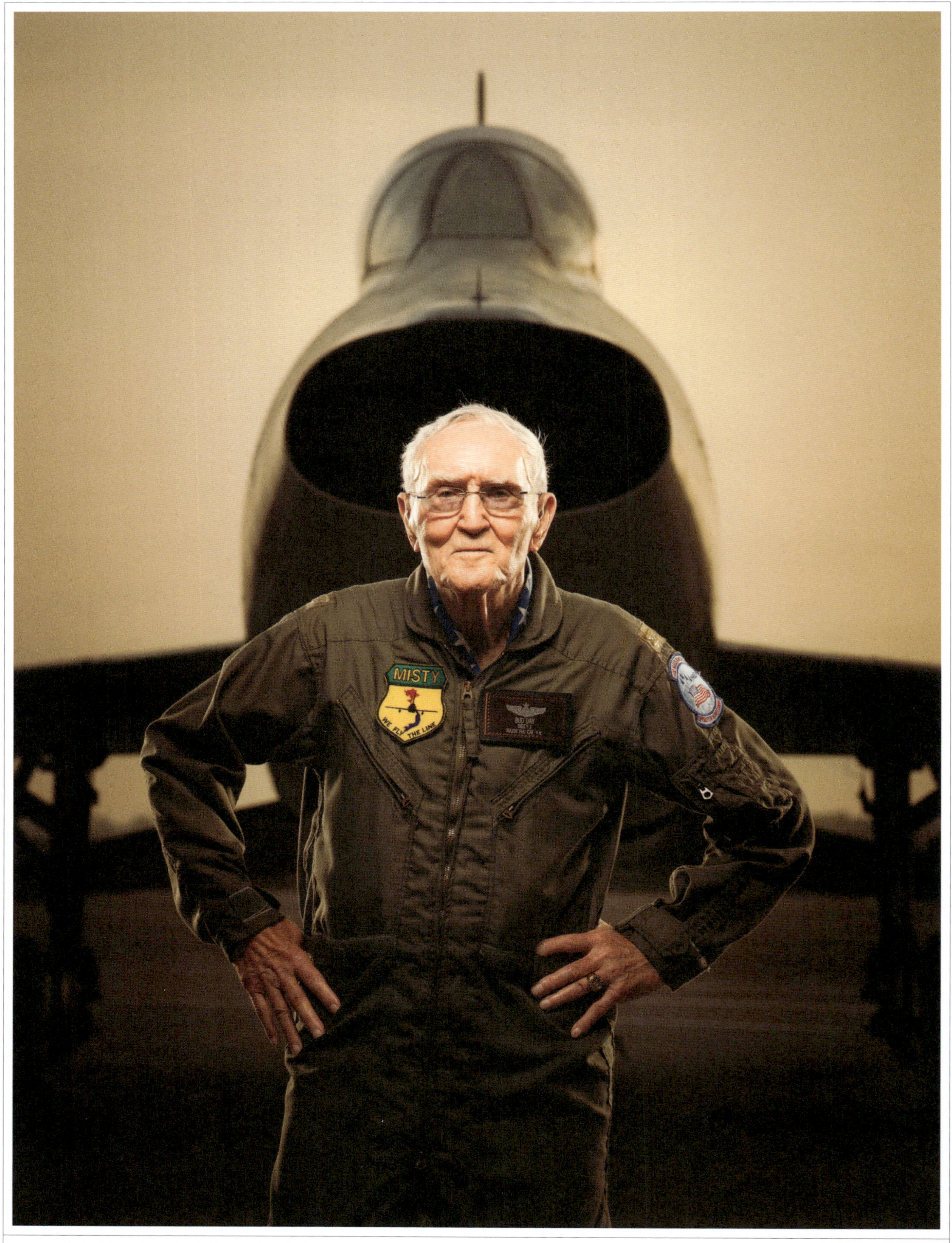

Retired US Air Force Col. Bud Day with the Collings Foundation North American F-100 Super Sabre at Ellington Field in Houston, Texas on Wednesday, June 6, 2012. Bud is a veteran of WWII, Korea, and Vietnam and was awarded the Congressional Medal of Honor after serving over five years as a POW in North Vietnam.

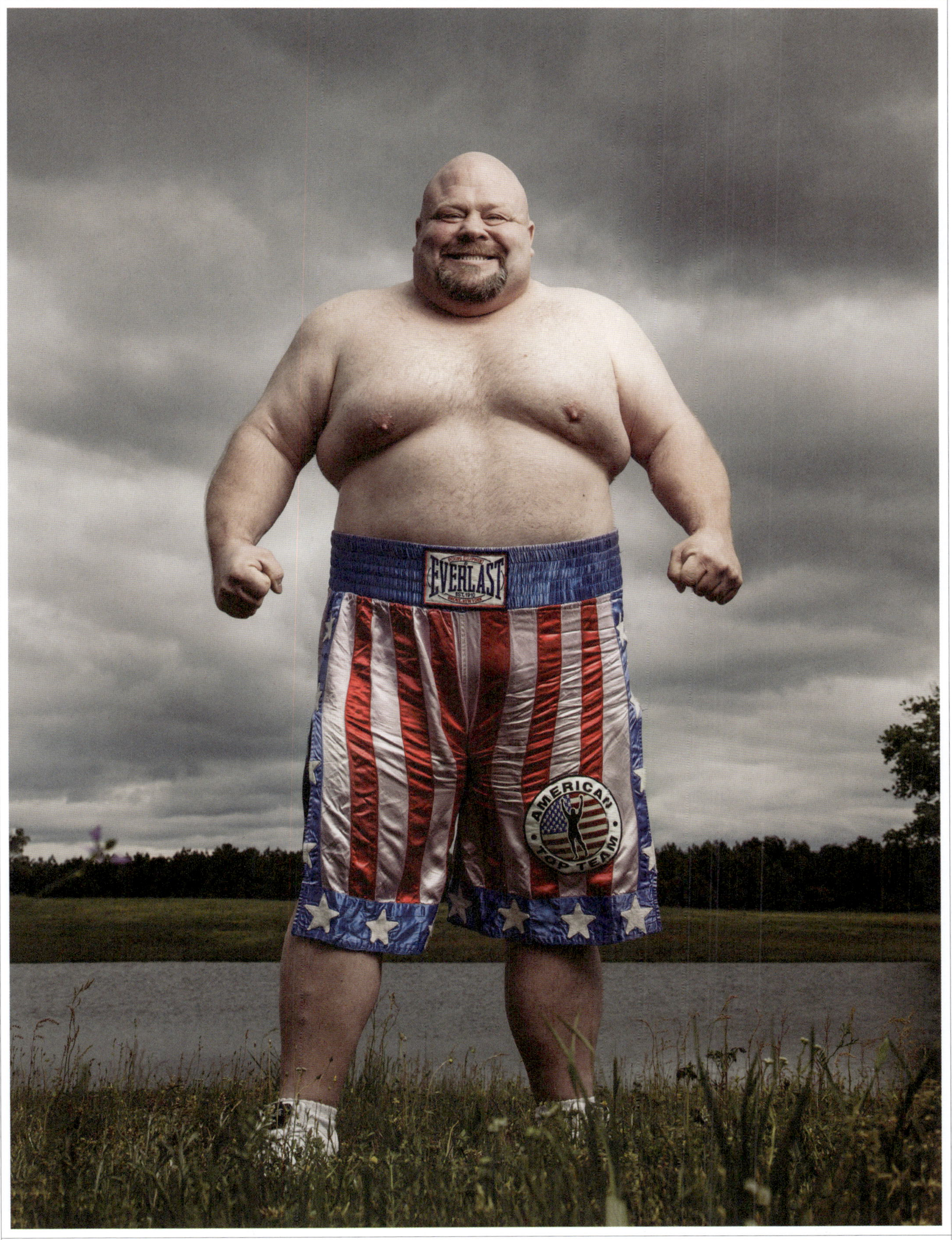

Portrait of former heavyweight boxer, kickboxer, and MMA fighter Eric "Butterbean" Esch near Jasper, Alabama.

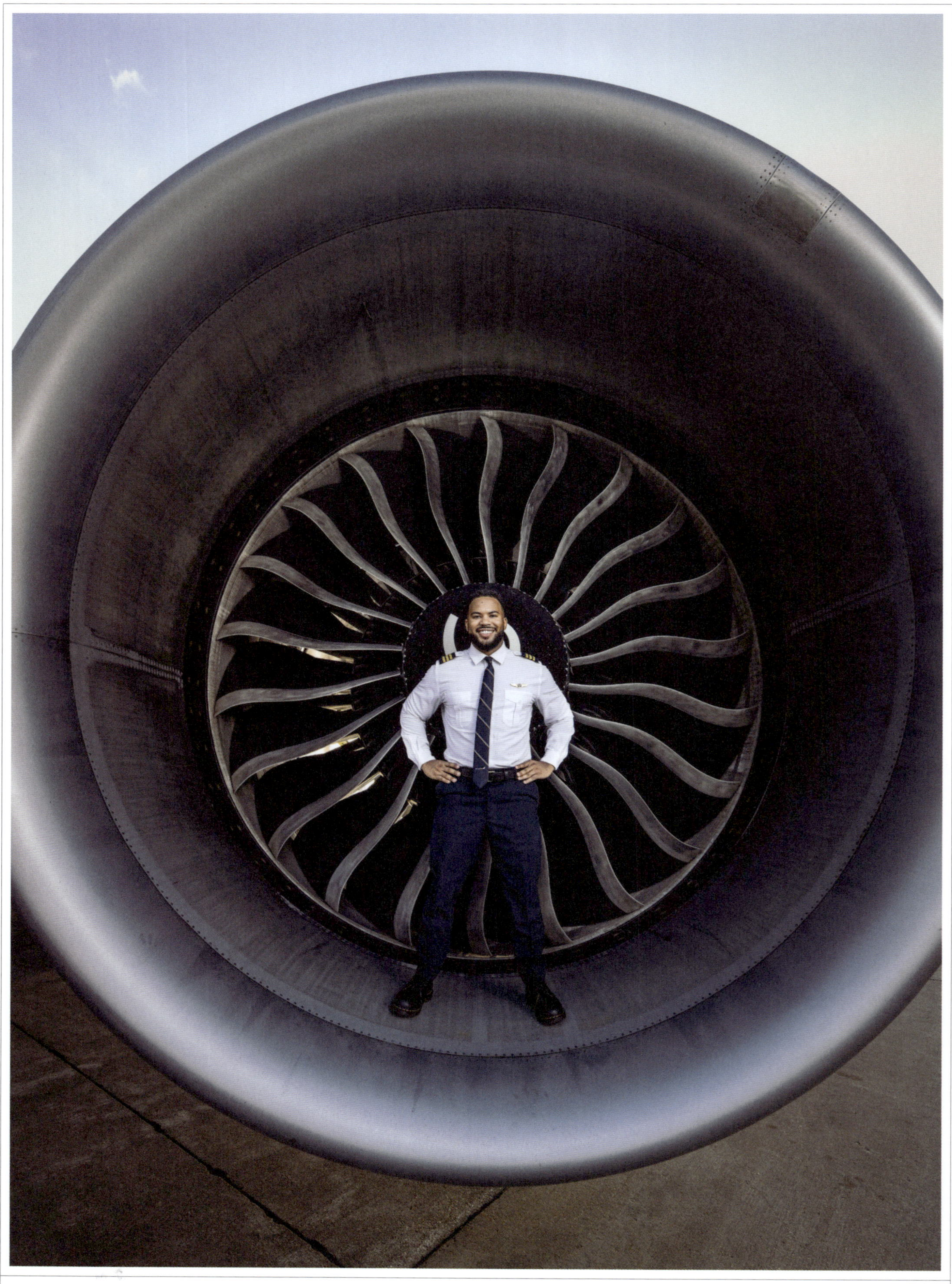

Portrait of a 777 pilot for Atlas Air Cargo at the Cincinnati/Northern Kentucky International Airport (CVG) in Hebron, Kentucky.

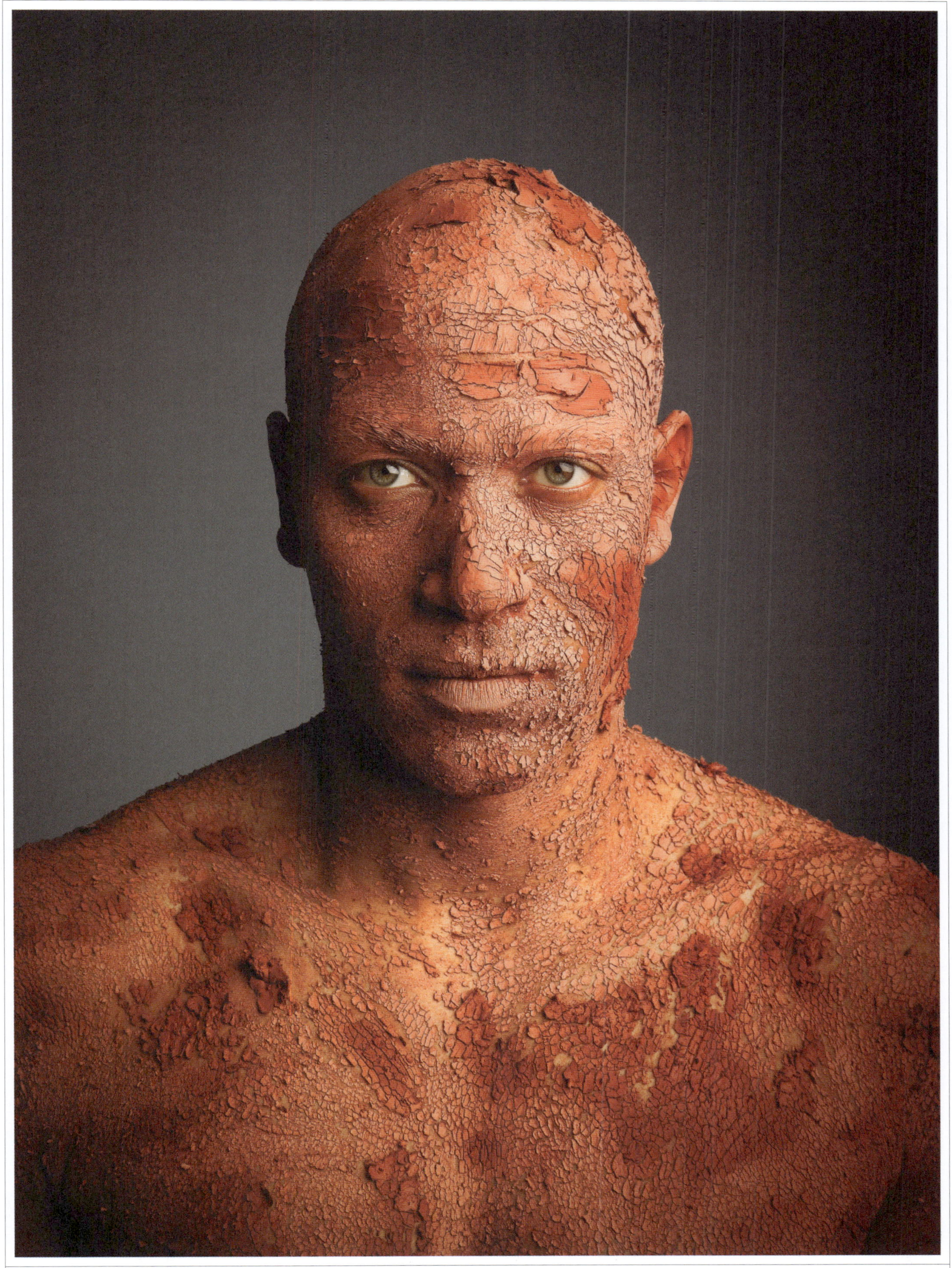

Cracked Earth Portrait. Fitness model Curtis Brown was photographed in studio as a personal project with makeup artist Wendy Martin.

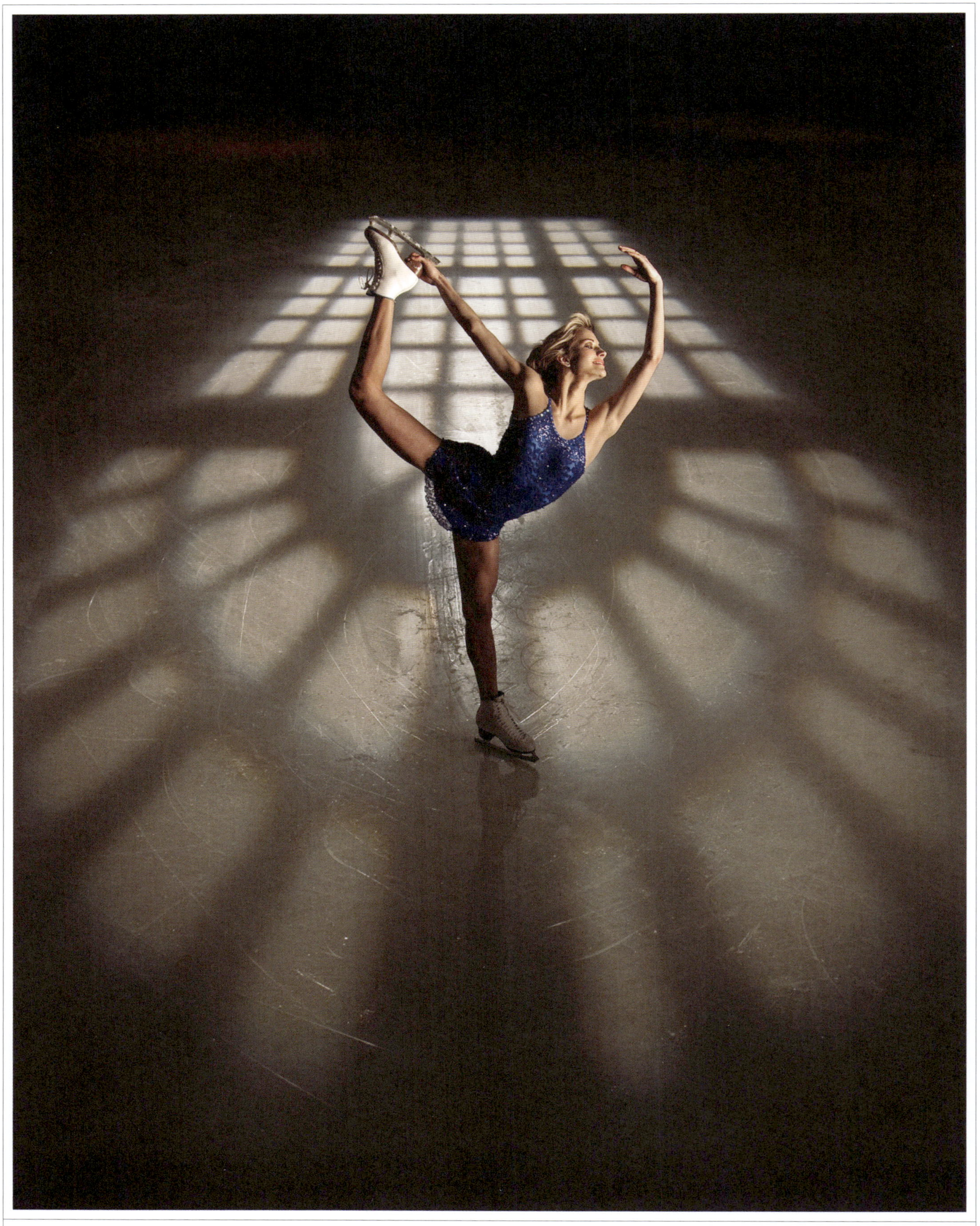

Figure skater Becky Bereswill at the Galleria ice rink in Houston, Texas, on February 2, 2010.

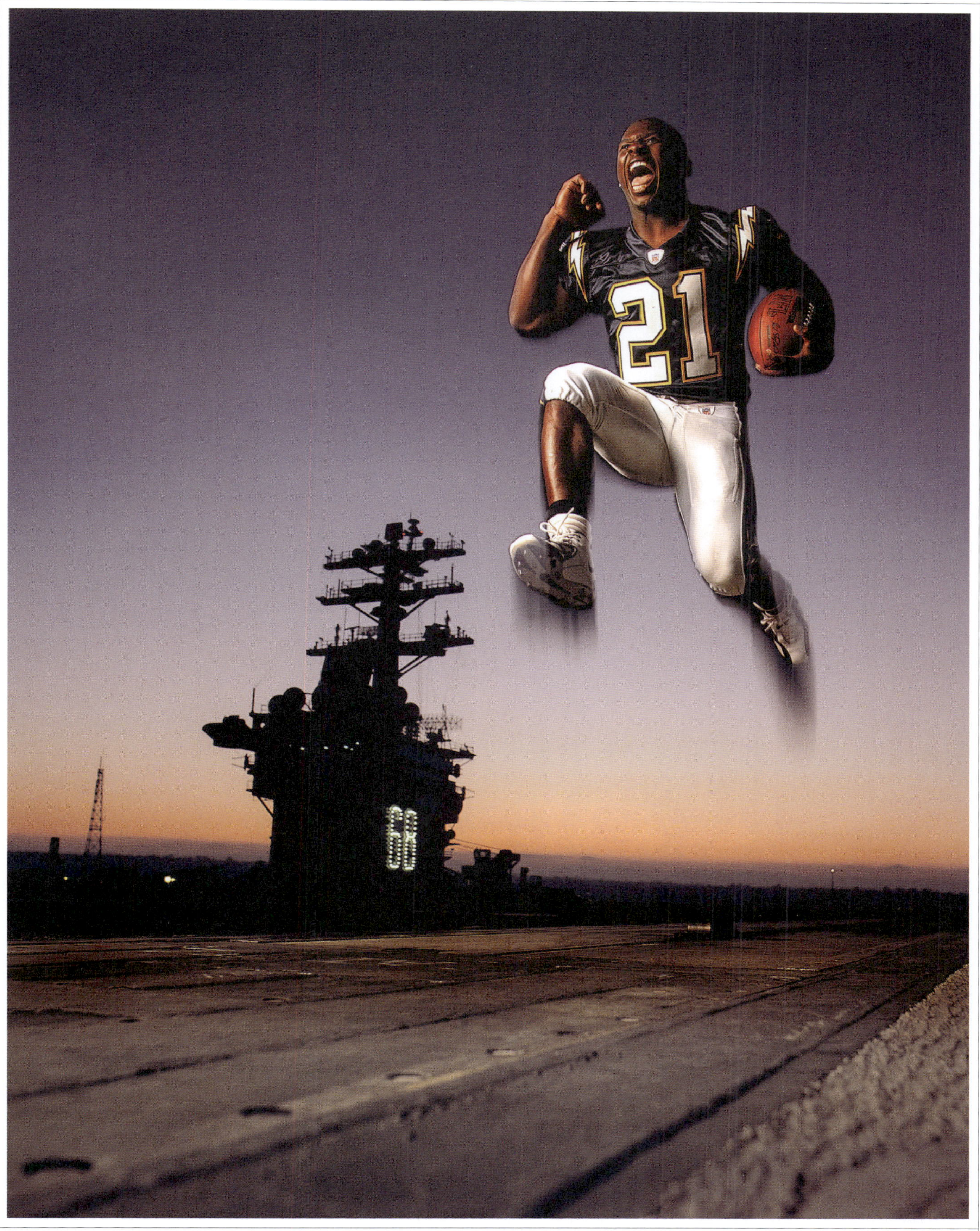

LaDainian Tomlinson, running back of the San Diego Chargers onboard the USS Nimitz, San Diego, California.

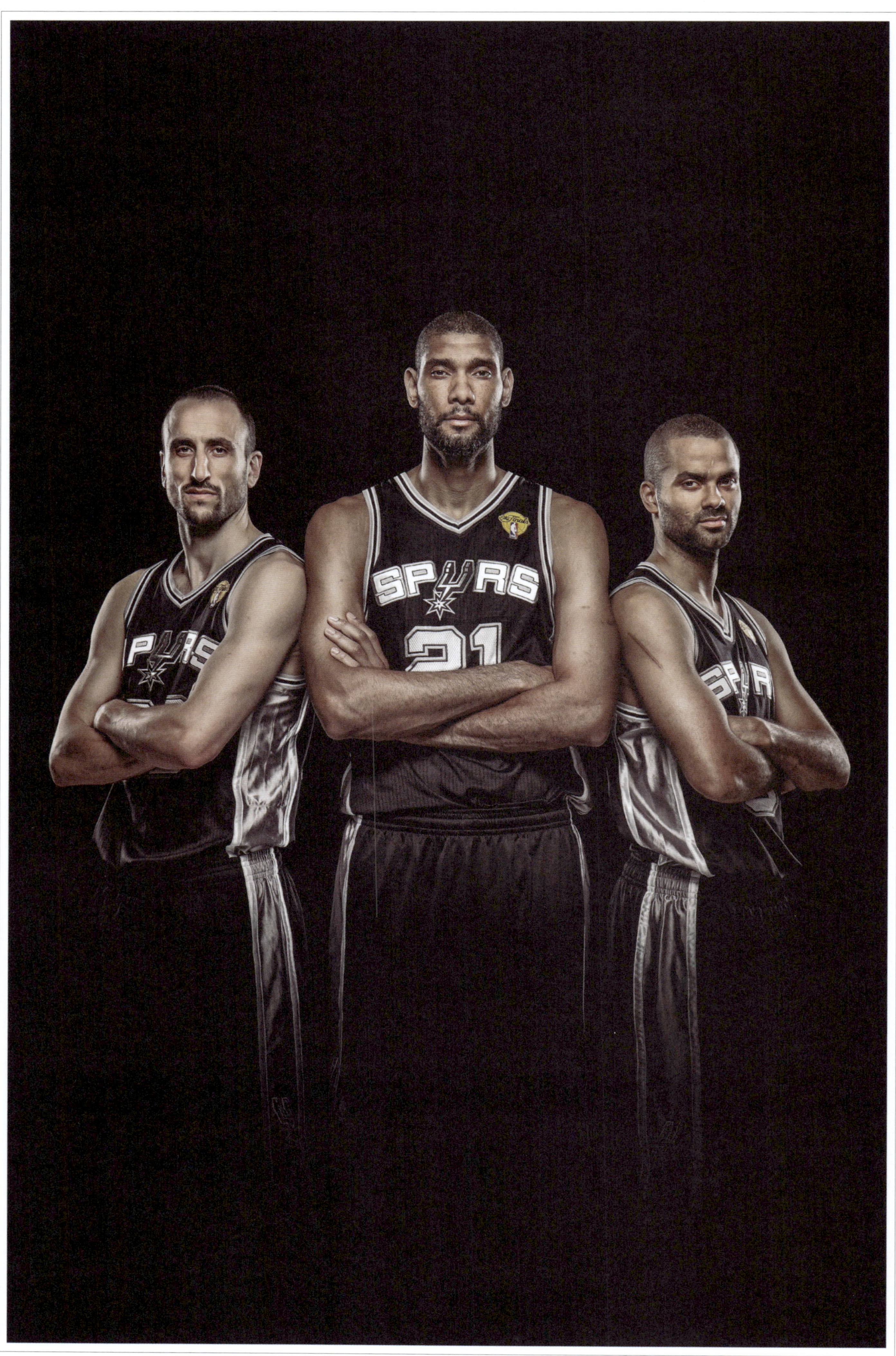

Manu Ginóbili, Tim Duncan, and Tony Parker of the San Antonio Spurs in San Antonio, Texas.

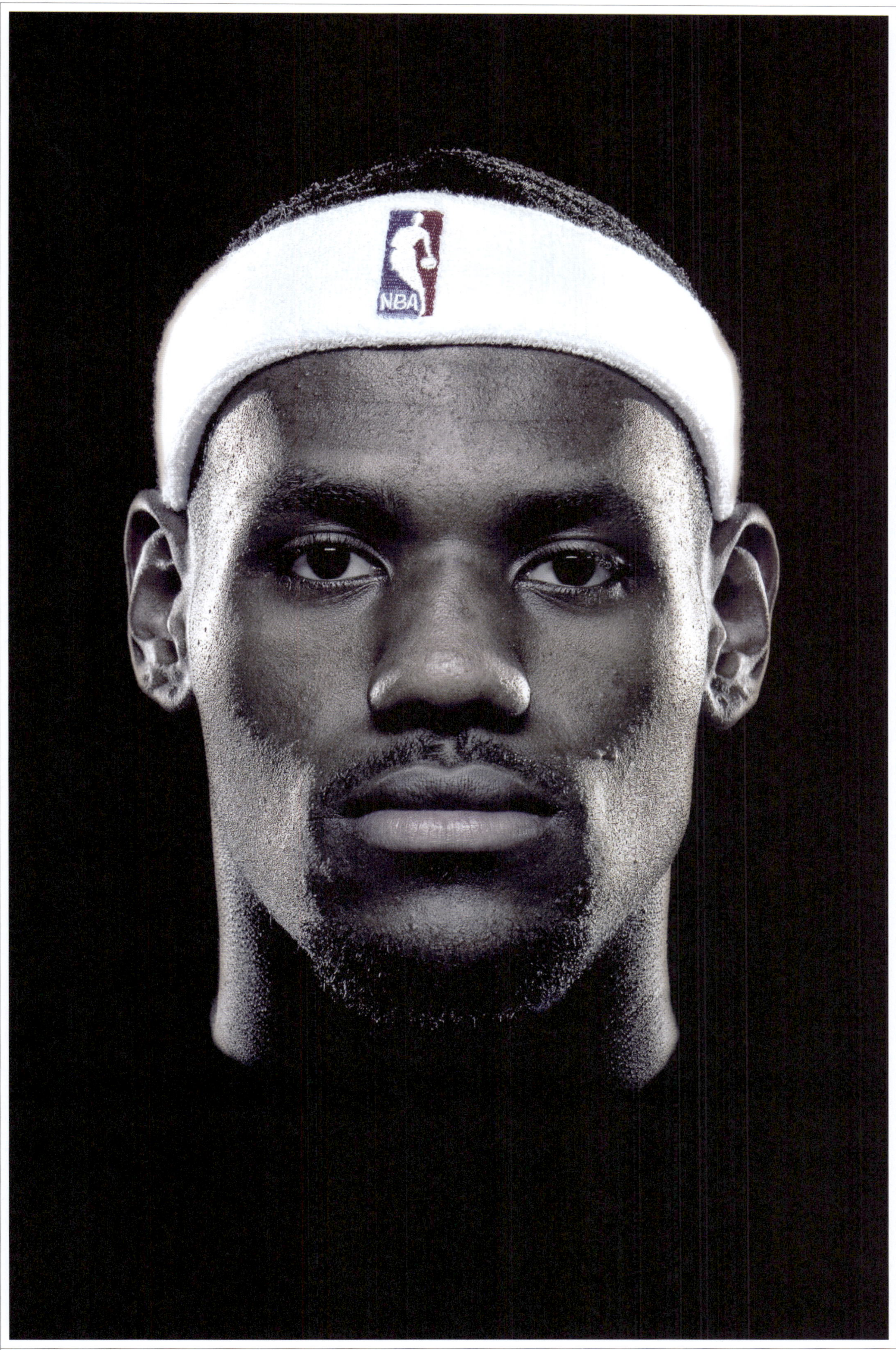

Portrait of NBA star LeBron James, Cleveland, Ohio.

TIM IS AN INCREDIBLE PHOTOGRAPHER, COLLABORATOR, AND ARTIST. IT WAS AN HONOR TO WORK WITH HIM ON THE NINJA X ADIDAS CAMPAIGN.

Evan DeHaven, *Co-owner & Head of Creative, Random Folk*

TIM'S ABILITY TO BLEND PHOTOGRAPHIC PRECISION WITH BOLD, OFTEN PROVOCATIVE IDEAS SETS HIM APART IN AN INDUSTRY CROWDED WITH IMITATORS.

Mike Campau, *President & Creative Director, Mike Campau Digital Imagery*

TIM WAS AWESOME TO WORK WITH AND CREATED SPECTACULAR IMAGES FOR ONE OF MY FAVORITE CLIENTS.

David Stevenson, *Founder & Chief Executive Officer, TwoXFour*

TIM'S PROFESSIONALISM, CREATIVITY, AND CUSTOMER-ORIENTED APPROACH CONTRIBUTED SIGNIFICANTLY TO OUR POSITIVE EXPERIENCE.

Sotiris Aggelou, *Vice President of Global Brand Partnerships, Ready Nutrition*

TIM IS A CREATIVE FORCE TO BE RECKONED WITH. HE BRINGS VISION, TECHNICAL EXPERTISE, AND TOP-TIER EXPERIENCE, AND I'M STOKED I WAS ABLE TO WORK WITH HIM ON OUR ADIDAS PROJECT.

Andy Burdin, *Staff Visual Product Designer, Crunchyroll*

(Opposite page) Nothing To See, Untitled #2 2017

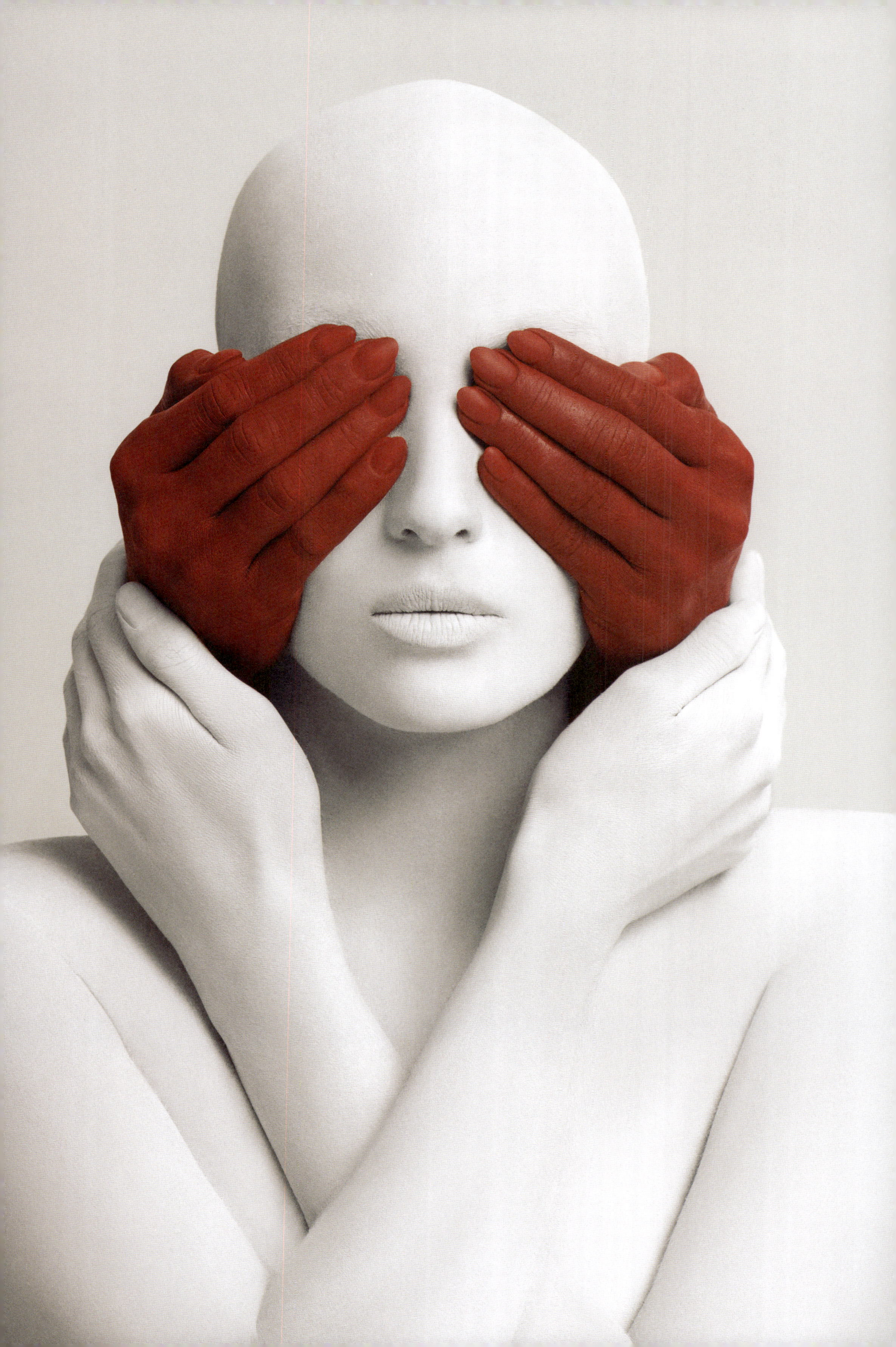

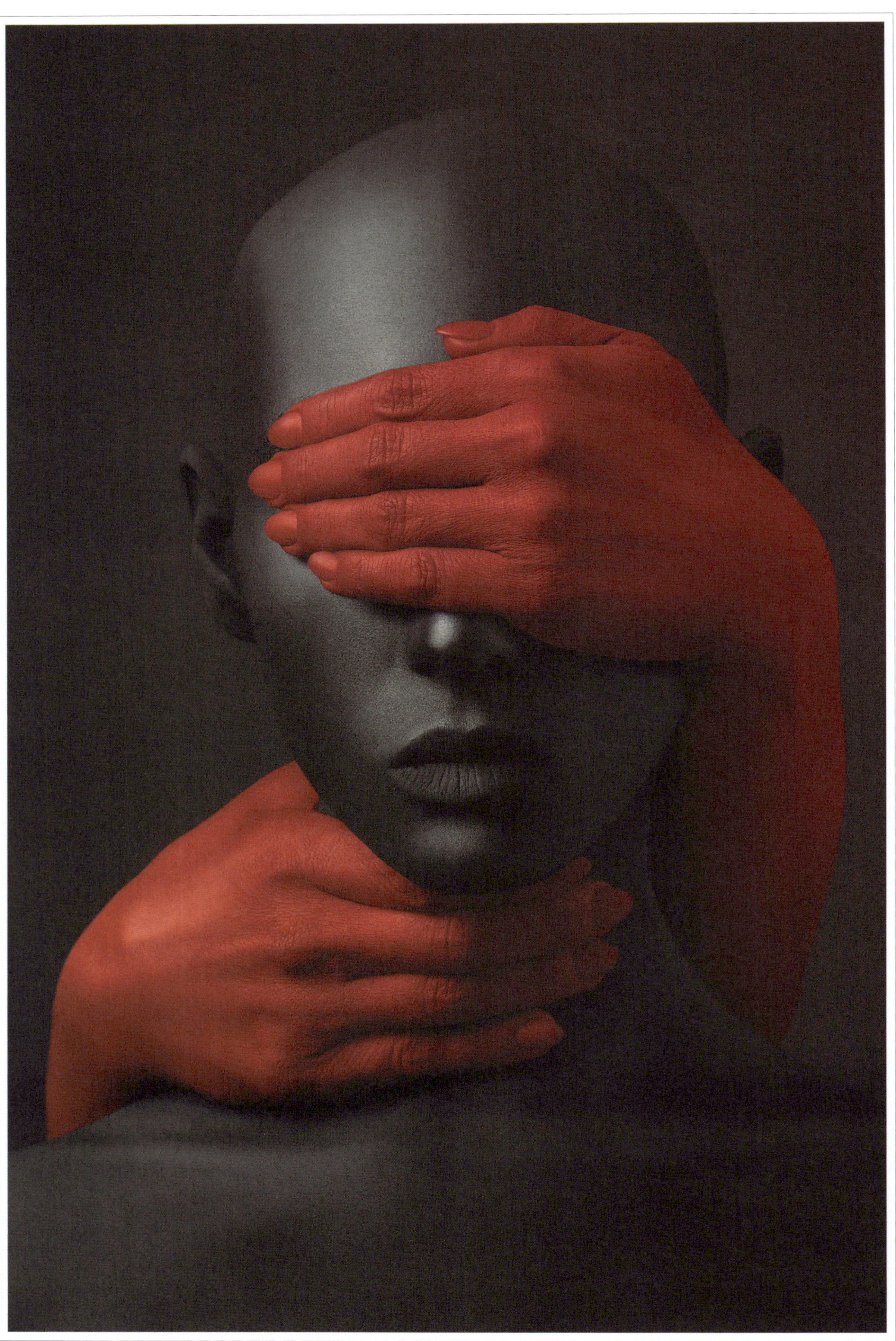

Title: Nothing To See, Untitled #12 2017. Fine art. "Nothing To See is a moment of resistance against a 'new normal' in which dishonesty functions as the currency of political success. With powerful imagery and a striking utilization of color, these works compel viewers to break free from the ever-present narratives."

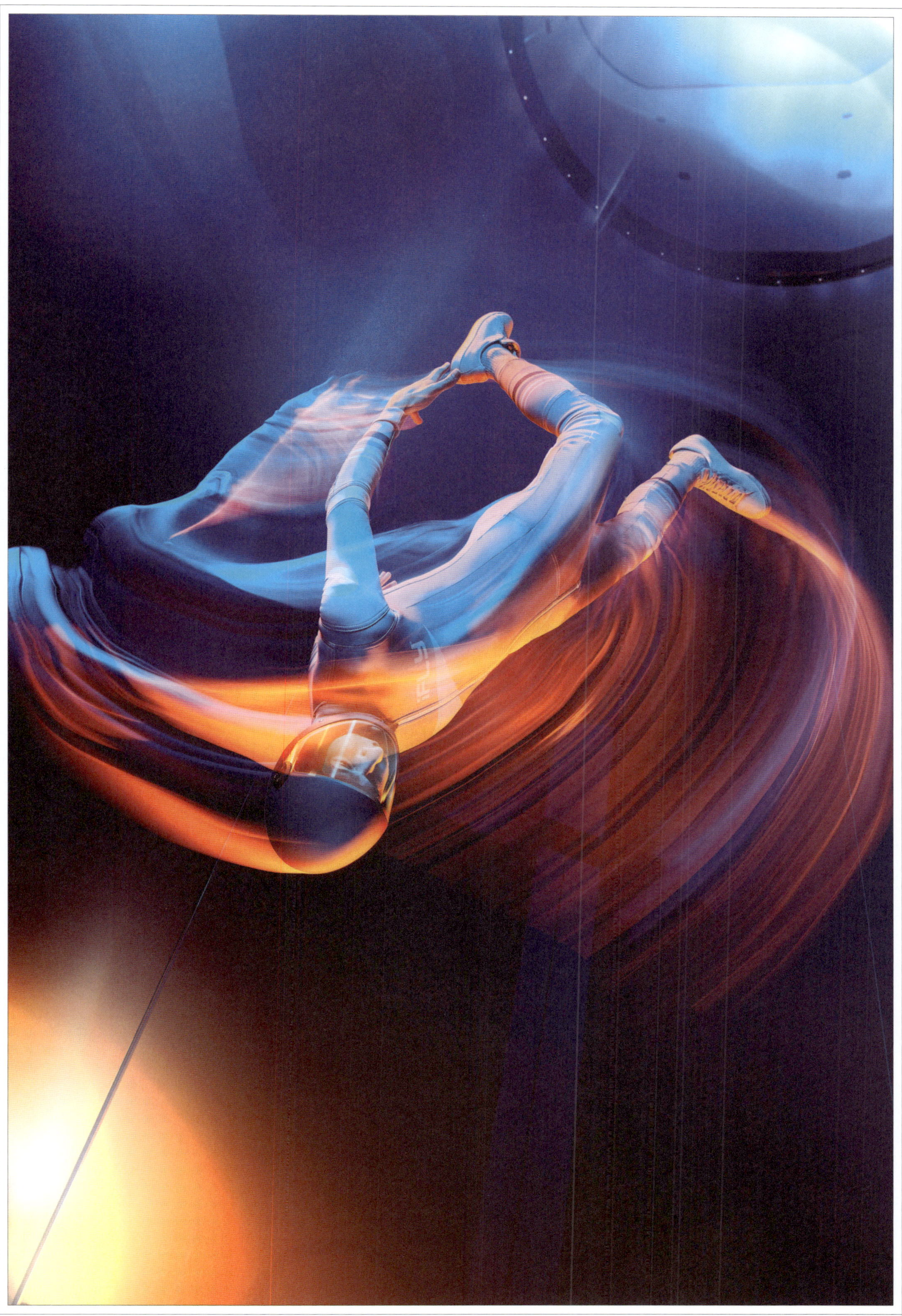

Title: IFly. Art Director: BJ Heinley. Executive Creative Director: John Trahar. Producer: Cassie Collin. Ad Agency: Greatest Common Factory. Client: iFLY.
"If you have ever seen images of indoor skydiving, it is very difficult to capture the essence, excitement, and joy. We shot these flyers in a studio with a suspension flying system, where subjects could move three-dimensionally through the space. We wanted the images to have a sense of movement, so we shot with one-second exposures. All trails and blurs were shot in camera, and those images were dropped into CGI backgrounds."

Introduction by **Michael Christopher Brown** *Photographer, National Geographic*

Tim is the best example of someone who, despite his talent, has worked hard for every ounce of his success. He is always pushing the boundaries of his genre, always relentlessly creative, and never afraid to try new tools, even amidst great criticism. On set, he connects with everyone and is a natural leader and director. I have learned so much while working on his sets over the years. He is also a great friend and the older brother I never had, as he always tells it like it is and pushes me to never settle for anything but the best.

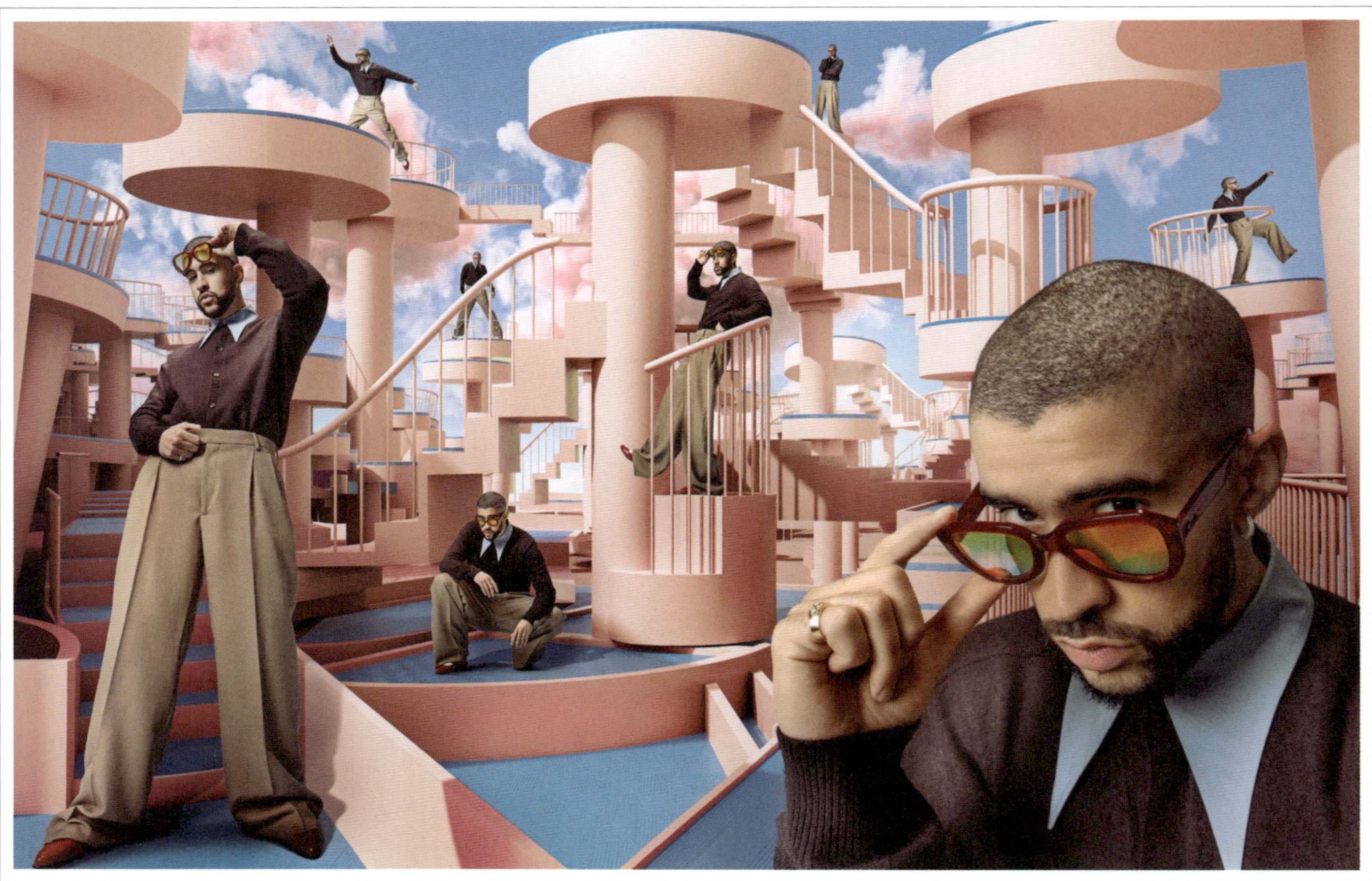

Title: Bad Bunny Forbes 30 Under 30. Photographer: Tim Tadder. Design Director: Alicia Hallett-Chan. Director of Photography: Robyn Selman. Client: Forbes. "Bad Bunny gives an exclusive tour of his budding sports, fashion, and entertainment empire. The Puerto Rican artist has expertly harnessed the power of music streaming and social media to become one of the most famous musicians on the planet. After partnering with companies like Gucci, Adidas, and WWE, he's wielding his fame to become a global brand."

I LOVE THE STORYTELLING POWER OF VIDEO, BUT STILLS ARE MY FIRST LOVE: MORE INTIMACY, MORE CONTROL.

Tim Tadder, *Photographer, Tim Tadder Stills & Motion*

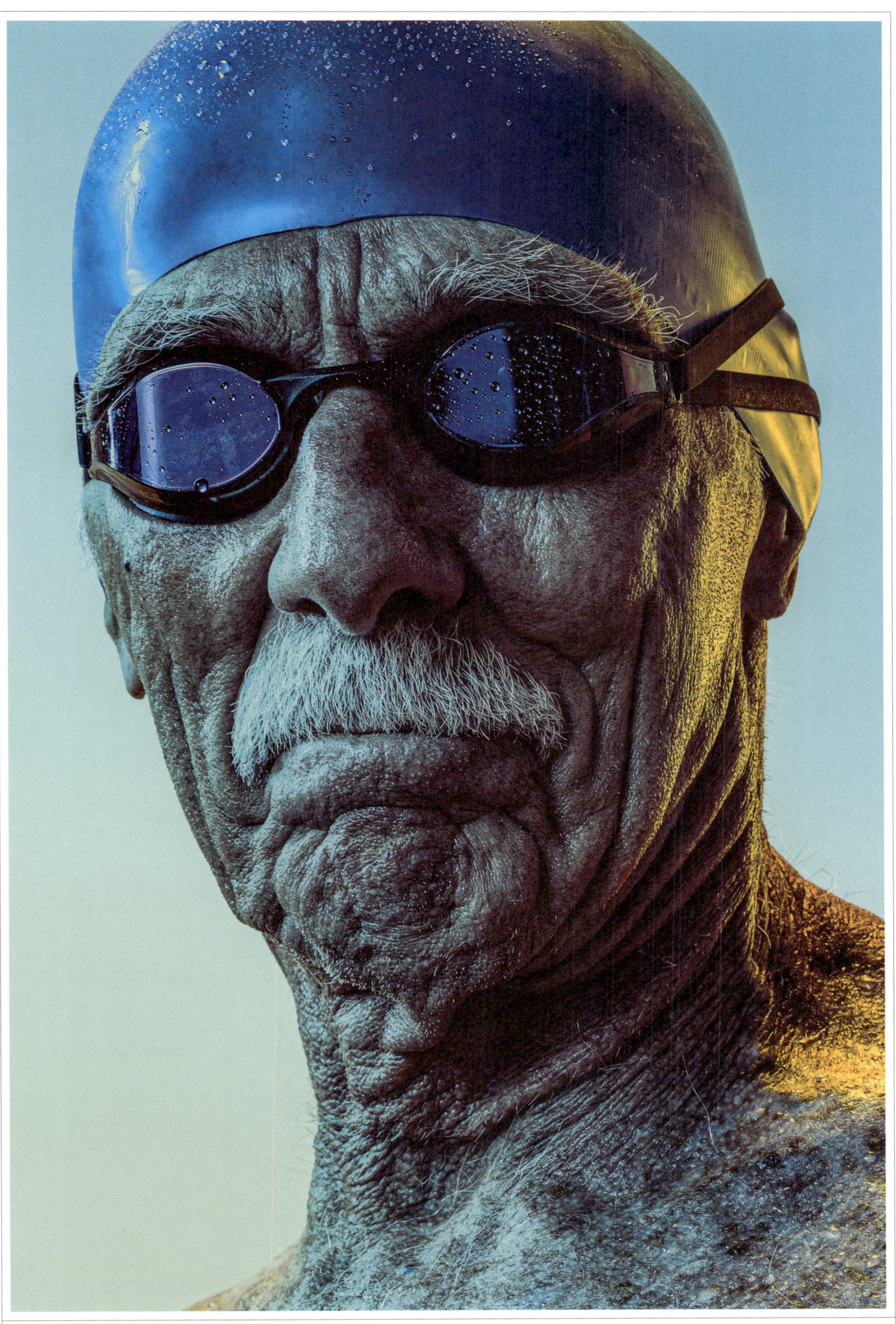

Title: Cav Cavanaugh, Senior Olympic Athlete for Humana Commercial Advertising Project. Creative Director: Kari McCarthy. Ad Agency: Golin. Client: Humana. "Key art celebrating the National Senior Games by Humana, featuring champion senior Olympic athletes shot on location. Used in public relations and blogs to promote the games and celebrate wellness in seniors."

What inspired or motivated you to pursue a career in photography and be a photographer?
My father was a commercial photographer, so I grew up around a studio, constantly watching him work. When I was 13, he gave me a film camera, and I started photographing my friends skateboarding. When I finished my first roll, he didn't just hand me the next one—he made me learn how to develop and print it. Taking an image from idea to tangible print felt like magic. I was hooked from that moment on.

What is your philosophy when it comes to taking photographs?
Originality. I'm not trying to out-execute anyone technically—I'm trying to create something unique that moves people. Whether it's through lighting, color, composition, or concept, I want my work to stop people in their tracks and make them feel something. Surprise them. That's the bar.

Who among your contemporaries do you most admire and think the world hasn't heard enough from?
There's so much content today chasing algorithms over impact. One person I deeply admire is Michael Christopher Brown—a conflict photographer and a close friend. His work is soulful, emotional, and powerful. He doesn't seek attention—he just creates for the right reasons. That's rare. And it matters.

Who have been some of your favorite colleagues or clients, and how have they shaped your career?
My career really kicked off with a Gatorade campaign. Since then, I've worked with big names such as Nike, AT&T, McDonald's, Reebok, and Pepsi, but it's never been about the logos. It's about the people—the creatives who believe in you, challenge you, and push you further than you thought you could go. The "additive creatives" make it all worth doing.

Who has been your greatest mentor?
My dad. He always pushed me to be different—not just in my work but in how I think. His relentless work ethic and belief that most solutions are hidden behind the hard work we tend to avoid shaped how I approach every shoot and every challenge.

Your father photographed the Baltimore Orioles for almost 45 years. How did that influence your own work?
He introduced me to great photography early, especially Neil Leifer's sports photography, which was interpretive, not just documentary. That idea stuck with me: Don't just be there with a camera—see differently, bring something new. My dad shared that philosophy. It wasn't about copying him—it was about learning to see.

Tell us about Tim Tadder Stills & Motion. How did it start, and how has it evolved?
It started out of necessity. As I grew, I needed an assistant, then a producer, then a retoucher. Over time, it became a full team. I wanted control over quality, consistency, and delivery. The more you outsource, the more cracks appear. A tight in-house team created trust—and that trust built the studio.

How did you get into shooting film?
It wasn't a choice—it was survival. When the Canon 5D came out, suddenly every photographer had to be a filmmaker. I learned the medium from scratch. I love the storytelling power of video, but stills are my first love: more intimacy, more control. But I'm glad I know both.

How do your fine art and commercial work influence each other?
Advertising is a career, but fine art is who I am. One funds the other. Commercial work is structured and high-pressure, while fine art is introspective and meditative. But there is some overlap. The technical discipline of my commercial work sharpens my fine art, and the soul-searching from my fine art keeps my commercial work alive.

You're called a "pioneer, innovator, and disrupter" in tech. What's impacted your work most recently?
AI, without question. I have mixed feelings about it. It's built on the backs of photographers like me, and it devalues real image-making. But it's a tidal wave. Refusing to engage with it today is like refusing to learn digital photography 20 years ago. I don't love what it represents, but I can't ignore it.

Do you have concerns about using AI in your work?
Absolutely. It's ethically murky and will disrupt the industry. But the debate is over—it's already happening. Commercial content will be generated with prompts. Productions will become novelties. It's a shift as big as the internet. You evolve, or you get left behind.

Tell us about the people who are in your studio. What influence do they have?
Pre-COVID, we had a full team—highly creative and collaborative. Since then, I've scaled back to make space for fine art and personal projects. But collaboration is always at the core. Great ideas rarely come from isolation. The people make the studio.

How do you balance your creative vision with client needs?
Some clients give you the freedom to create; some don't. I've experienced both. The best work always comes from trust. With brands like Hyperice and Ready Nutrition, I've been involved from the start—vision, concept, execution. That kind of deep collaboration leads to the best results.

Has your background in math and teaching influenced your photography in any way?
Definitely. Math taught me structure and problem-solving. Photography is deeply technical—light ratios, exposure, composition—they're all mathematical. Teaching gave me confidence. Running a production is like conducting an orchestra. Teaching taught me how to lead.

Your first big break was shooting Gatorade's global campaign. What was that like?
It was wild. I was too early in my career to realize how big it was. But I delivered. The creative director believed in me and let me run with it. That campaign opened the floodgates. I rode that wave for years before evolving again. It changed everything.

Can you tell us if there's a project you're currently working on that excites you?
I'm experimenting with AI to go beyond image generation into video storytelling. Animations, sequences, evolving narratives. I'm not aiming for polish right now—just discovery. It's exciting, terrifying, and frustrating all at once.

What do you want people to take away from your photographs?
A feeling. That's it. Joy, discomfort, nostalgia, confusion—I don't care what it is. But if they feel nothing, I missed. I want to move people. That's the point.

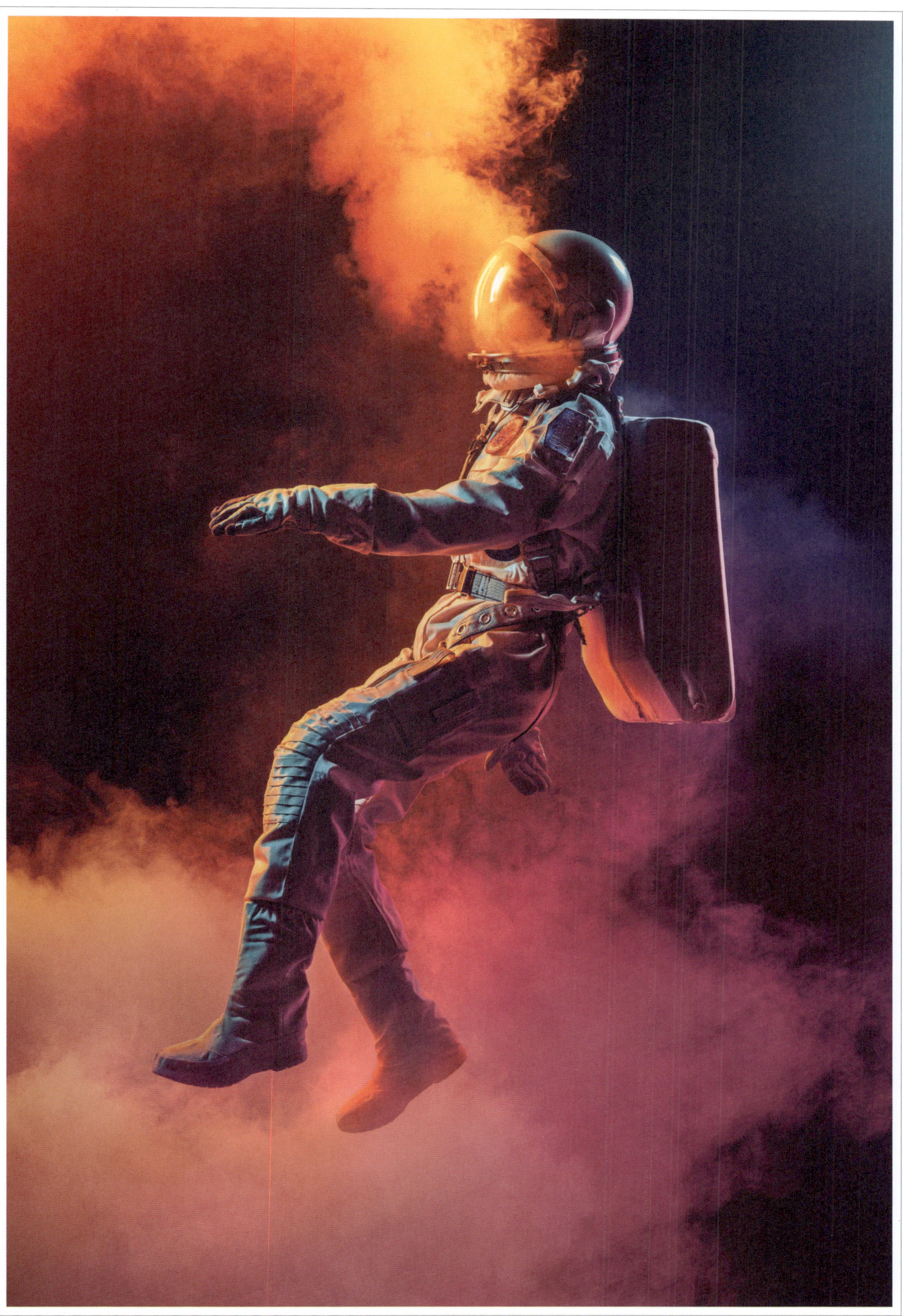

Title: THE ASTRONAUTS COMPANY. Agency: Jane & Jay Brands, Encinitas, USA. Creative Director: Marcelo Kertesz.
"This series was key art for the launch of the cannabis brand, The Astronauts Company. The ads ran as posters at events announcing the brand with tag lines such as 'Houston, We Have No Problem,' and the campaign landed on the cover of Archive Magazine. The concept behind this launch was to use the long-held stoner tradition of hotboxing inside the iconic Apollo-era spacesuits."

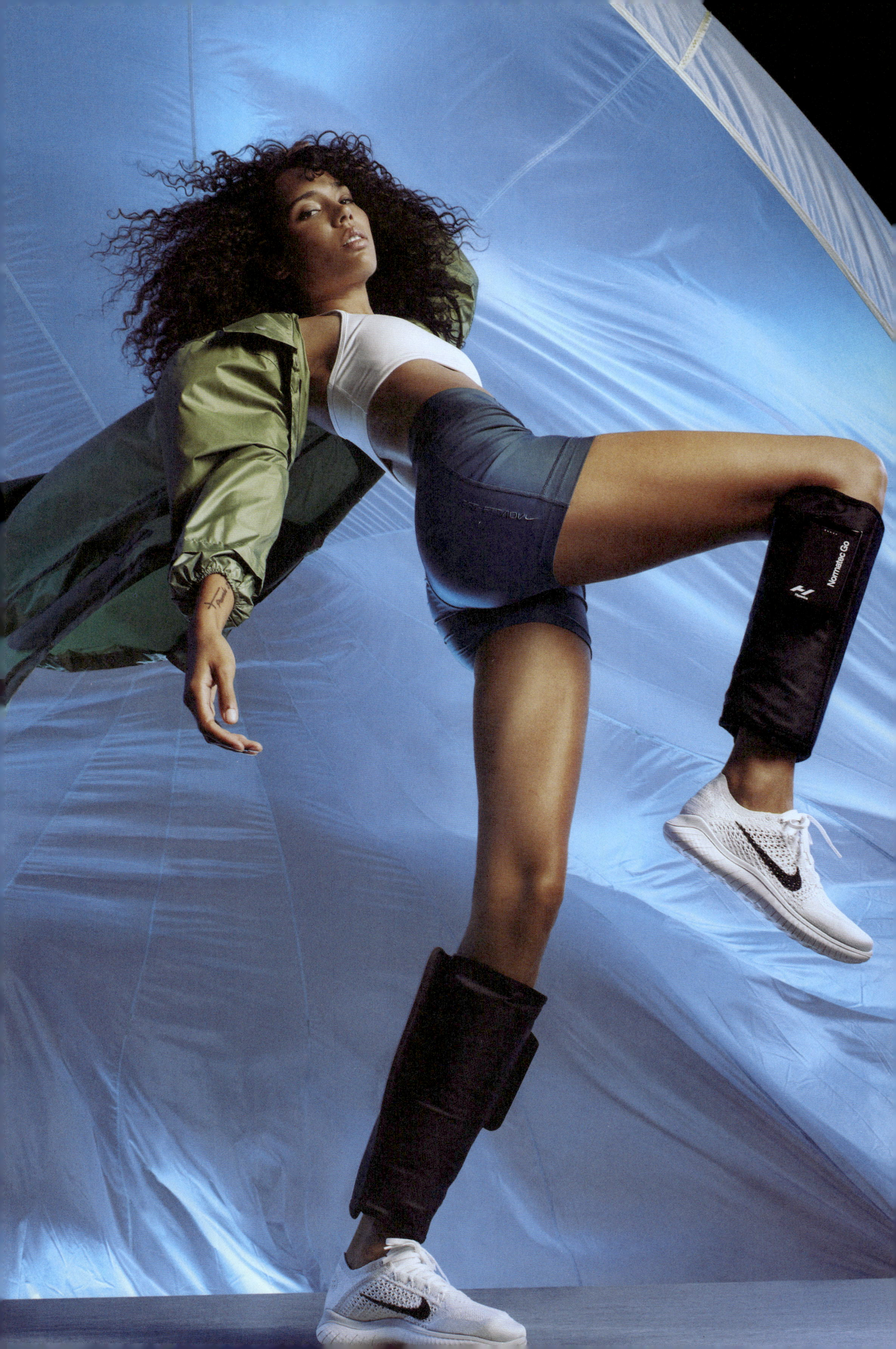
Normatec Go

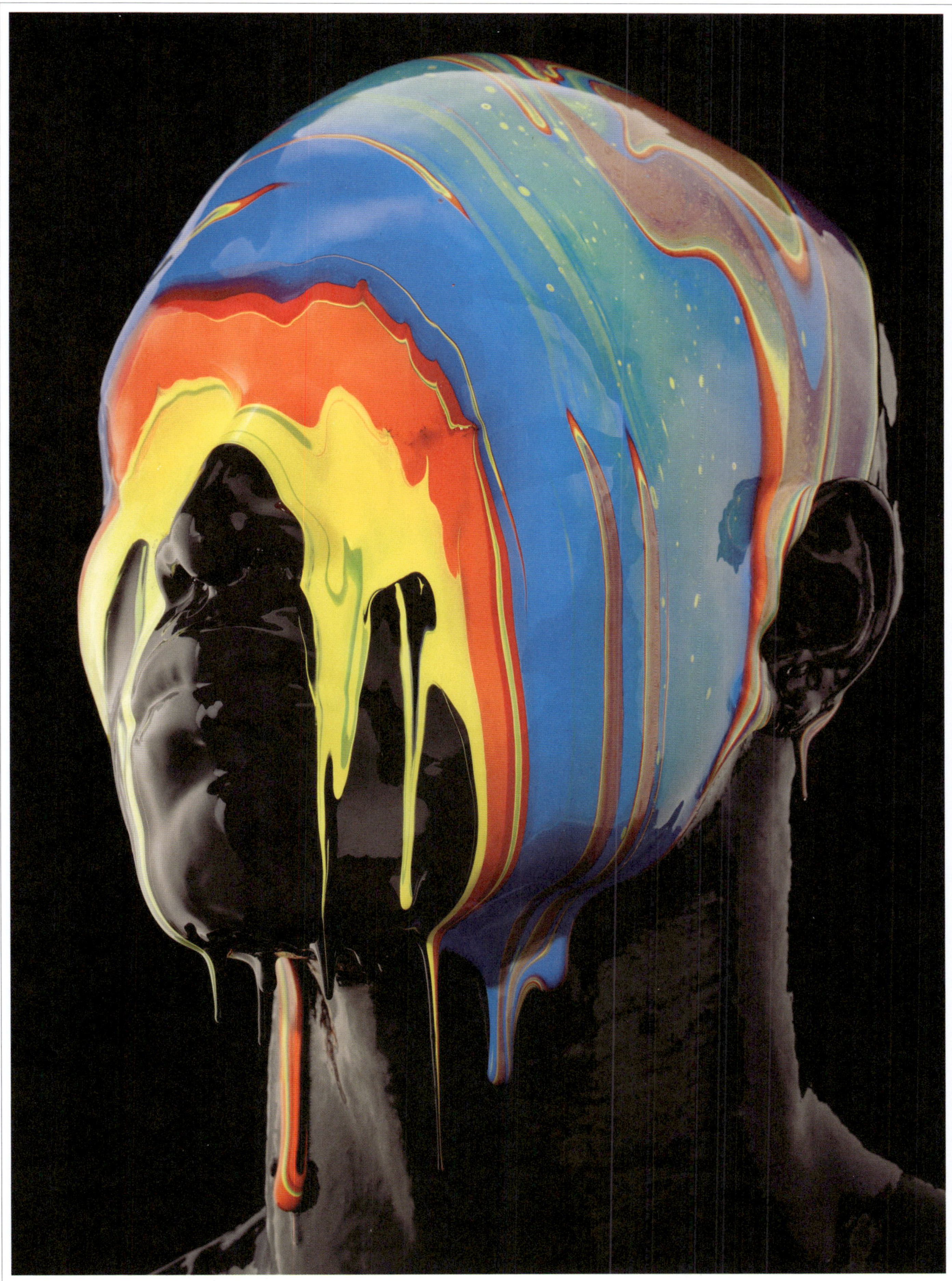

(Above) Title: Black is a Color. Fine art. "Part of my exhibition at Avant Gallery in New York City. When primary colors are mixed in equal parts, black is ultimately the precipitating color. Black is a Color challenges us to see past race as binary and into beautiful, infinitely complex humans." Used as gallery prints. (Opposite page) Title: Hyperice. Client: Hyperice. "Hyperice's innovative products are recognized and used by the most influential athletes, professionals, and corporations worldwide. Our team helped create the visual feel for its 2020 product catalog and redefine its brand imagery. The work had to be as clean, innovative, and just as powerful as its smartly designed products."

How do you approach working with startups vs. legacy brands?
Startups have small budgets but big freedom. Legacy brands have layers—agencies, approvals, red tape. Startups let you help define the brand from day one. That's personal. That's fulfilling. That's why I started.

What's next for you and your studio?
Adaptability and nimbleness. Media is shifting fast—formats are shorter, and attention spans are shorter. We're producing faster and simpler for less permanence. It's about efficiency, scale, and relevance.

What's your constant source of inspiration?
Honestly, Instagram. It's exhausting, but it's also a firehose of ideas. The algorithm knows what excites me. I'm also inspired by the edges—what's emerging, especially AI. It scares me, but it also fuels me. That tension drives a lot of my work.

Tell us about shooting the Amazon Business campaign "Buy Smarter. Dream Bigger."
It was a great shoot. James Sablin, who is an amazing producer I've worked with before, brought me on. They had a solid concept, and I pushed it visually—new lighting, bold color, and strong profiles. When I showed them both versions, they immediately knew: This is it.

Have you shot your dream assignment yet?
Not yet. I've shot dreamy projects, but the dream assignment is still out there. Believing that is what keeps me going.

What advice would you give students starting out today?
Master AI. Understand how it's reshaping storytelling. Learn to use it to pitch, to ideate, to create. This shift is bigger than the internet. If you're just starting now, you're either riding the wave or getting buried by it.

How does your personal life influence your work?
It's all connected. When I'm grounded personally, I show up stronger professionally. I take about four months a year off to do something completely different. That keeps me sharp. The work doesn't matter if you're not living fully.

What do you love most about photography?
The ability to freeze a feeling, to take something fleeting and make it permanent. That still feels like magic.

Other than new tech, how do you keep your work relevant?
I stay uncomfortable. I experiment. I surround myself with people who push me. Staying relevant isn't about trends—it's about curiosity. That's what keeps the fire lit.

How do you stay creatively energized while juggling commercial and personal projects?
Personal work is my passion. Commercial work has structure—creative, strategic, and legal limitations. That structure can drain you if you never step out. I always keep something personal running in the background. One fuels the other.

How do you blend CGI, photography, and video into a cohesive visual narrative?
It starts with intention. What's the core emotion? What world are we building? Once that's clear, the tools—CGI, stills, AI—are just methods. I think in layers: light, texture, motion, depth. Everything has to feel like it lives in the same universe.

Has embracing AI changed your workflow or mindset?
Absolutely. AI lets me visualize faster, experiment with light, create mood boards, and push into surreal ideas without wasting days in pre-production. It's like a sketchpad for your imagination. It's broken my linear thinking—and that's huge.

What have you learned about building a personal brand in today's saturated visual world?
Clarity wins. If people can't instantly understand what you stand for, they'll scroll past. Your brand isn't your logo—it's how your work makes people feel. For me, that's bold, conceptual, and human. That thread has to run through everything.

Is there a way for commercial photographers to future-proof their careers today?
By being more than a technician. Understand brand strategy. Think like a creative director. The "just show up and shoot" model is dead. You need to bring value on multiple levels. Gear won't save you. Adaptability will.

How important is it for a photographer to also be both a storyteller and strategist?
Being a storyteller and strategist is everything. Without a story, your image is just decoration. Without strategy, it's just noise. The best photographers think upstream—what's the message, who's the audience, and what do we want them to feel? If you can answer that and still deliver stunning visuals, you're not just a photographer—you're indispensable.

Tim Tadder Stills & Motion www.timtadder.com

WHETHER IT'S THROUGH LIGHTING, COLOR, COMPOSITION, OR CONCEPT, I WANT MY WORK TO STOP PEOPLE IN THEIR TRACKS AND MAKE THEM FEEL SOMETHING.

Tim Tadder, *Photographer, Tim Tadder Stills & Motion*

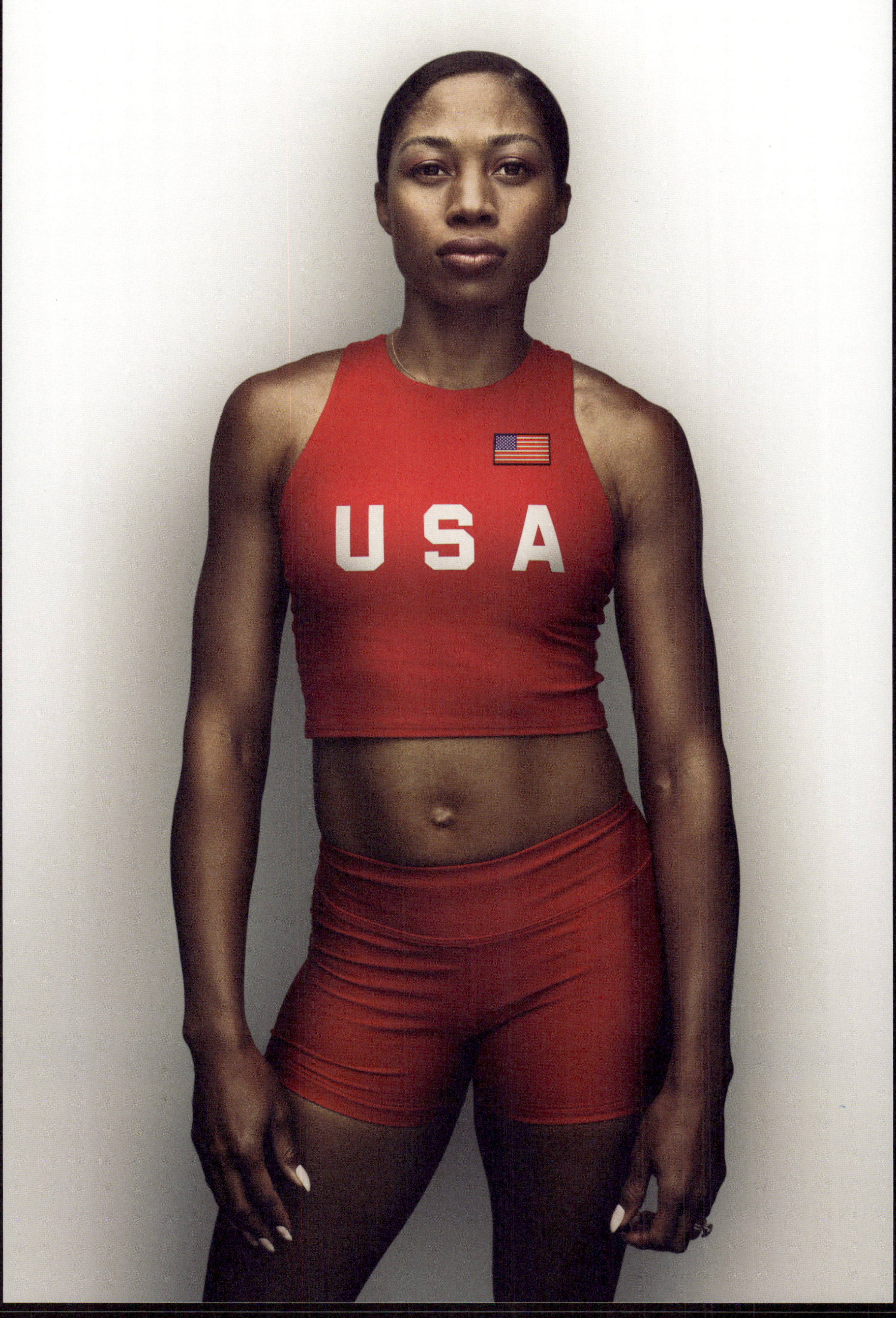

Title: Allyson Felix. The most decorated American track and field athlete ever.
"For Bridgestone Olympic campaign. Commercial project shot for ads surrounding Bridgestone Tires' partnership with Team USA."

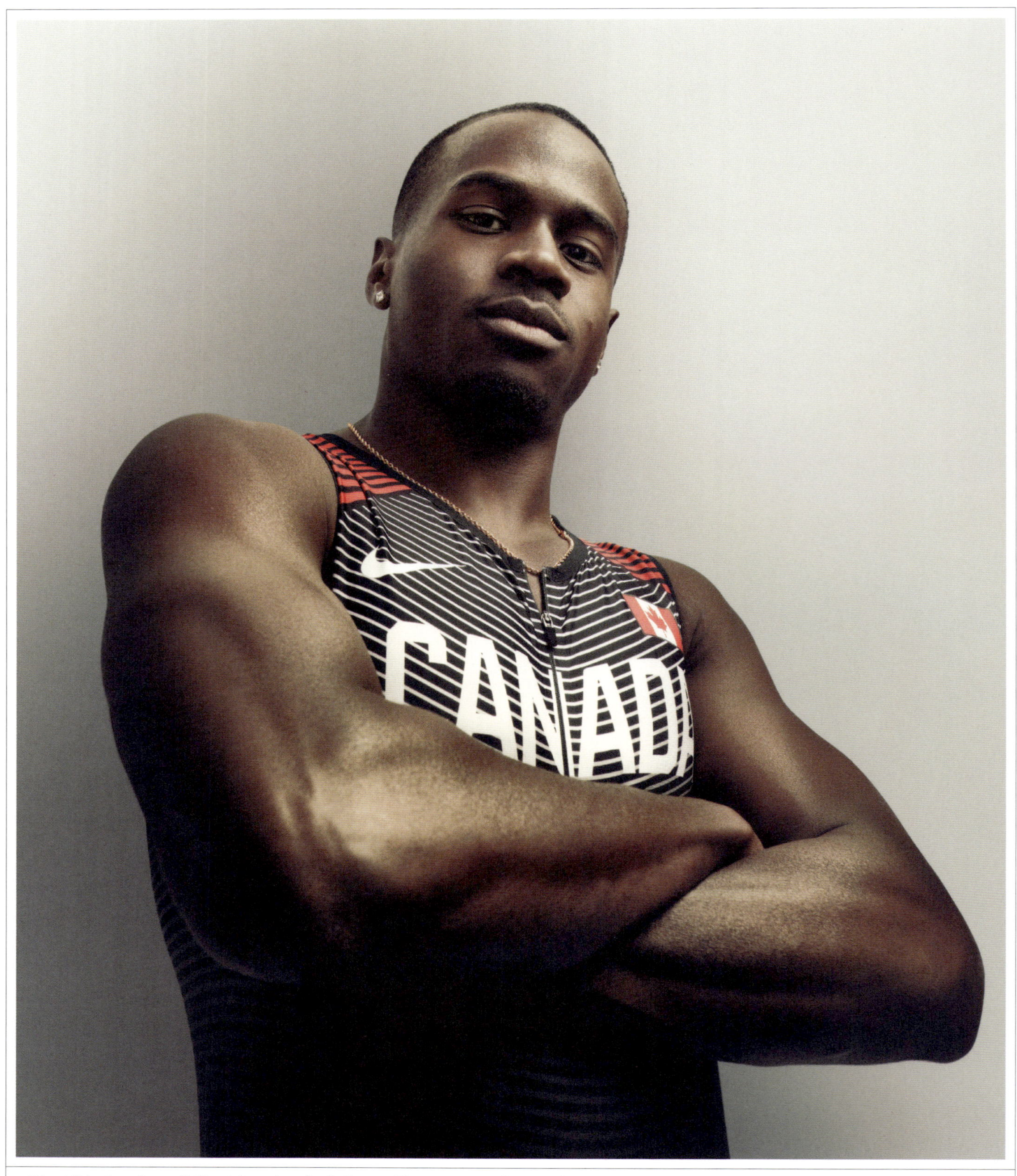

(Above) Title: Aaron Brown. Gold medalist sprinter. For Bridgestone Olympic campaign. Commercial project shot for ads surrounding Bridgestone Tires' partnership with Team USA."
(Opposite page) Title: TikTokers. "Personal work with TikTok influencers."

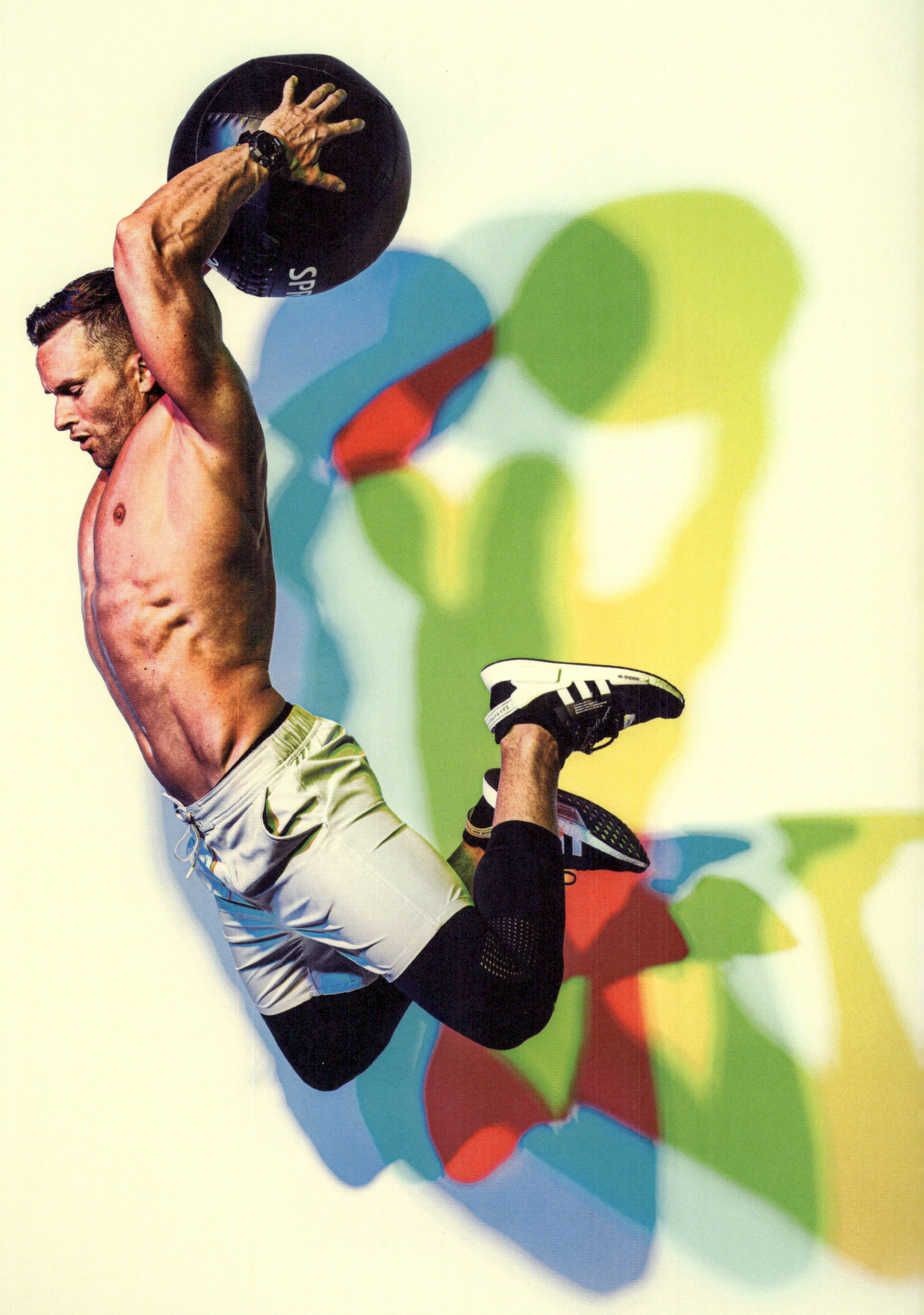

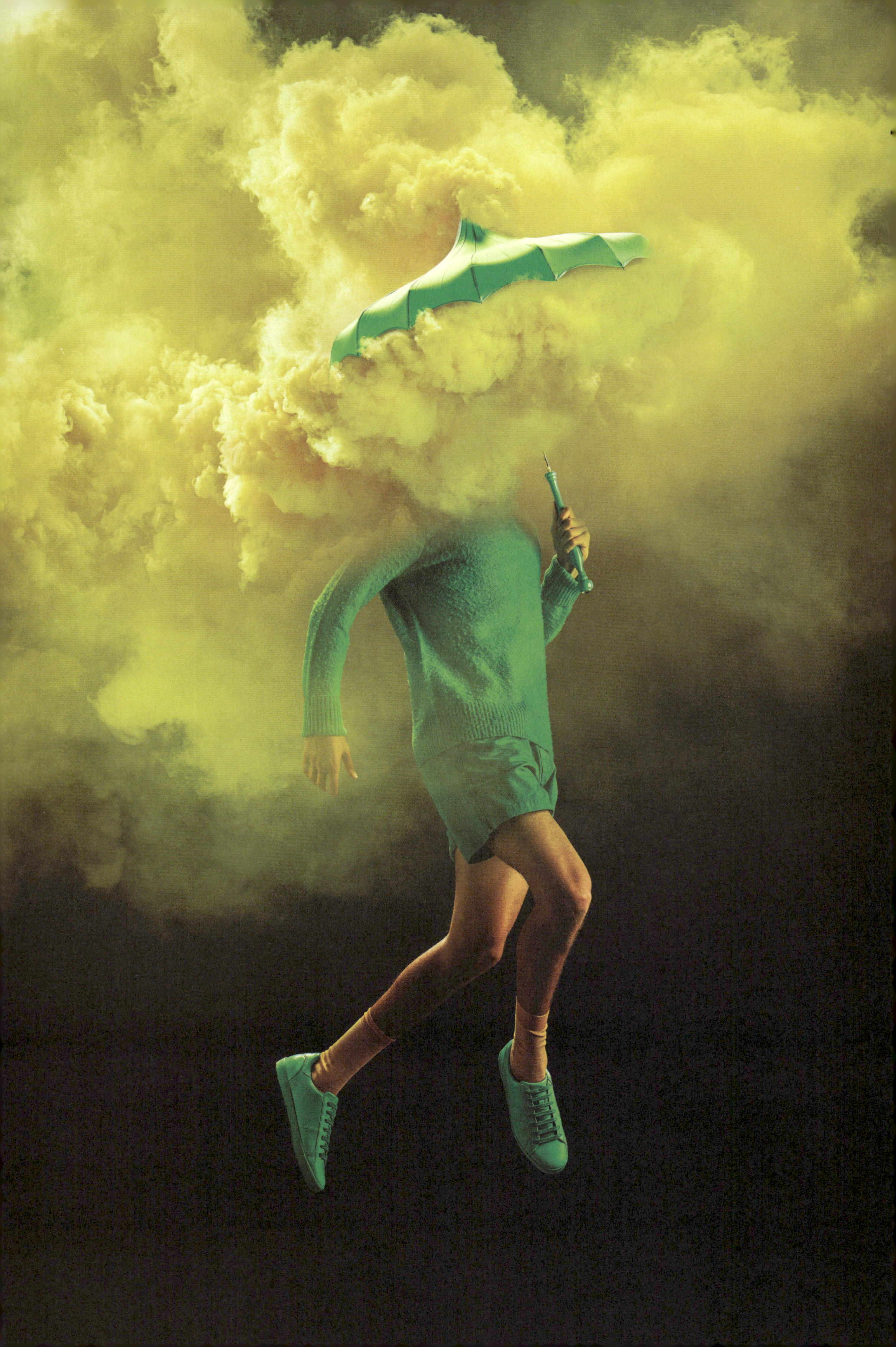

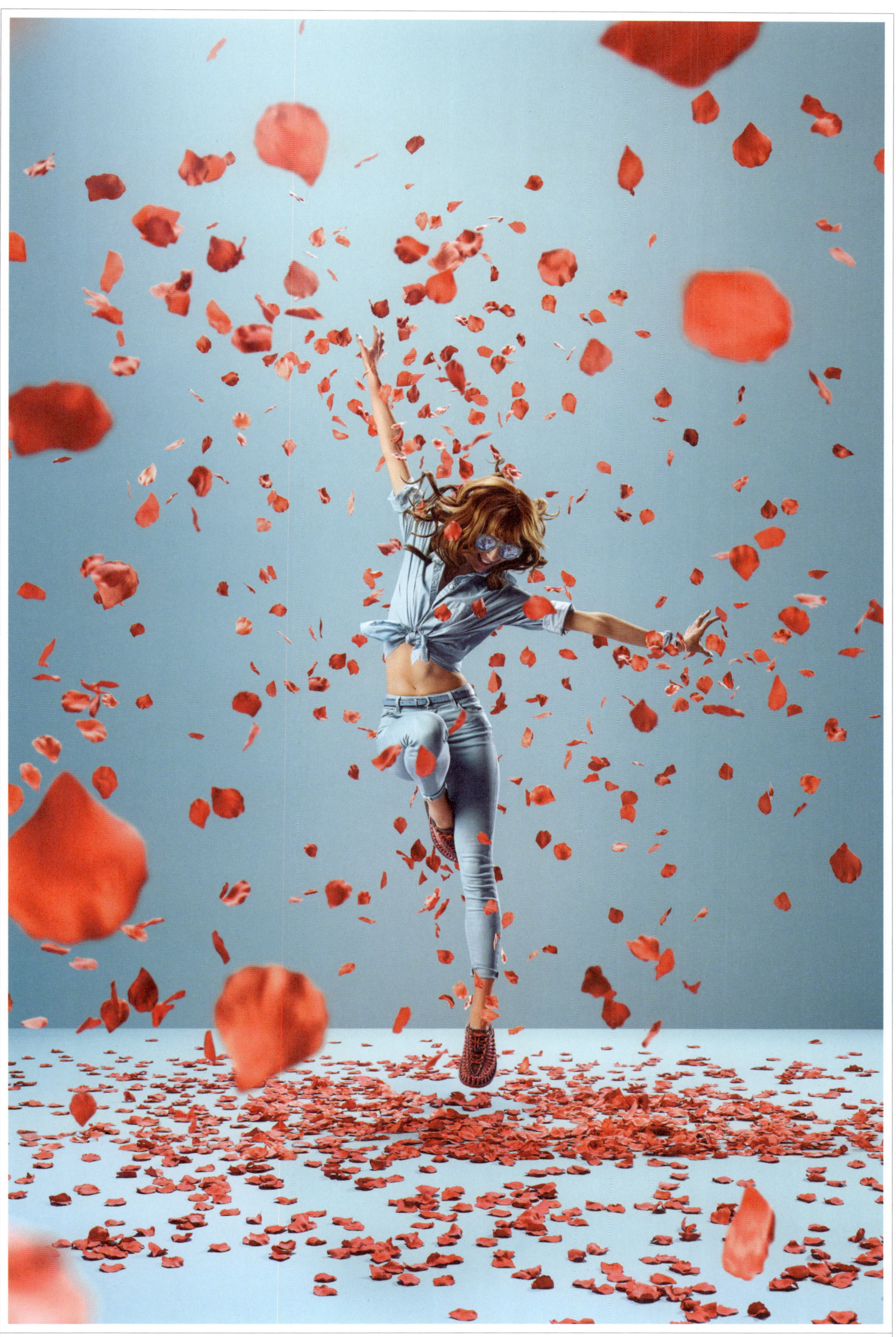

(Above) Title: KEEN Flowers. Commercial advertising. Creative Direction: Michael Minter. Brand: KEEN Footwear. Creative Direction & Photography: Tim Tadder. Digital Art: Mike Campau / (Opposite page) Bella Umbrella.

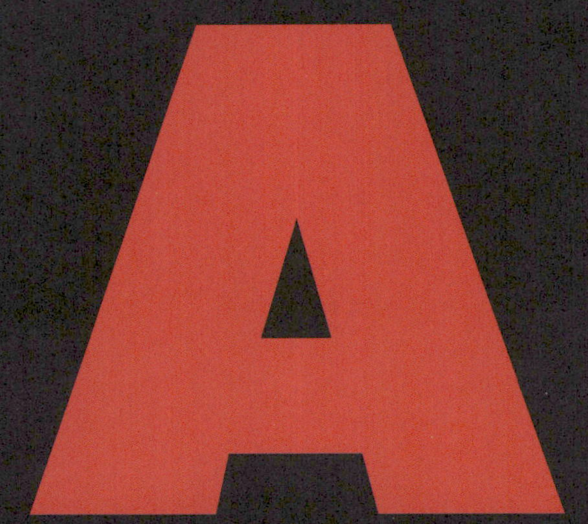

ART/ILLUSTRATION

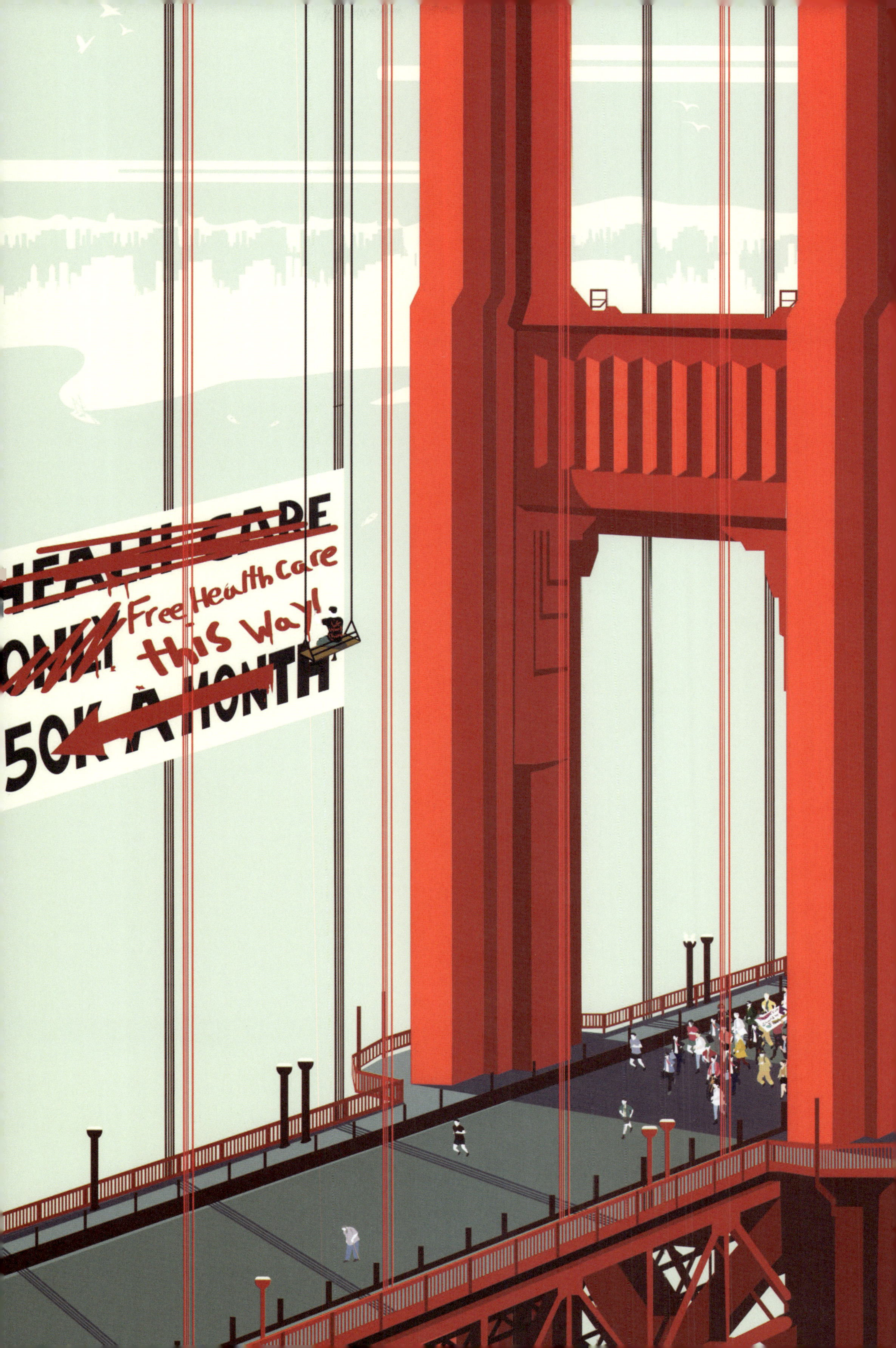
Free Health care
this way!
50K A MONTH

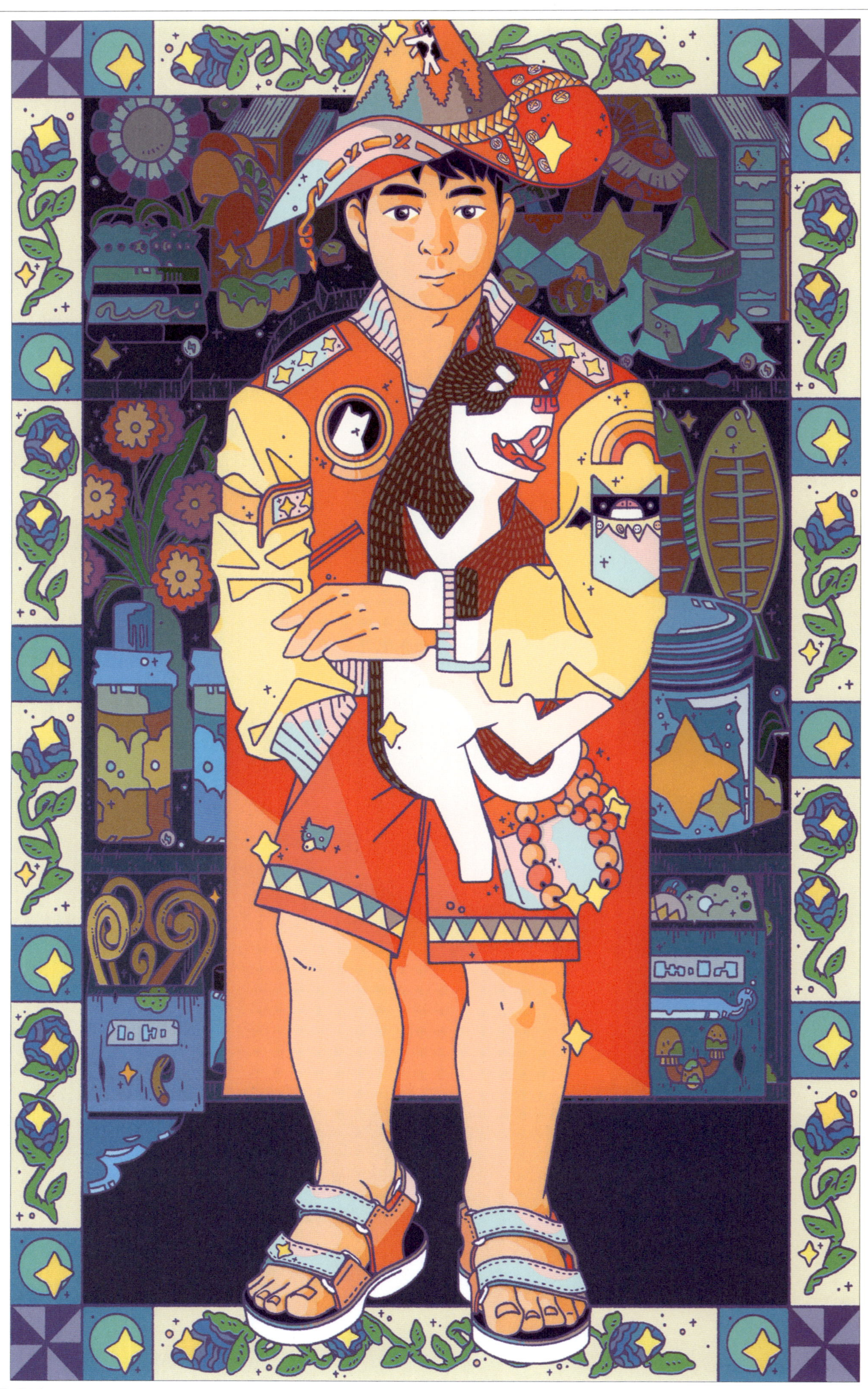

(Page 99) SDG's Poster Series, New Talent Annual 2025. Gold-winning student: Jackson Fojut. School: Colorado State University. Professor: John Gravdahl.
(Above) My BF, New Talent Annual 2025. Gold-winning student: Jianfei Sun. School: ArtCenter College of Design. Professor: Jim Salvati.

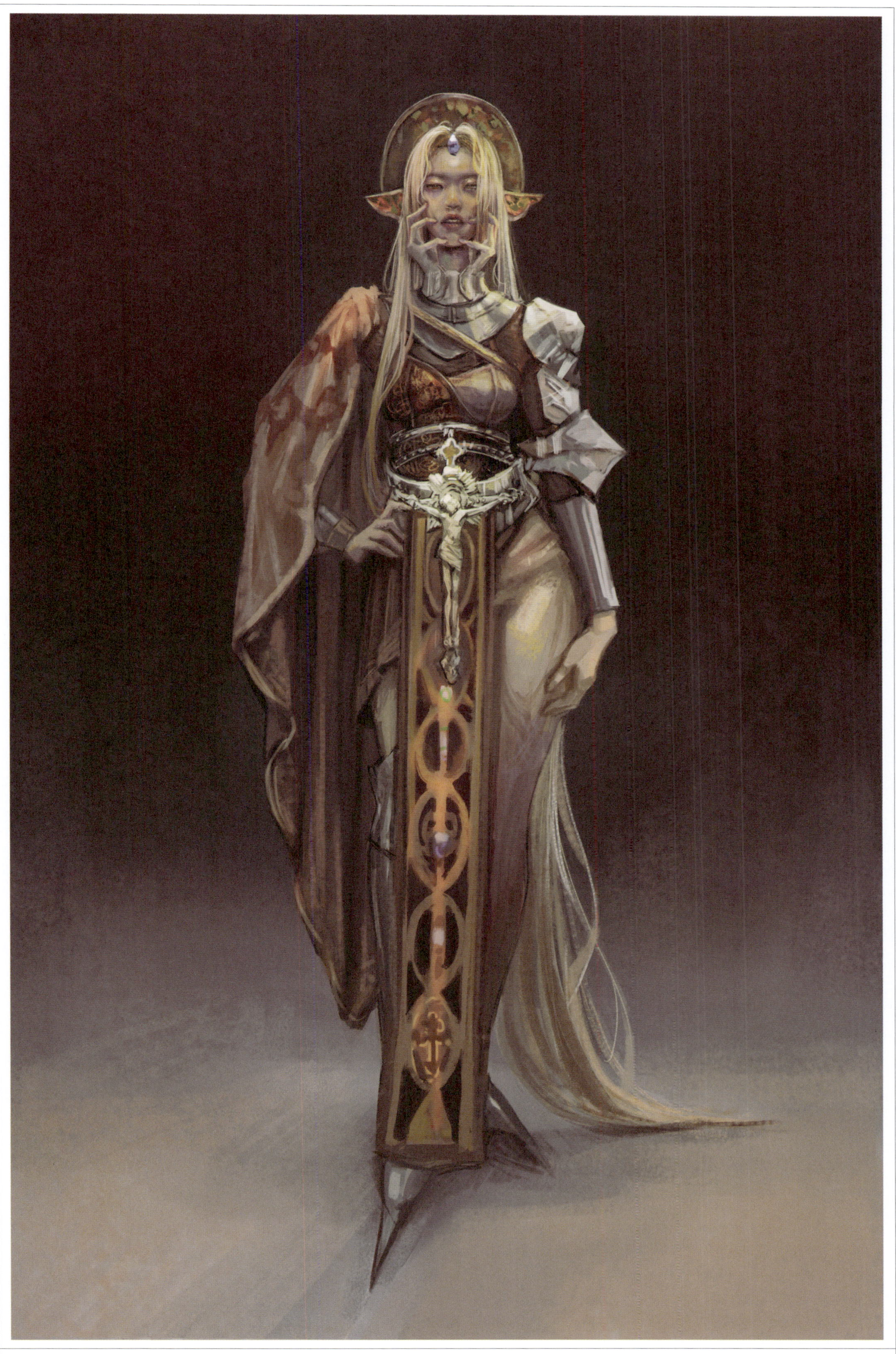

Byzantine Witch, New Talent Annual 2025. Platinum-winning student: Jingwen Zhang. School: School of Visual Arts. Professor: Eliott Lilly.

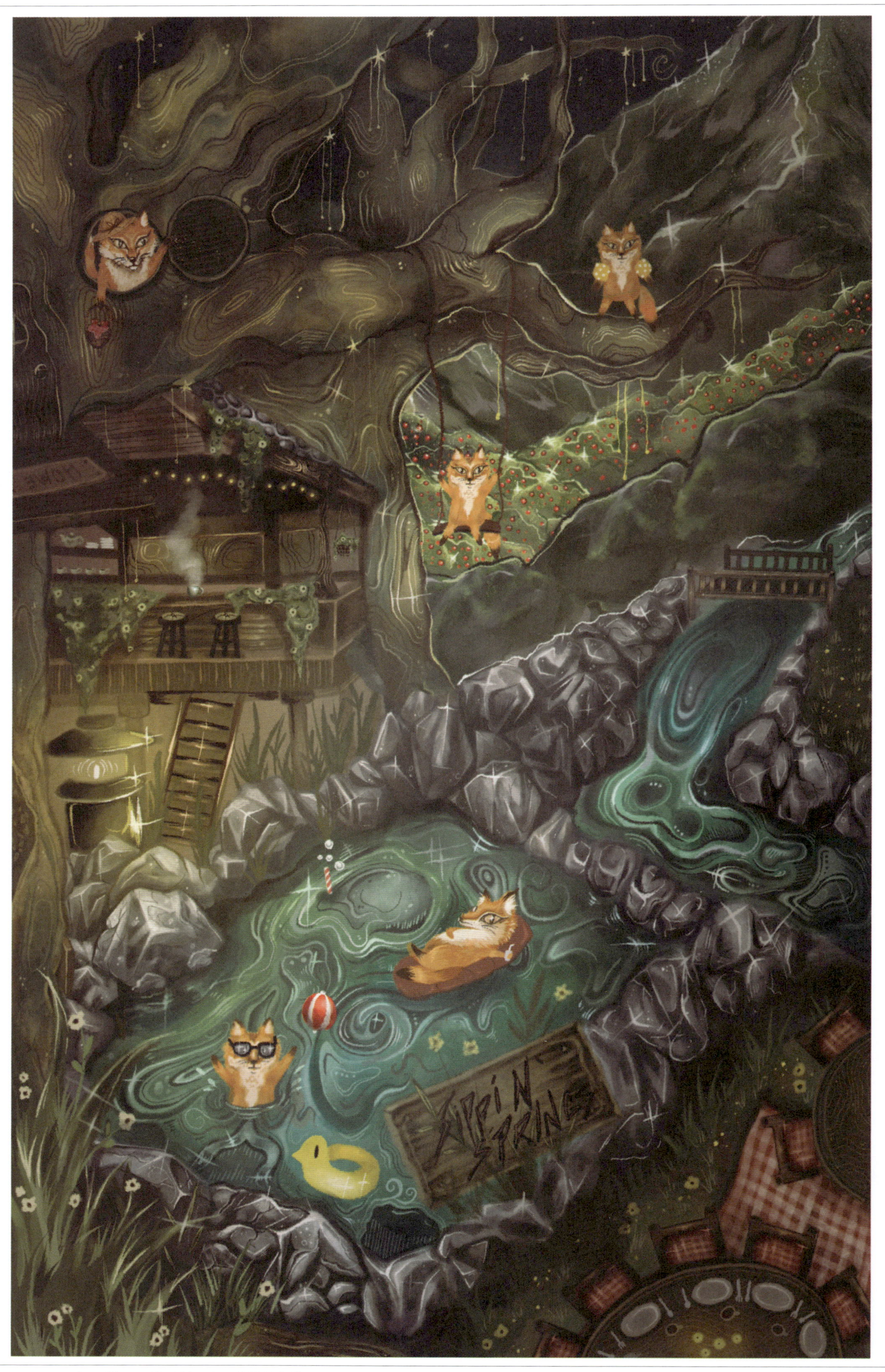

Sippin' Springs, New Talent Annual 2025. Gold-winning student: Emma Blomiley. School: Kutztown University of Pennsylvania. Professor: Elaine Cunfer.

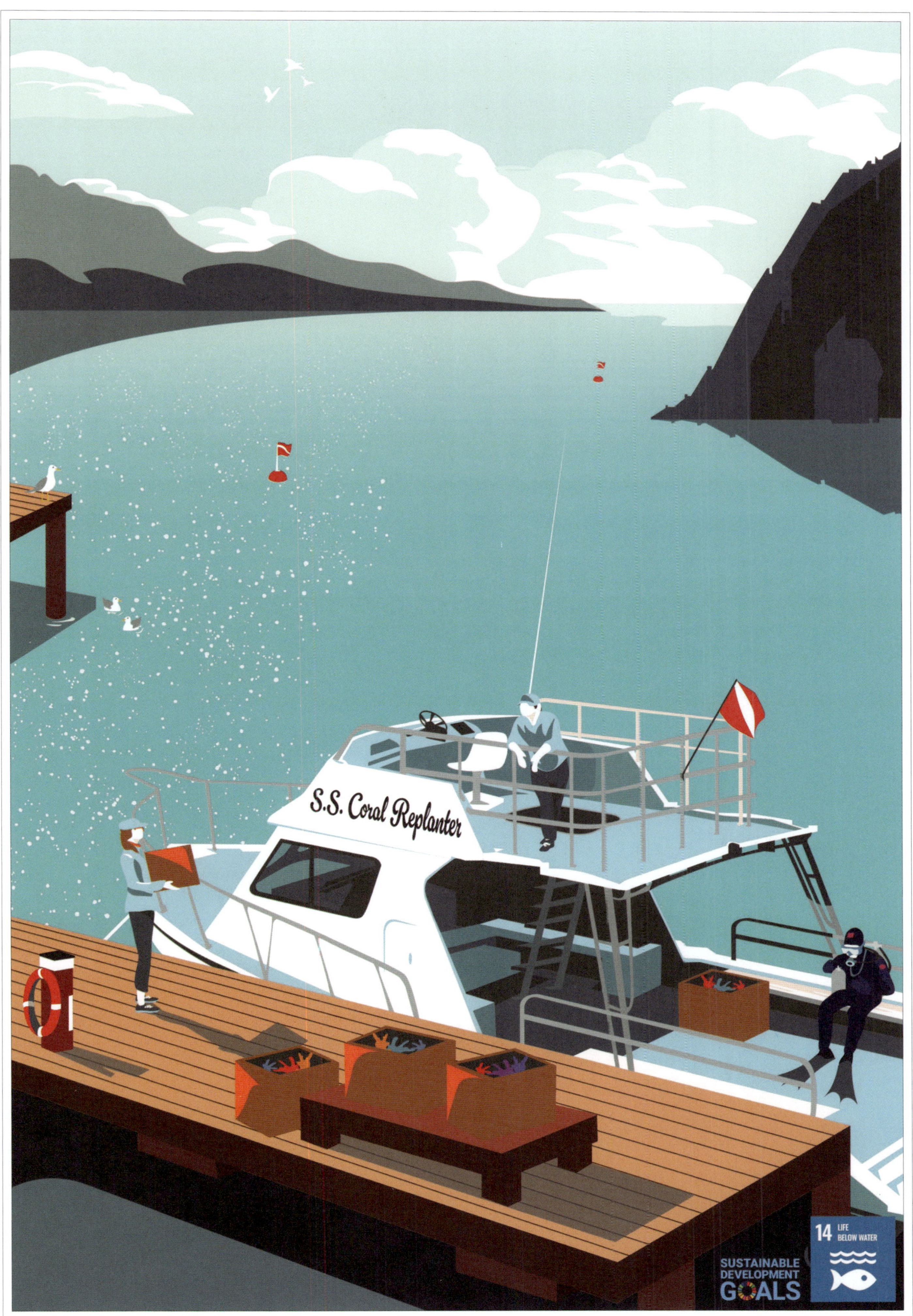

SDG's Poster Series, New Talent Annual 2025. Gold-winning student: Jackson Fojut. School: Colorado State University. Professor: John Gravdahl.

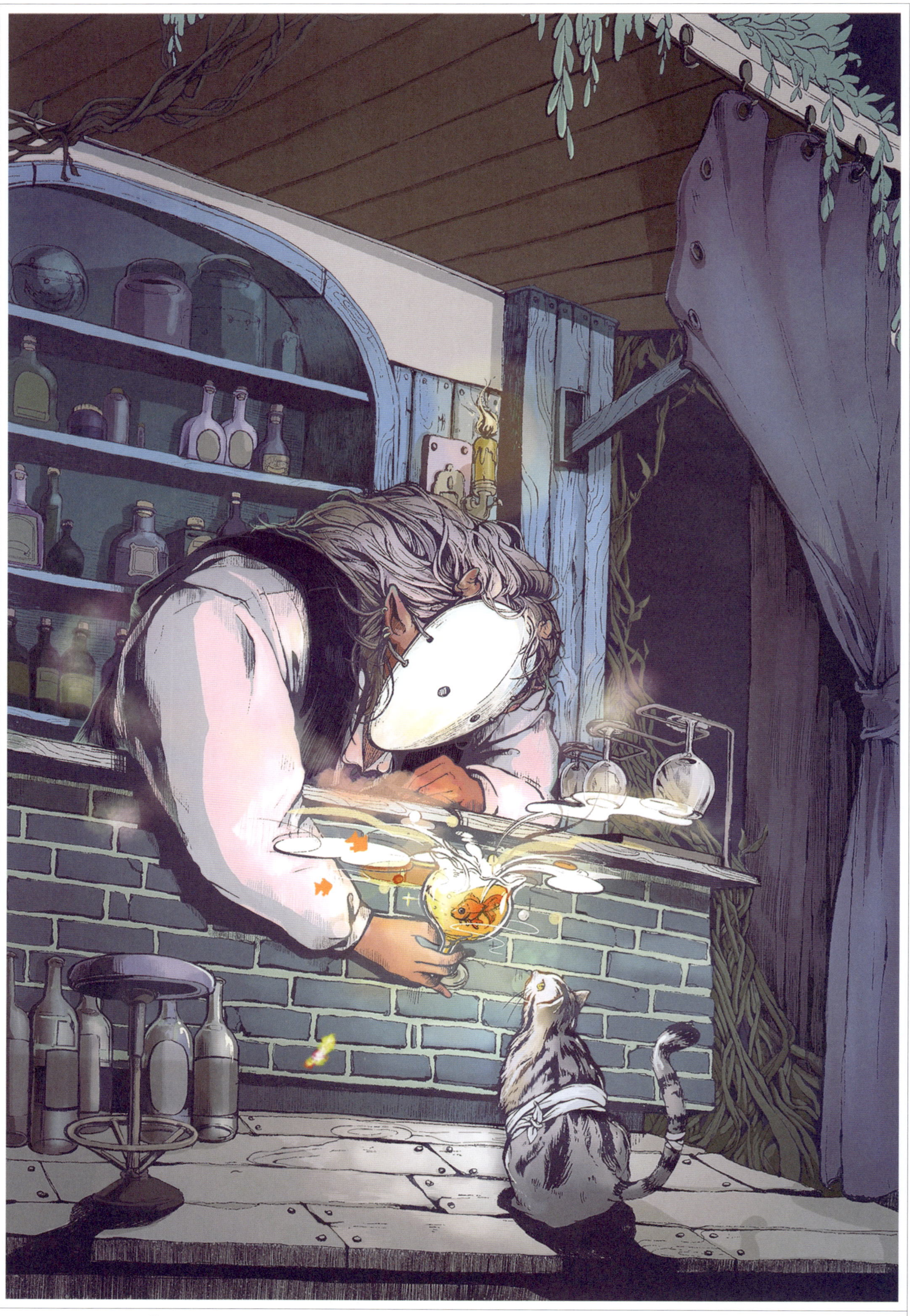

The Lure, New Talent Annual 2024. Gold-winning student: Jenna Park. School: School of Visual Arts. Professor: Josh Cochran.

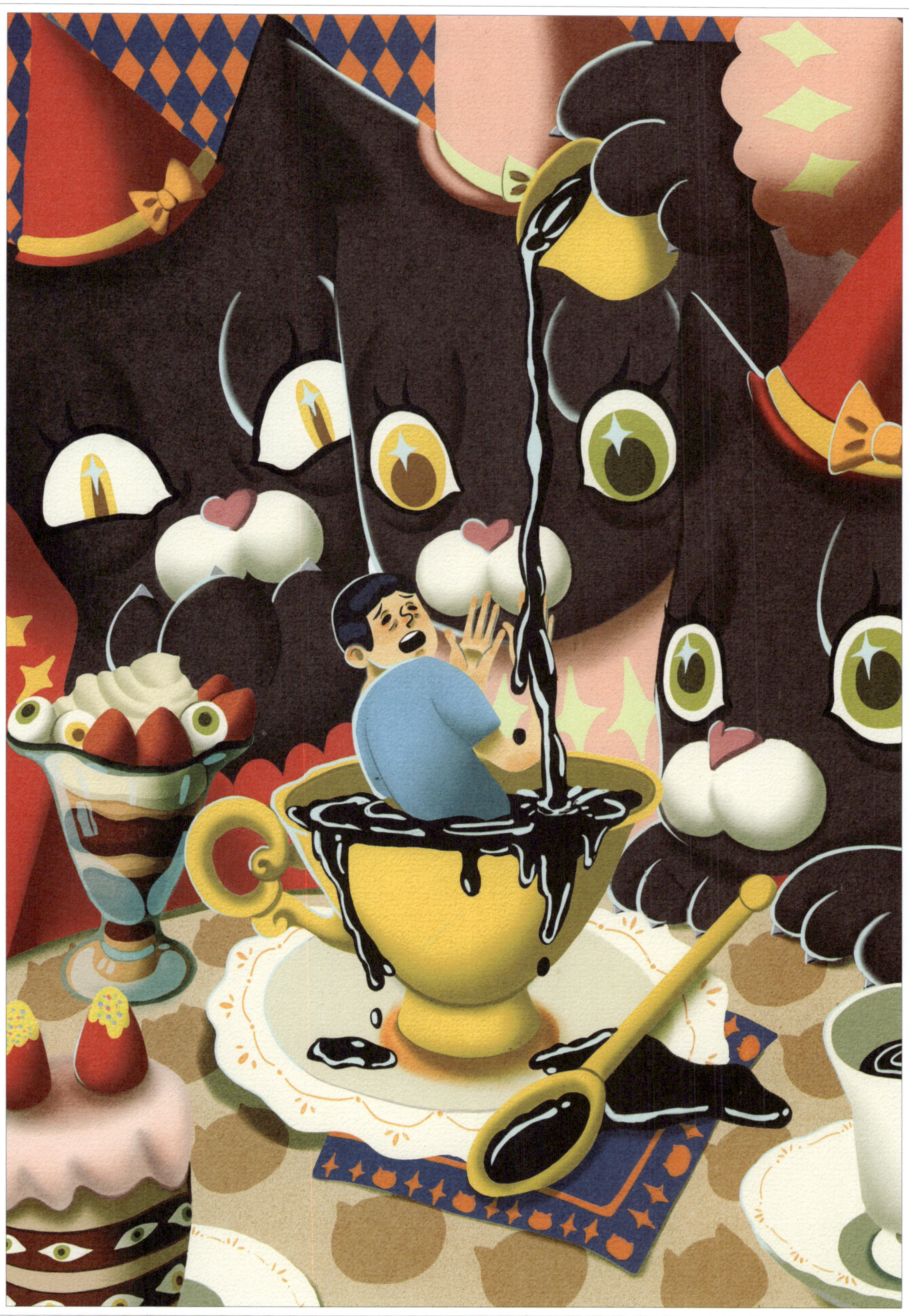

Behind the Eyes, New Talent Annual 2025. Gold-winning student: Tianyi Zhang. School: Rochester Institute of Technology. Professor: Anne Jordan.

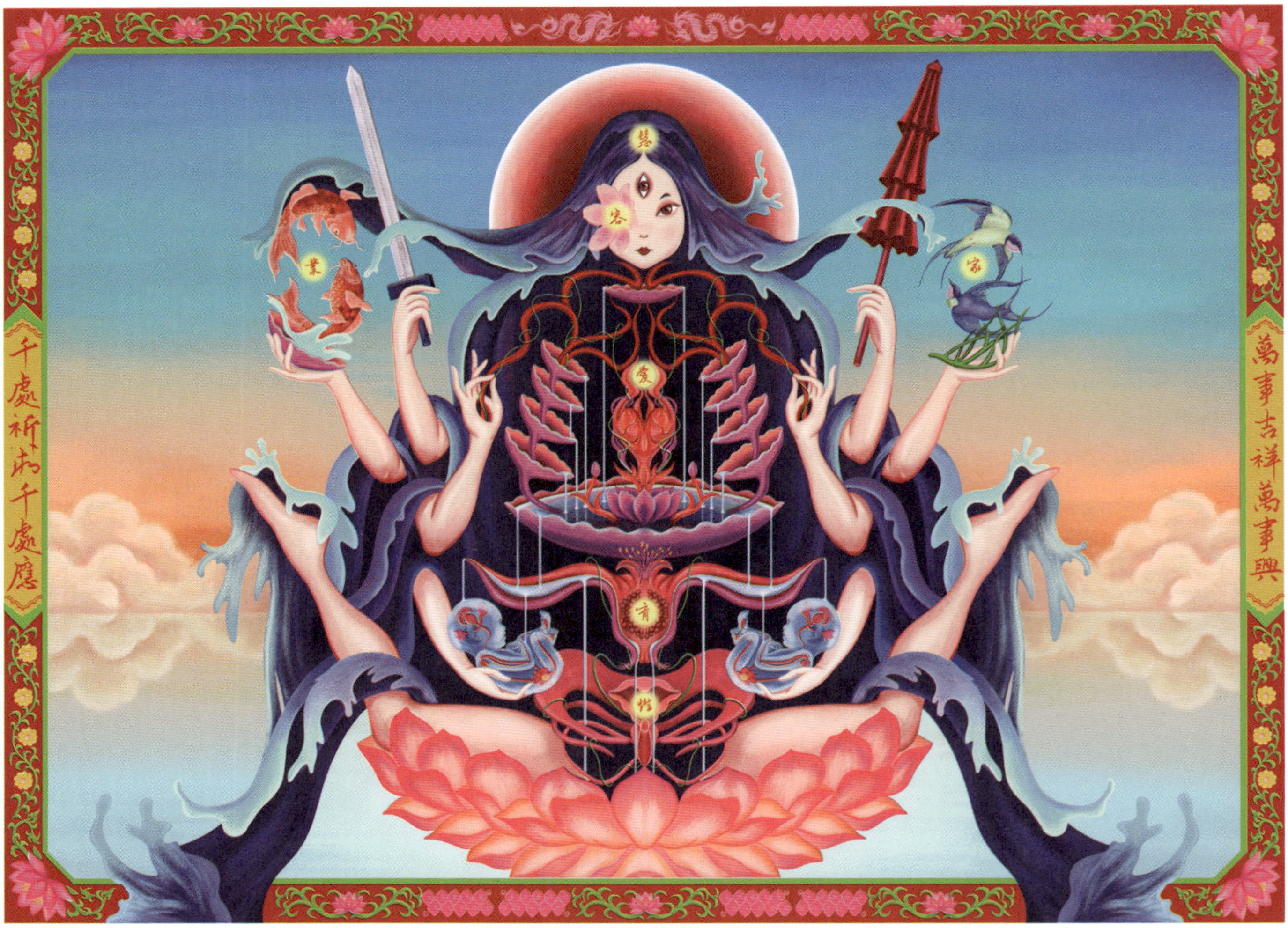

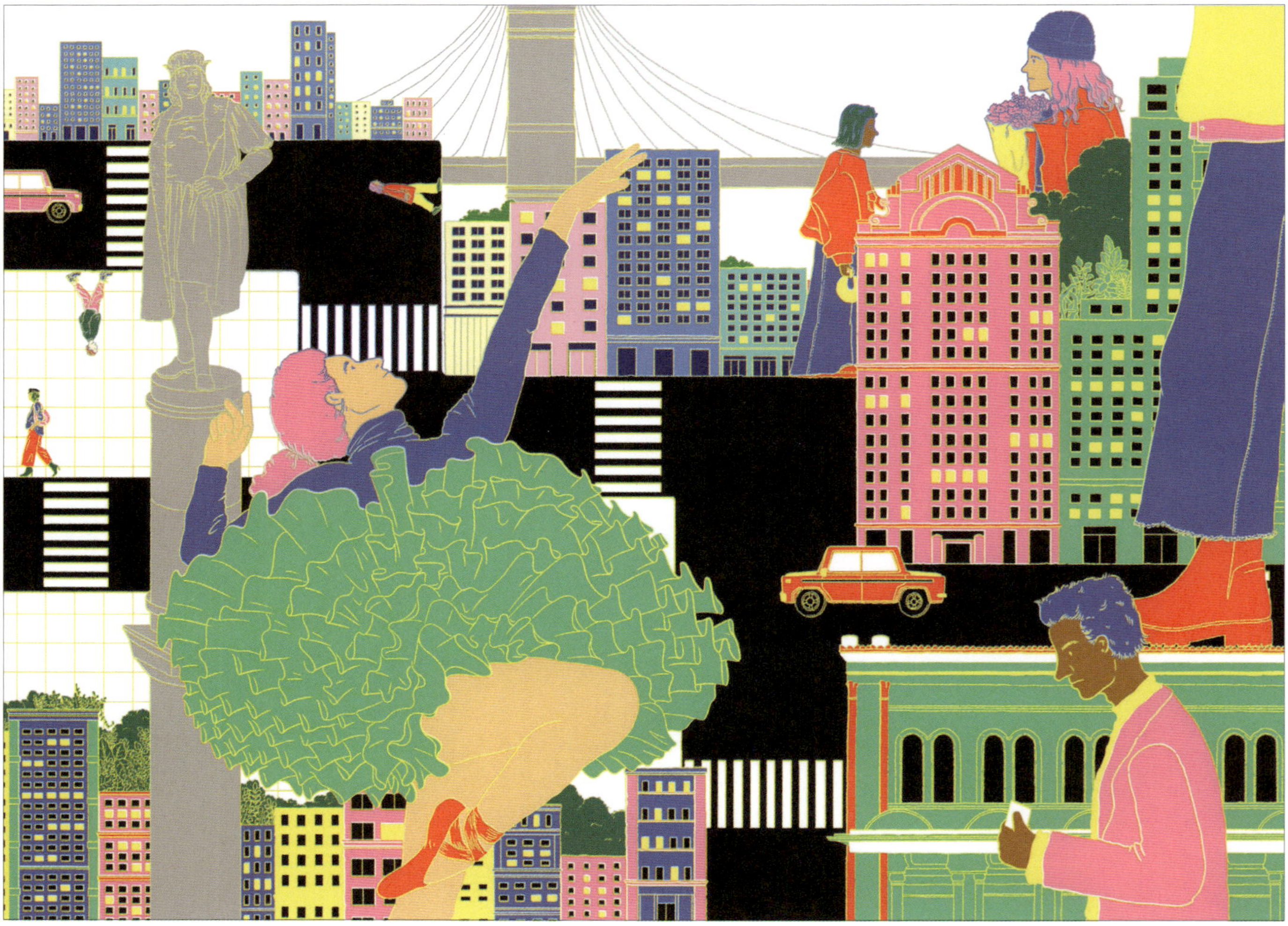

(Top) The New Goddess, New Talent Annual 2025. Platinum-winning student: Scarlett Yang. School: University of Brighton. Professor: Lizzie Finn.
(Bottom) Metropolitan Diary, New Talent Annual 2024. Gold-winning student: Samantha Wang. School: School of Visual Arts. Professor: Lily Padula.

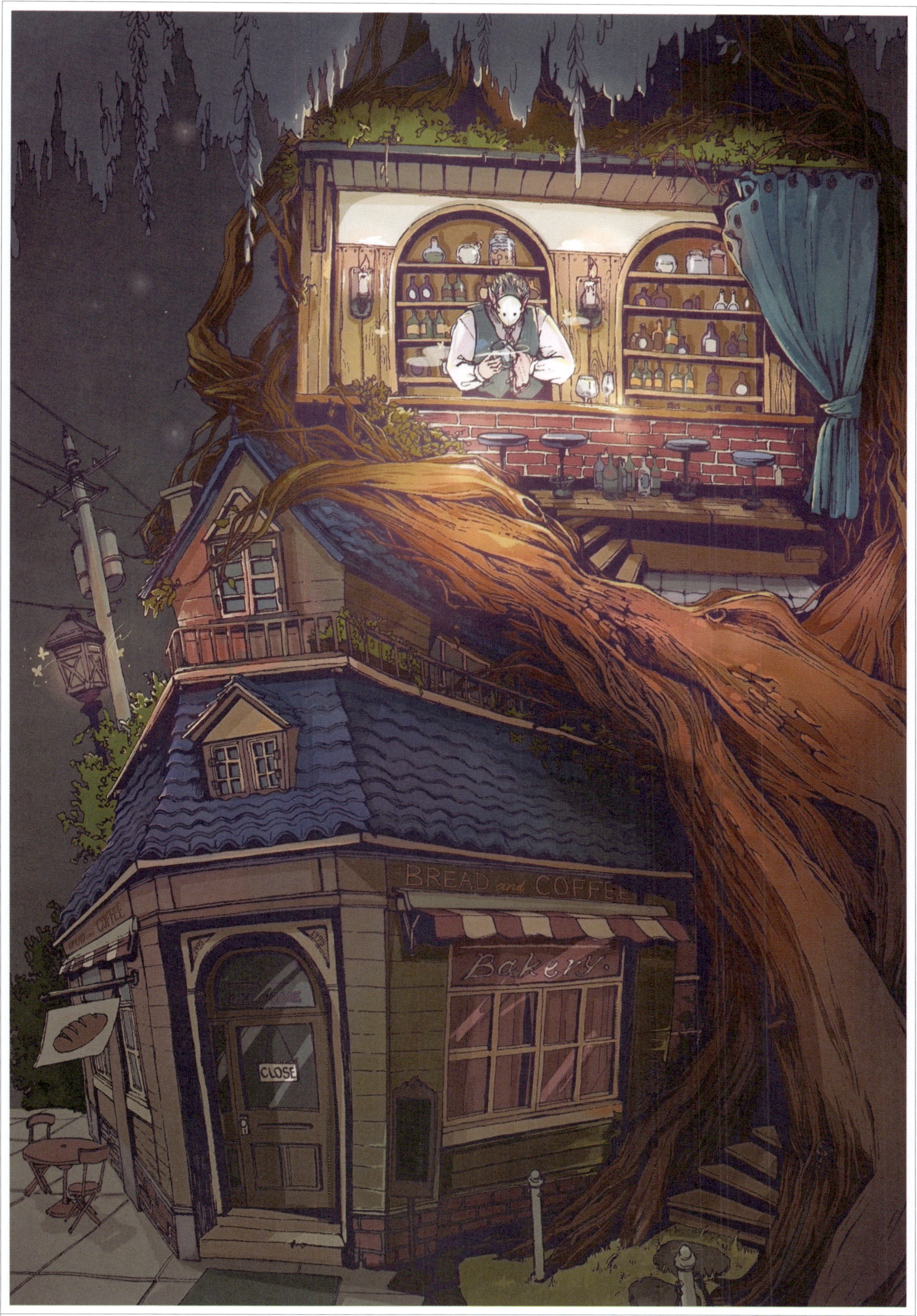

The Lure, New Talent Annual 2024. Gold-winning student: Jenna Park. School: School of Visual Arts. Professor: Josh Cochran.

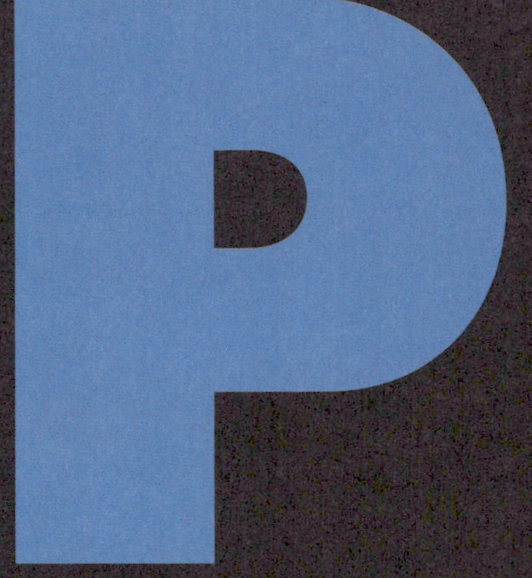

PRODUCTS

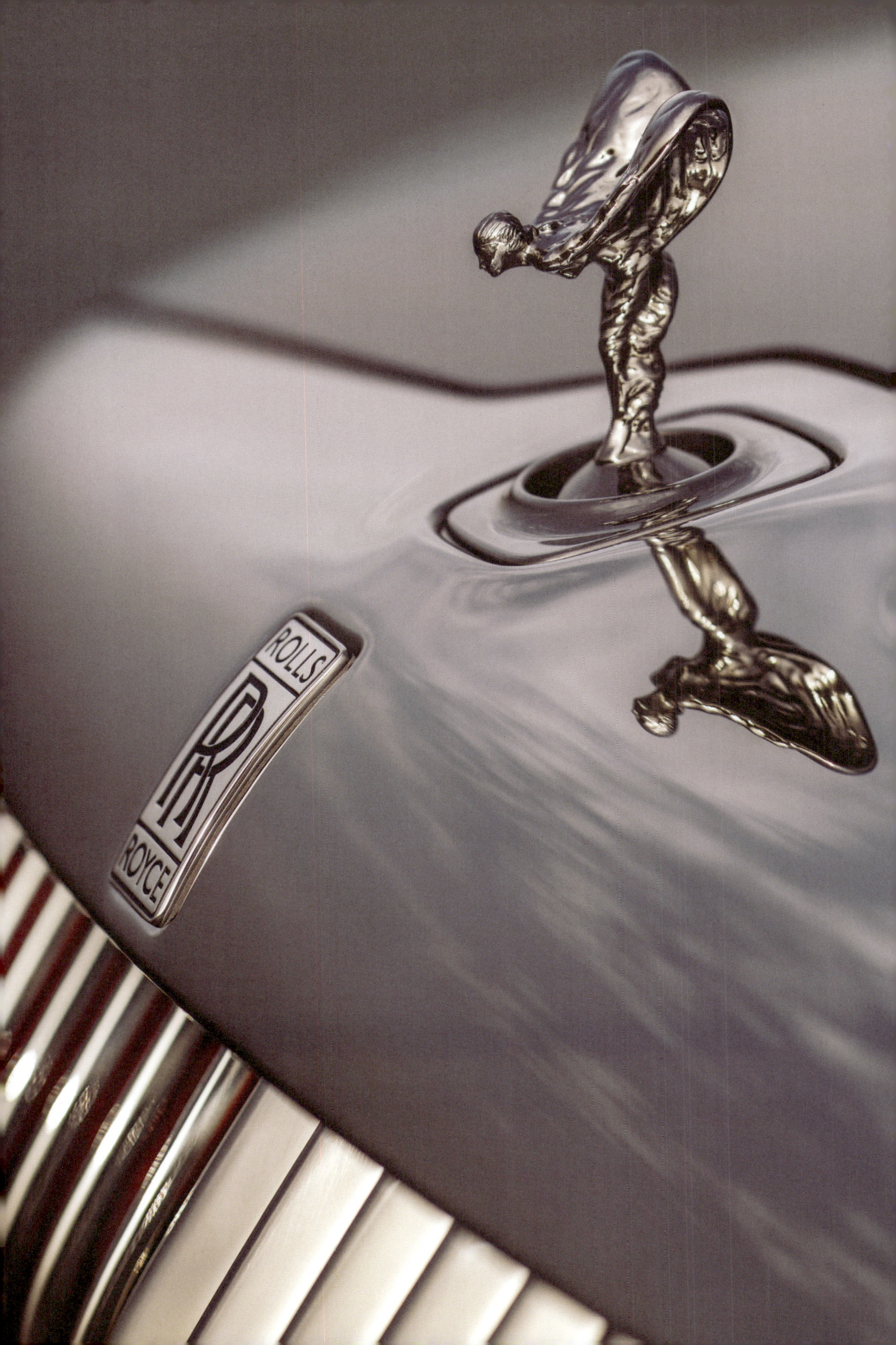
ROLLS
RR
ROYCE

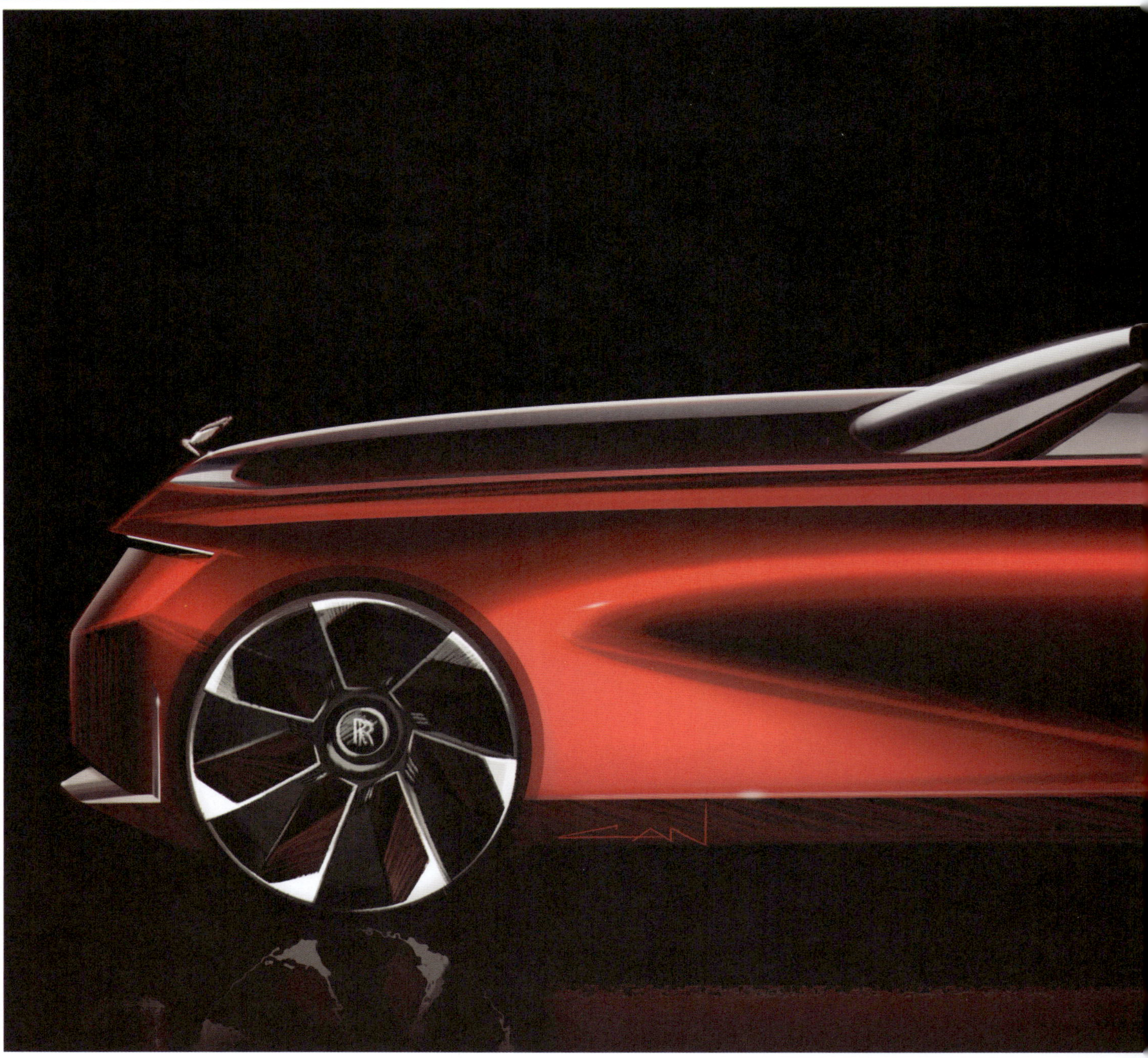

LA ROSE NOIRE DROPTAIL BY ROLLS-ROYCE MOTOR CARS LIMITED $30M+

Length: 5.3 m (17.4 ft)
Width: 2 m (6.6 ft)
Height: 1.5 m (4.9 ft)
Engine: Twin-turbocharged 6.75-L V12
Power output: 563 bhp at 5,250 rpm
Torque: 820 Nm (625 lb-ft) at 1,500 rpm

Within the hallowed workshops of Goodwood, where quintessential British craftsmanship meets boundless imagination, Rolls-Royce Motor Cars Limited has orchestrated perhaps the most profound meditation on bespoke luxury ever conceived. La Rose Noire Droptail transcends mere transportation to become a rolling manifesto for what occurs when design constraints are entirely abandoned, and artisanal excellence becomes the sole governing principle.

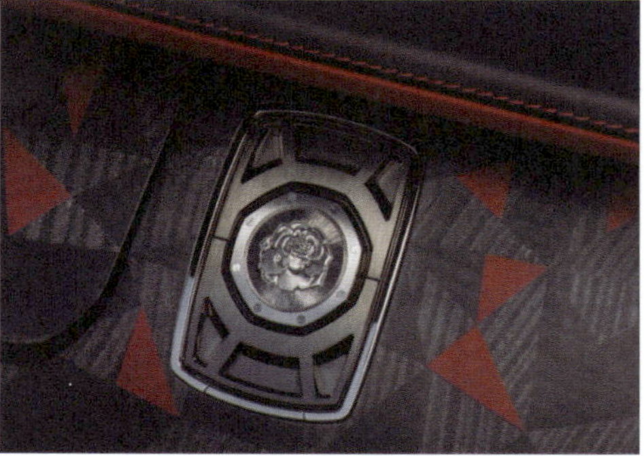

Stretching an impressive 5.3 meters in length with a commanding 2-meter width and purposefully low 1.5-meter height, La Rose Noire Droptail occupies space with the presence of a sculptural installation rather than a conventional automobile. The carefully considered proportions speak to mid-century racing prototypes while embracing contemporary luxury paradigms—a sophisticated synthesis that required a complete reimagining of Rolls-Royce's traditional aesthetic vocabulary.

The Droptail's silhouette represents a radical departure from the marque's typical upright stance. This dramatically horizontal emphasis creates visual tension between raw power and refined elegance, suggesting movement even when static. Every surface has been meticulously hand-formed to eliminate visual interruption, creating a seamless flow from nose to tail that speaks to aerodynamic efficiency and pure aesthetic ambition.

Beneath the exquisitely hand-crafted bodywork lies Rolls-Royce's legendary twin-turbocharged 6.75-liter V12 engine, producing an impressive 563 horsepower and a substantial 625 pounds per foot of torque. The sophisticated powertrain achieves 0-62 miles per hour in five seconds—truly remarkable for a vehicle prioritizing supreme refinement over raw performance. Maximum velocity reaches 155 miles per hour, though such specifications hardly capture the experiential reality of piloting this mechanical artwork.

The eight-speed automatic transmission features manual override capability, acknowledging that owners of such rari-

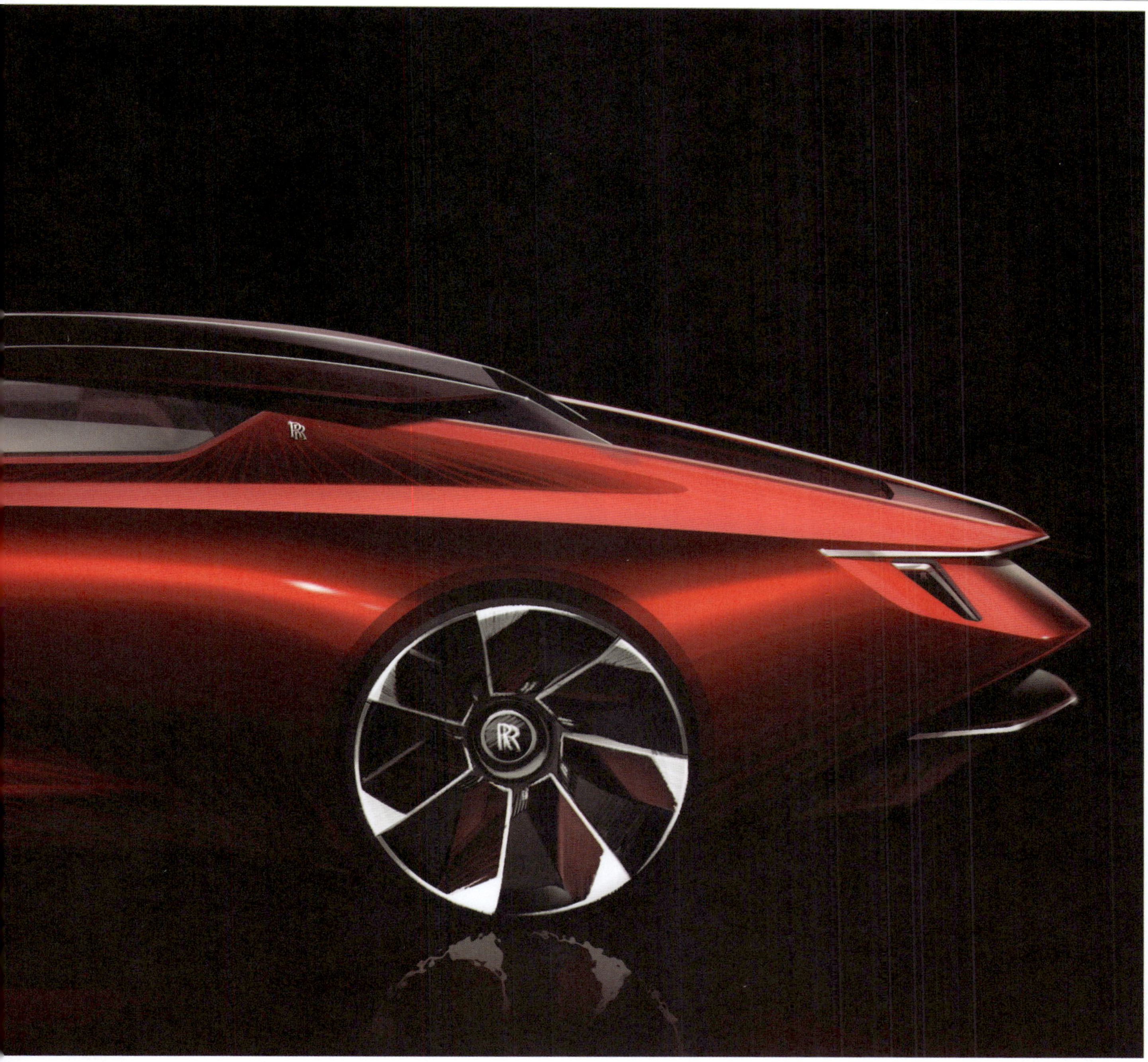

Transmission: 8-speed automatic gearbox with manual override
Acceleration: 0-100 km/h (0-62 mph) in 5 s
Top speed: 250 km/h (155 mph)
Body style: Cabriolet
Layout: FR layout
Wheels: 22 in

fied machinery occasionally desire direct mechanical connection. 22-inch wheels provide the substantial contact patch necessary for both handling and driving while maintaining the astounding visual impact befitting a statement piece such as this.

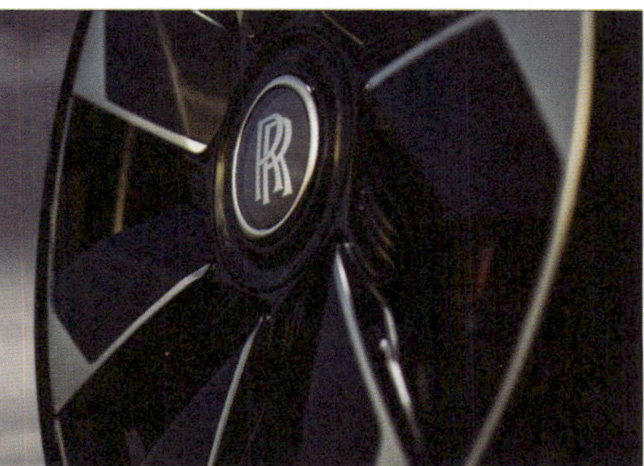

La Rose Noire Droptail represents the absolute apotheosis of Rolls-Royce's prestigious Coachbuild program, where traditional automotive manufacturing yields entirely to atelier-style creation. Each individual component undergoes obsessive refinement: hand-stitched leather requiring weeks of careful preparation, wood veneers selected from trees that have been aging for decades, and metal surfaces polished to mirror-like perfection through techniques unchanged since pre-war craftsmanship traditions.

The interior becomes an exhibition space for extraordinary material mastery. Surfaces that will never be touched by human hands receive the same meticulous attention as primary contact points. This unwavering commitment to invisible excellence represents luxury's purest expression—where perfection exists for its own sake rather than a practical necessity.

The evocative "Black Rose" nomenclature suggests both beauty and darkness, romance and mystery—dualities that permeate every single design decision. This carefully developed concept influences everything from the precise color selection to the material texture choices, creating a cohesive aesthetic narrative that transforms mere conveyance into a profound emotional experience.

At an extraordinary $30 million, La Rose Noire Droptail occupies rarified territory where traditional value propositions become entirely irrelevant. Instead, it stands as the ultimate expression of automotive design as pure art form—definitively proving that when budgets become unlimited and creativity unconstrained, the resulting objects transcend their functional origins to become cultural artifacts worthy of museums rather than merely garages.

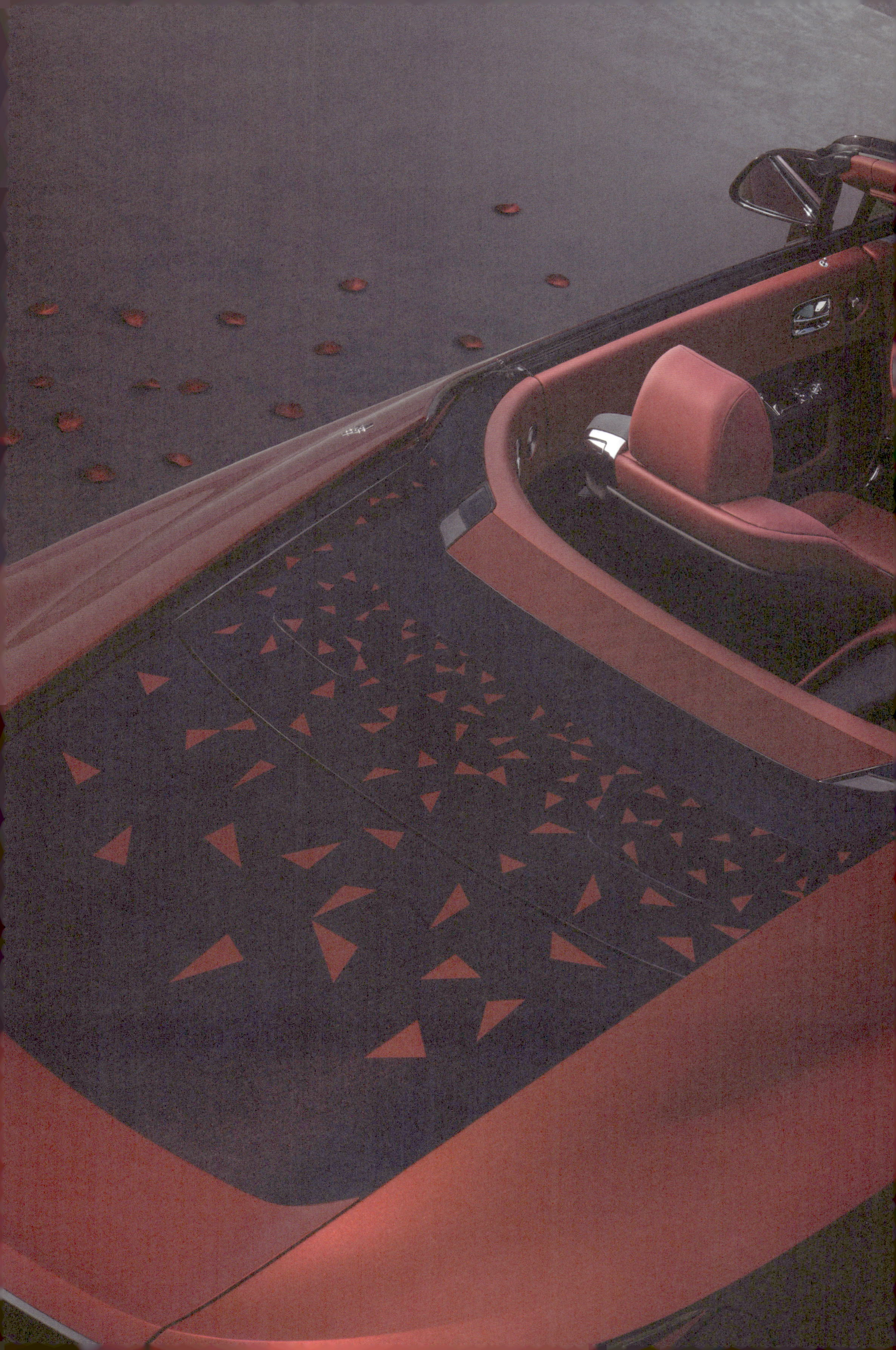

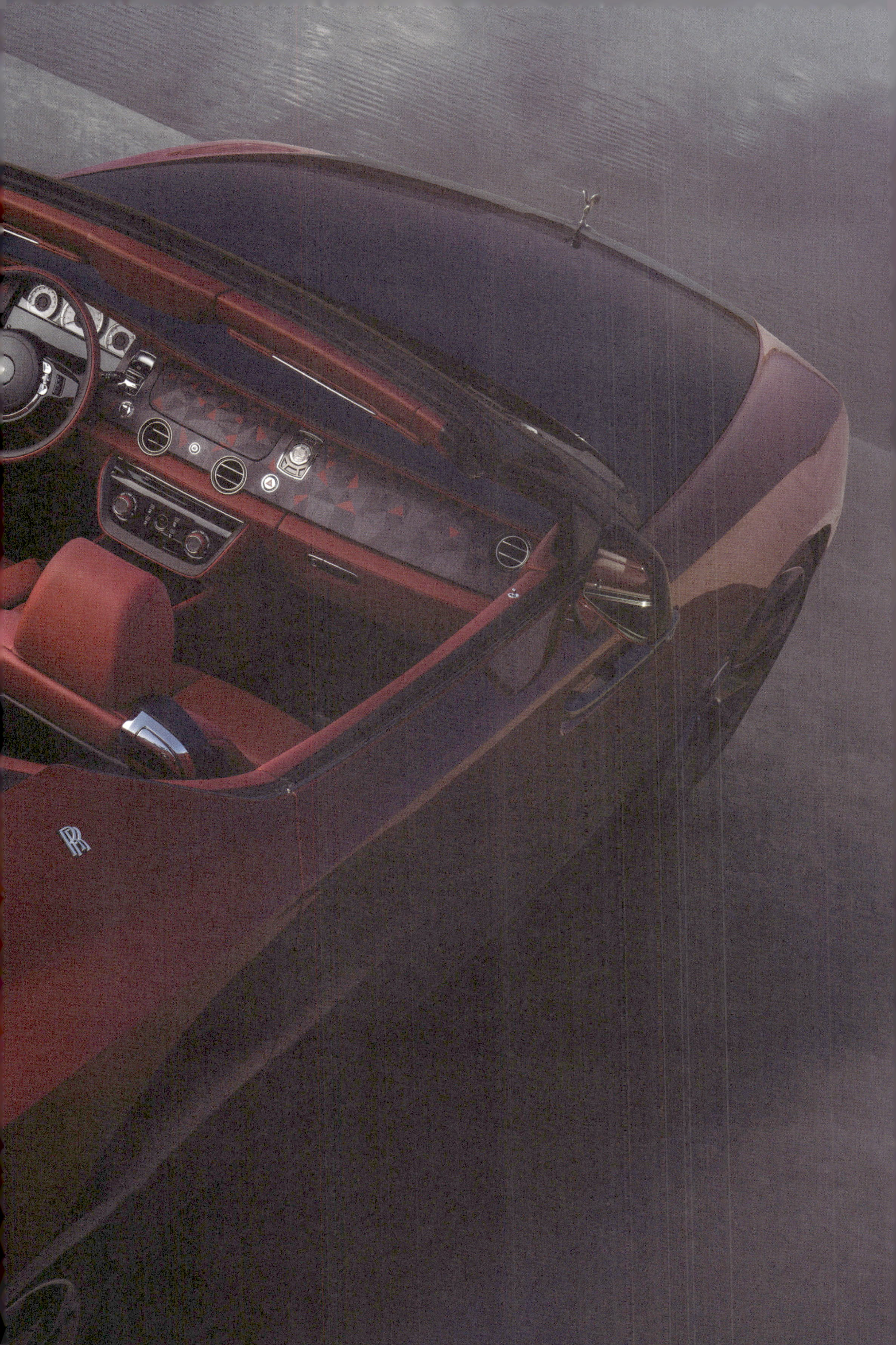

OWLET ONE BY OWLET BIKES **$3-4000**

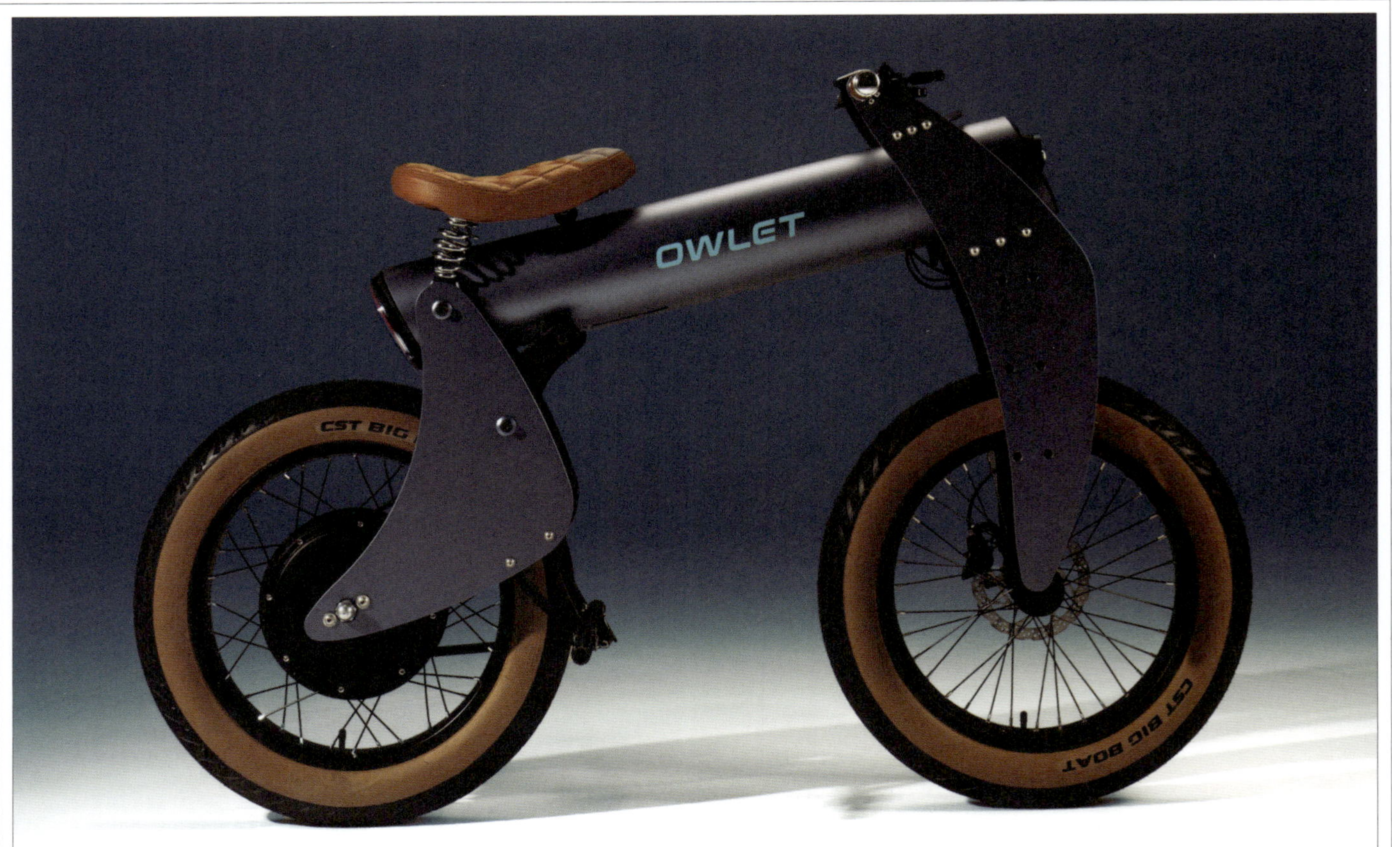

Dimensions: 58-63 in* x 37 in x 21 in
(*Depending on wheelbase setting)
Folded dimensions: 44 in x 37 in x 21 in
Weight: 84 lbs
Seat height: 31 in

Wheels: 20 in fat bike
Wheelbase: 25-40 in
Travel front fork: 3.5 in
Lights: 30 W LED
Brakes: Shimano hydraulic disc brakes

Top speed: 30 mph with 3 easily accessible modes (15mph, 20mph, 30mph)
Motor: 3,000 W peak direct drive motor
Torque: 180 Nm
Battery power: 1,500 Wh (56V 30 Ah)

Charger type: 350 W 6A+
Charging time: 2.5 h
Range: 40-60 mi

In a time where congestion meets environmental consciousness, Owlet Bikes has engineered a profound reimagining of how you get to places. The Owlet One is not just an electric bicycle (e-bike) but also as a sophisticated design statement that addresses the intersection of mobility, sustainability, and spatial efficiency in whatever contemporary metropolitan environment you live in.

The Owlet One's defining characteristic lies in its revolutionary folding mechanism, achieving dramatic dimensional transformation from 58-63 inches to a compact 44-inch folded profile. This engineering marvel weighs just 84 pounds while maintaining structural integrity sufficient to support 30 miles per hour speeds—a remarkable achievement in material optimization and mechanical design. The wheelbase system, adjustable from 25 to 40 inches, demonstrates a smart understanding of riding dynamics versus storage requirements.

20-inch fat bike wheels allow for plenty of stability without impeding the folding capabilities. This tire choice represents a careful balance between rolling efficiency, ride comfort, and spatial constraints—design decisions reflecting deep consideration of user experience across different urban terrains. The 31-inch seat height accommodates a variety of diverse rider anthropometrics while maintaining the low center of gravity needed for confident handling.

The Owlet One's 3,000-watt peak direct drive motor delivers 180 Newton meters of torque through elegantly integrated packaging that avoids the visual clutter typical of electric mobility devices. This enables three distinct speed modes—15, 20, and 30 miles per hour—acknowledging that mobility requires adaptability to varied contexts and regulatory environments. The motor's direct drive configuration eliminates mechanical complexity while providing the silent operation important for citywide acceptance.

The 1,500-watt-per-hour battery system achieves remarkable energy density, delivering a 40-60 mile range while maintaining reasonable charging parameters. The 350-watt charger completes replenishment in 2.5 hours—perfectly aligned with typical working hours. This electrical setup demonstrates how technical specifications can serve aesthetic goals: Power delivery remains invisible until it's used, preserving the visual cleanliness essential to modern design sensibilities.

Shimano hydraulic disc brakes provide stopping power commensurate with the Owlet One's performance capabilities while reflecting the design team's commitment to proven, reliable components. The 30-watt LED lighting system integrates seamlessly into the overall design, providing safe illumination without compromising the bike's appearance. The 3.5-inch front fork travel balances comfort with performance, acknowledging that riders encounter various surface conditions.

With pricing between $3,000-4,000—if you pay a $50 reservation fee—the Owlet One is sophisticated enough to satisfy design-conscious consumers while remaining attainable compared to other alternatives. The fee suggests confidence in the product's appeal while enabling equal access to advanced mobility solutions. Furthermore, this pricing strategy reflects an understanding that transformative design must achieve broad adoption to create a meaningful impact.

The Owlet One is an evolution beyond traditional bicycle models toward genuine urban mobility solutions. Its folding capability addresses the spatial constraints of city living, while its performance specifications acknowledge that personal transportation has to compete with automotive convenience. By solving storage, performance, and aesthetic challenges simultaneously, Owlet Bikes demonstrates how thoughtful design can make sustainable mobility genuinely affordable rather than merely desirable, proving that environmental responsibility and design excellence are complementary rather than competing objectives.

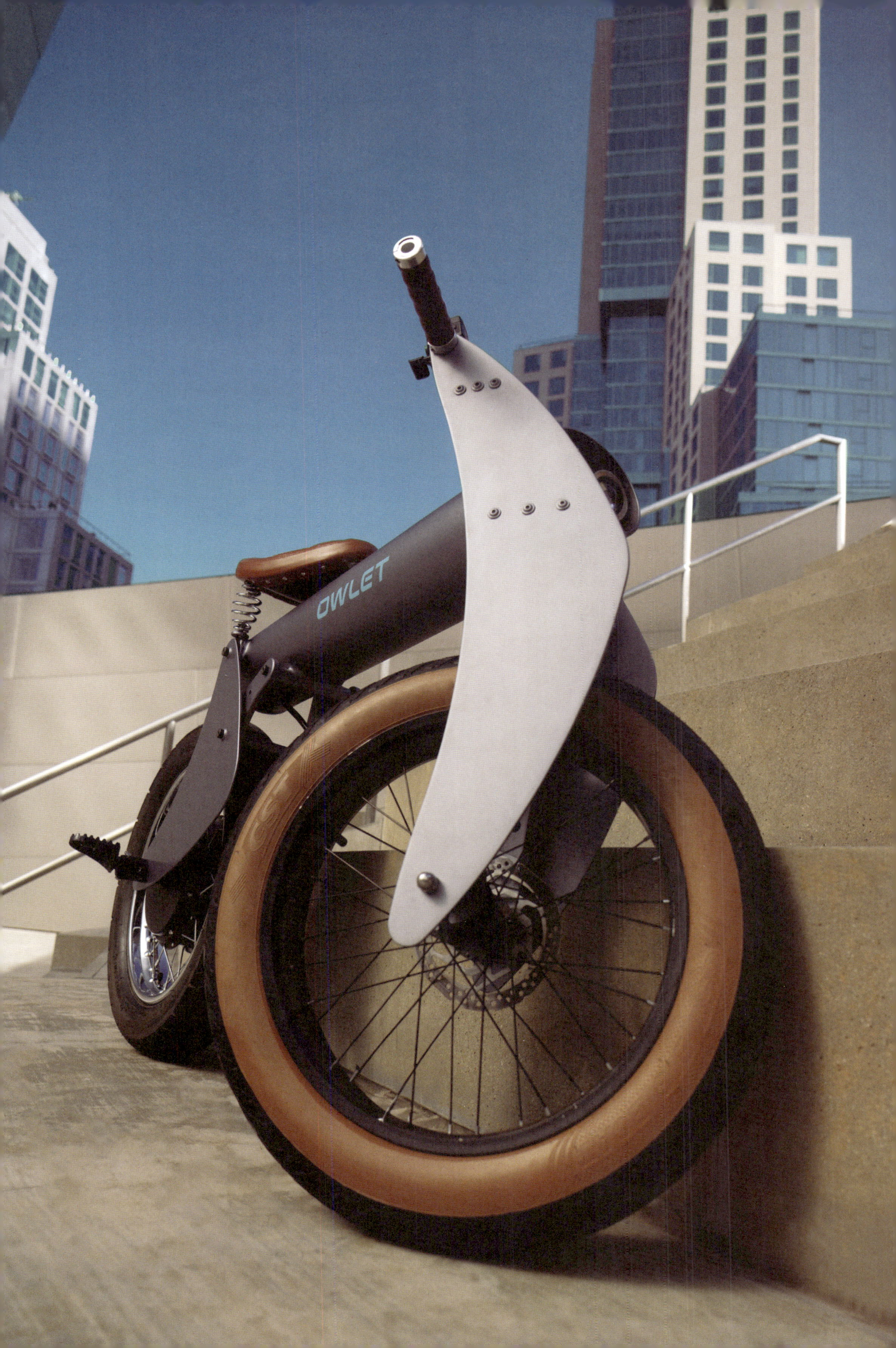
OWLET

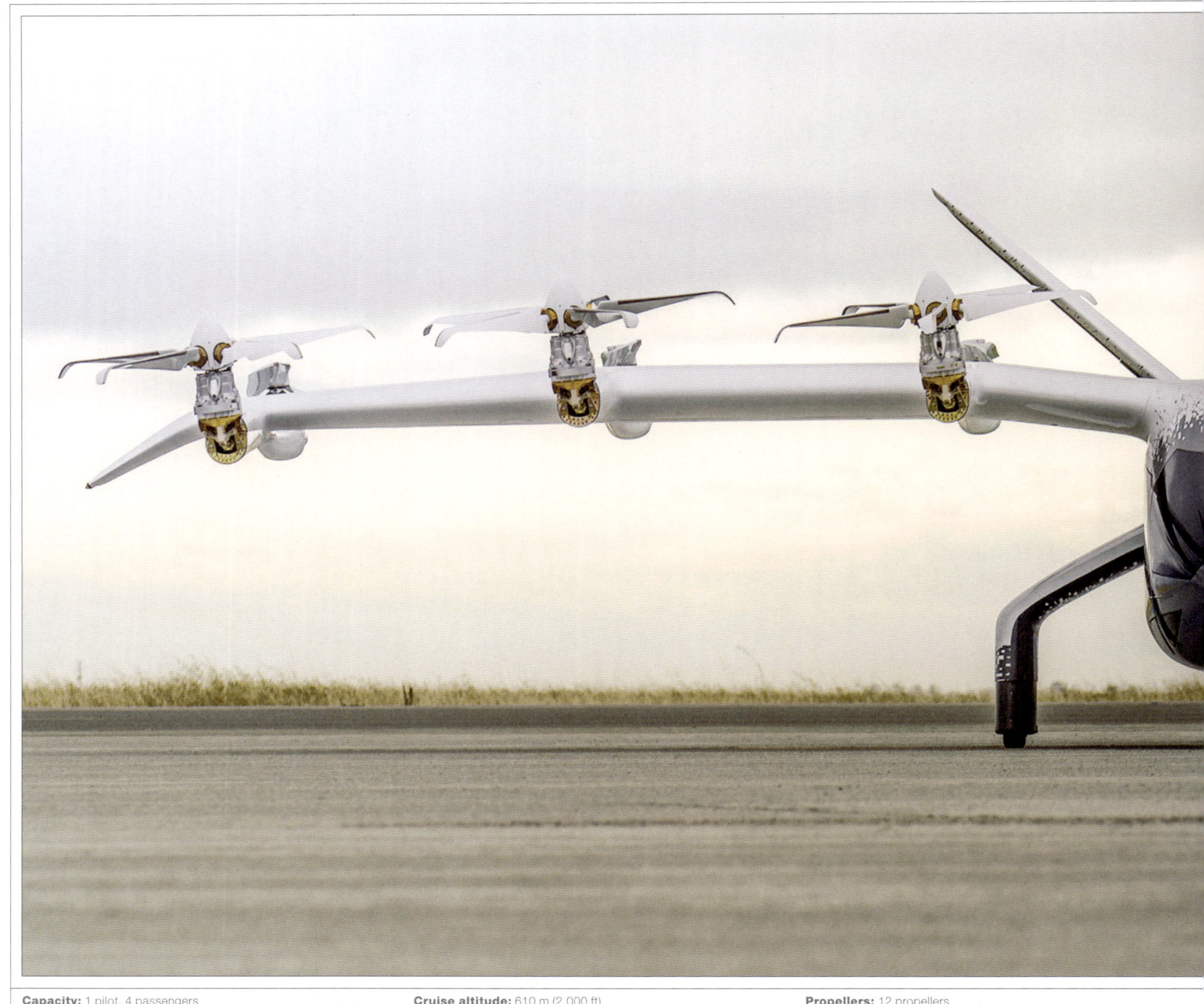

Capacity: 1 pilot, 4 passengers
Cruise speed: 150 mph (241 km/h)
Range: 20-50 mi (32-80 km)
Cruise altitude: 610 m (2,000 ft)
Maximum payload: 1,000+ lbs (456+ kg)
Maximum takeoff weight: 7,000 lbs (3,175 kg)
Propellers: 12 propellers
Electric motors: 12 electric motors
Power source: 6 independent battery packs

Above the gridlocked arteries of cities everywhere, a revolution is silently unfolding. Archer Aviation's Midnight represents more than aerial transportation; it embodies a fundamental reimagining of urban movement, transforming three-dimensional space into navigable infrastructure. This electric vertical takeoff and landing (eVTOL) aircraft doesn't merely promise to ferry passengers above traffic—it heralds the dawn of sky taxi services that will redefine urban living.

Midnight's polished design language speaks to aerospace sophistication that is refined for civilian elegance. The high wing configuration paired with a distinctive V-tail creates visual harmony while optimizing aerodynamic efficiency. 12 precisely positioned propellers generate lift through distributed propulsion architecture that eliminates single points of failure while creating the whisper-quiet operation essential for citywide use. At just 45-65 decibels, Midnight operates more quietly than ground-based traffic, enabling seamless integration into dense metropolitan environments.

The panoramic windows transform this utilitarian transport into an awe-inspiring journey. Passengers inhabit a glass cathedral suspended above the landscape, experiencing their home from perspectives previously reserved for helicopters and private planes. This visual connectivity between occupant and environment represents a profound shift in transportation philosophy—from isolated transit to engaged observation.

Midnight's six independent battery packs power 12 electric motors set in a configuration that prioritizes redundancy and safety over simplicity. This lets the aircraft maintain a controlled flight even with multiple motor failures—a crucial feature for operating above populated areas. The 1,000-pound payload capacity accommodates four passengers plus the pilot while maintaining the 7,000-pound maximum takeoff weight that keeps Midnight within the regulatory frameworks designed for air mobility.

Operating at a 2,000-foot cruise altitude with a 150-mile-per-hour cruise speed, Midnight has a 20-50-mile range that is perfectly calibrated for intra-city travel. These specifications aren't arbitrary—they represent a careful balance between energy efficiency, regulatory compliance, and practical distances. For example, a Manhattan-to-JFK journey that requires a 45-90 minute trip with ground transportation becomes a 12-minute aerial commute, fundamentally altering time-distance relationships that govern urban sprawl.

If you're only taking a trip, Midnight's $170 fare means that aerial transport would be within reach of premium ride-sharing economics while establishing an entirely new market category. On the other hand, a $5 million fleet acquisition cost could let companies deploy sky taxi services that would transform inner-city mobility from two-dimensional street networks to three-dimensional aerial corridors. This represents the largest shift in

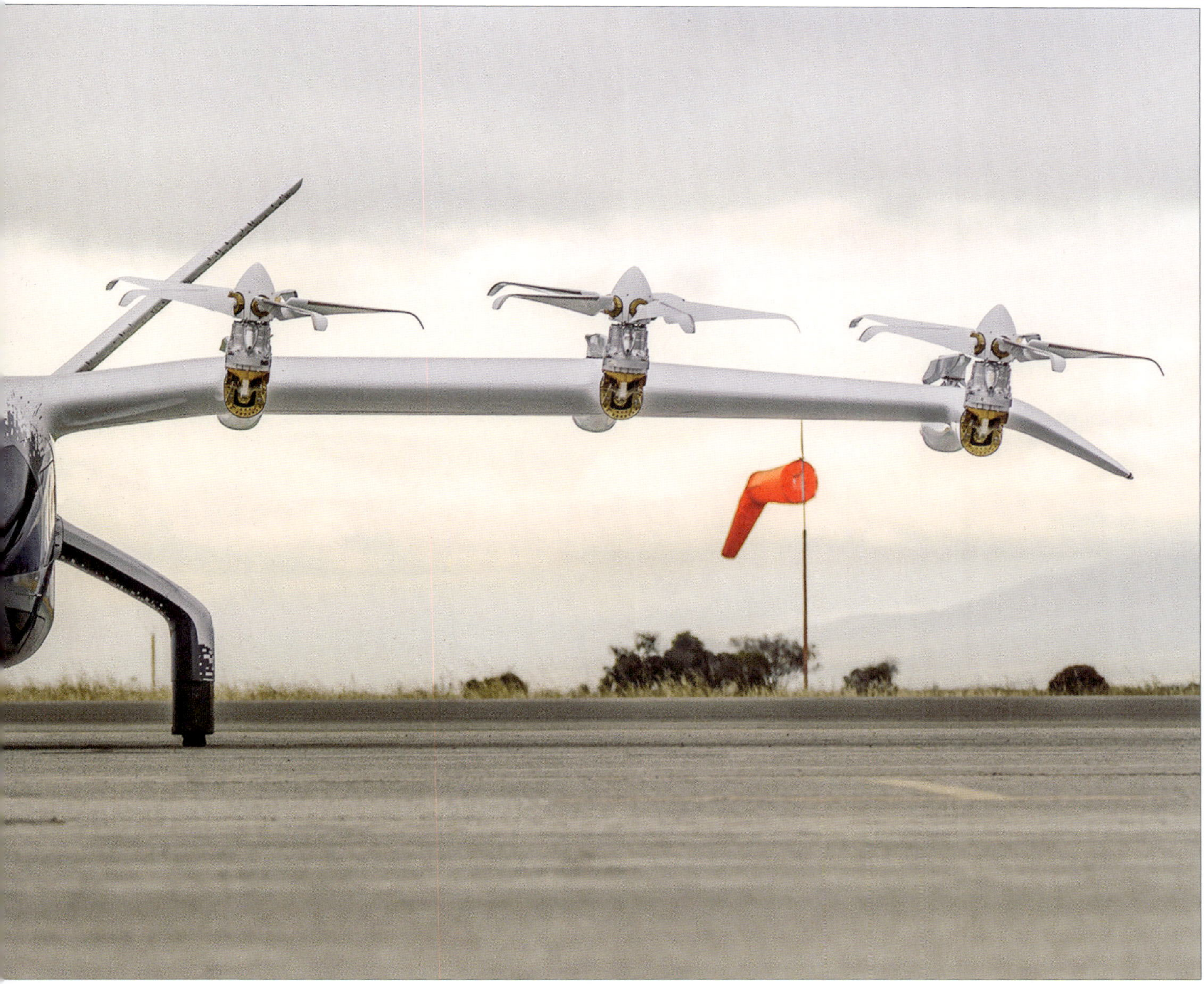

Noise level: 45-65 dB
Windows: Panoramic windows

Wing: High wing
Tail: V-tail with vertical stabilizer

transportation ever since the automobile displaced the horse.

Cities looking to integrate Midnight into their infrastructure—such as Miami and Los Angeles—are establishing vertiports that function as dedicated landing pads, creating new architectural typologies and zoning requirements. These elevated platforms become nodes in aerial transportation networks that bypass traditional infrastructure entirely, offering cities remarkable opportunities to reduce street-level congestion while expanding flight options.

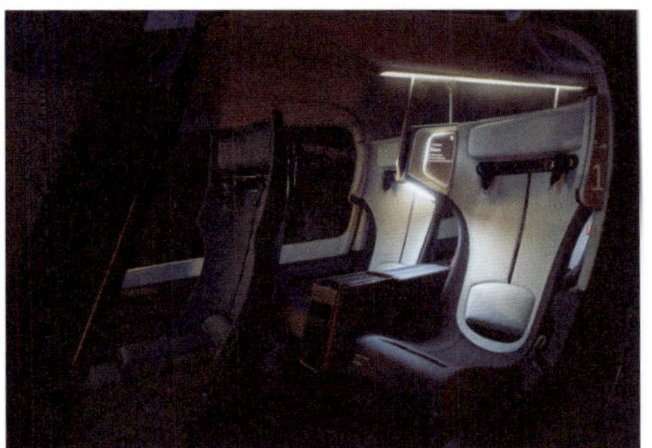

Archer Aviation has successfully democratized flying through design thinking that prioritizes safety, sustainability, and accessibility over regular aerospace conventions. Midnight proves that electric flight can achieve commercial viability while maintaining the visual and acoustic restraint necessary for integration. By solving noise, safety, and economic challenges simultaneously, Midnight demonstrates how thoughtful design can make revolutionary technology genuinely practical—transforming science fiction fantasy into imminent reality.

MIDNIGHT IS BELIEVED TO BE ONE OF THE LARGEST EVTOL AIRCRAFT EVER TO ACHIEVE TRANSITION AND ONE OF THE FIRST THAT IS PURPOSE-BUILT TO CARRY ENOUGH PASSENGERS TO OPERATE A SUCCESSFUL AIR TAXI BUSINESS. **Geoff Bower,** *Chief Engineer, Archer Aviation*

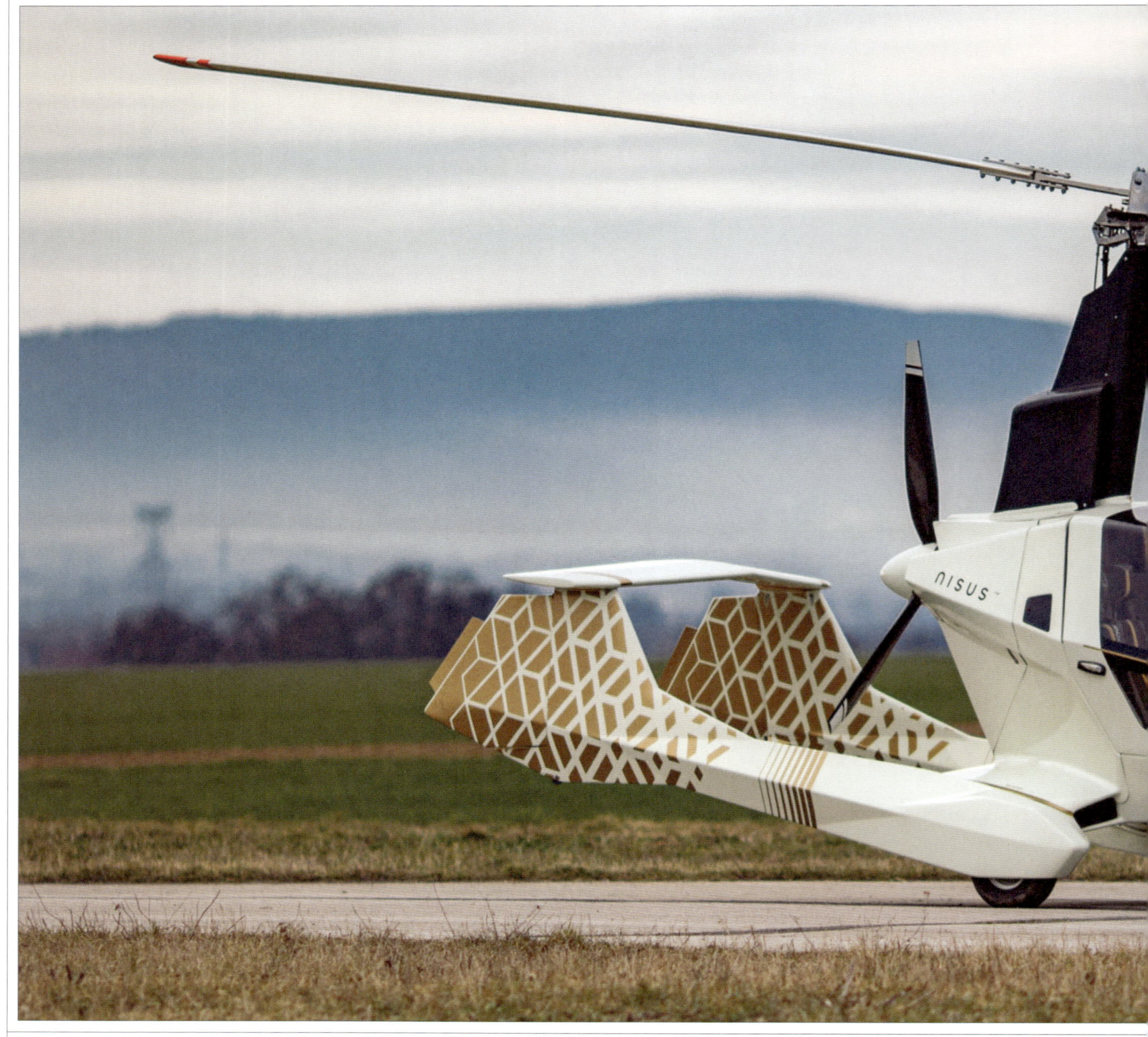

Length: 4.75 m (15.6 ft)
Width: 1.68 m (5.5 ft)
Height: 2.7 m (8.9 ft)
Cabin width: 1.3 m (4.3 ft)
Cruise speed: 130-160 km/h (70-86 KIAS)
Maximum speed: 195 km/h (105 KIAS)
Minimum speed: 30 km/h (16 KIAS)
Engine: Rotax 915 iS (141 Hp)
Rotor: Gyrotech 8600mm

Among the mighty mountains of Slovakia, where precision engineering meets sky-high ambition, NISUS AERO has orchestrated a remarkable convergence of recreational flying and professional aeronautics. The NISUS Gyroplane emerges from JokerTrike's mechanical expertise to represent a fundamental reimagining of personal aircraft design, proving that innovative solutions can emerge from the most unexpected geographic origins while challenging conventional assumptions about accessibility in general air transport.

Measuring 15.6 feet in length with a 5.5-foot width and an 8.9-foot height, the NISUS occupies compact dimensions that belie its manufacturing ancestry. The 4.3-foot cabin width provides a space for genuine two-person comfort while maintaining structural efficiency essential for flight. These proportions reflect a deep understanding of balancing aerodynamic necessities against practical operational constraints—design decisions informed by NISUS AERO's foundation in precision machining for aerospace applications.

The chrome-molybdenum steel tubes that make up the frame show a commitment to using proven aerospace materials while also assisting with weight optimization crucial for gyroplane performance. Moreover, this choice demonstrates how classic construction techniques can serve contemporary design goals, creating structures that achieve not just strength but also visual refinement. The composite three-blade propeller is more evidence of the careful material selection that characterizes serious aircraft development.

The Rotax 915 iS engine delivering 141 horsepower is the optimal power source, enabling cruise speeds of 81-100 mph with maximum velocity reaching 121 mph. These figures show how NISUS has practical cross-country potential while maintaining short-field performance that defines gyroplane advantages. The remarkably slow minimum speed of just 19 mph demonstrates inherent safety characteristics that make gyroplanes increasingly attractive for personal use.

The Gyrotech 8600mm rotor system provides the autorotational capability that fundamentally differentiates gyroplanes from conventional airplanes. This rotor diameter empowers the unpowered autorotation that allows gyroplanes to land safely even with complete engine failure, representing a significant safety advantage over traditional fixed-wing aircraft. The 656-foot takeoff distance and 492-foot landing requirement enable

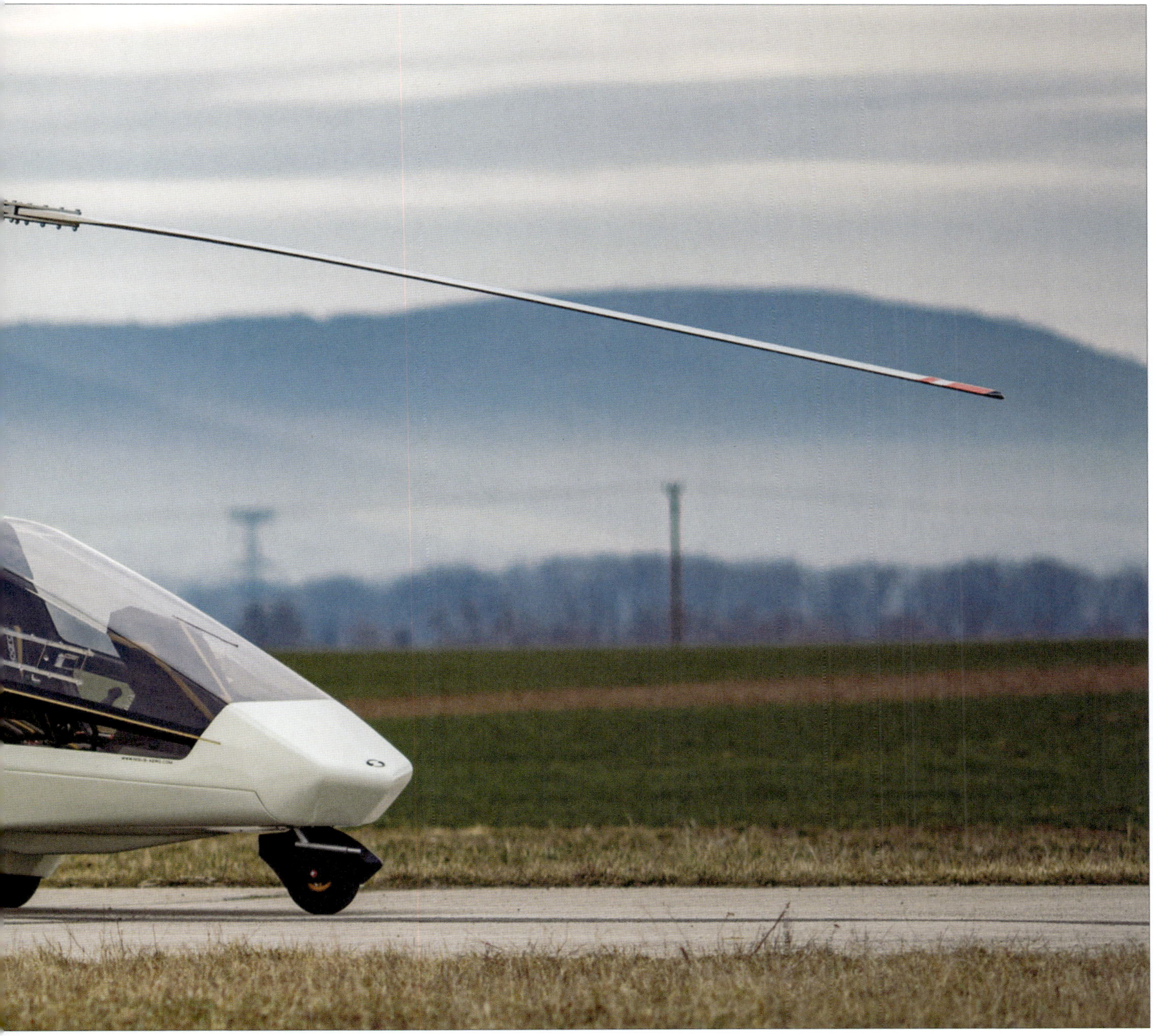

Fuel tank capacity: 92 L (2 x 46 L) or 24 gal (US)
Frame: Chrome-molybdenum steel tubes
Propeller: Composite, 3-blade
Takeoff distance: 200 m (656 ft)
Landing distance: 150 m (492 ft)
Takeoff roll: 70-120 m (230-393 ft)
Landing roll: 0-20 m (0-60 ft)

operations from fields that would challenge other types of planes.

NISUS AERO's positioning between recreational and professional flying reflects a broader equalization of aerospace technology. The 92-liter fuel capacity provides a wide traveling range while maintaining weight distribution optimal for handling. The 230 to 393-foot takeoff roll and virtually zero landing roll demonstrate operational flexibility that permits access to restricted airfields and private strips.

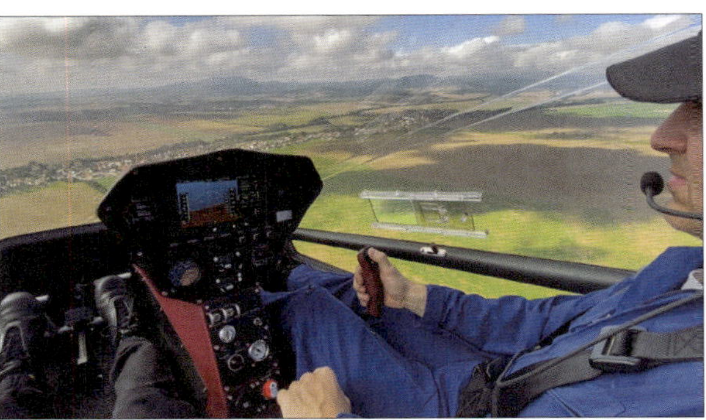

Costing between $151,000 and $184,000 dollars, NISUS firmly occupies the accessible luxury segment of personal aviation—on the one hand, it's enough to satisfy serious pilots while, on the other, remaining attainable compared to other, more expensive alternatives. This price range acknowledges that new, transformative aerospace technology needs to achieve broad adoption to create a meaningful market impact, positioning gyroplanes as a viable alternative to traditional aircraft.

NISUS AERO exemplifies the geographic dispersion of aerospace innovation beyond the normally accepted centers. Slovakia's engineering heritage—built through decades of precision assembly—provides the cornerstone for aeronautical development that rivals other, more well-known regions. JokerTrike's transition to complete aircraft development demonstrates how manufacturing competency can evolve into design leadership.

The NISUS Gyroplane stands as proof that creative solutions emerge from surprising sources when technological excellence meets visionary design thinking. By combining rotorcraft safety advantages with fixed-wing performance characteristics, NISUS AERO demonstrates how thoughtful engineering can make advanced aviation technology genuinely accessible—transforming personal flying from an exclusive privilege into an attainable reality.

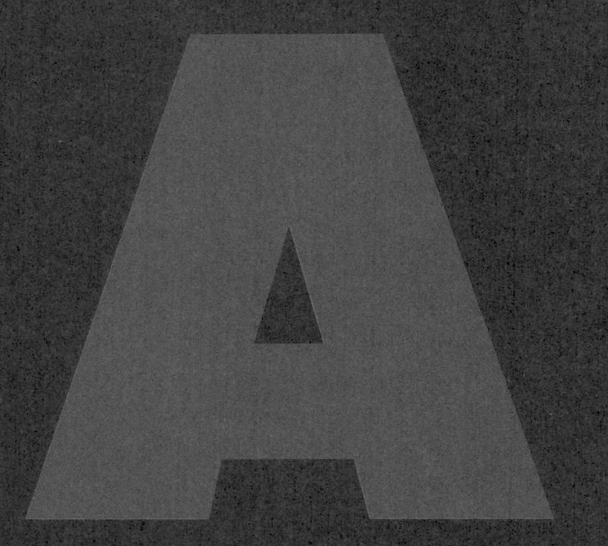

ARCHITECTURE

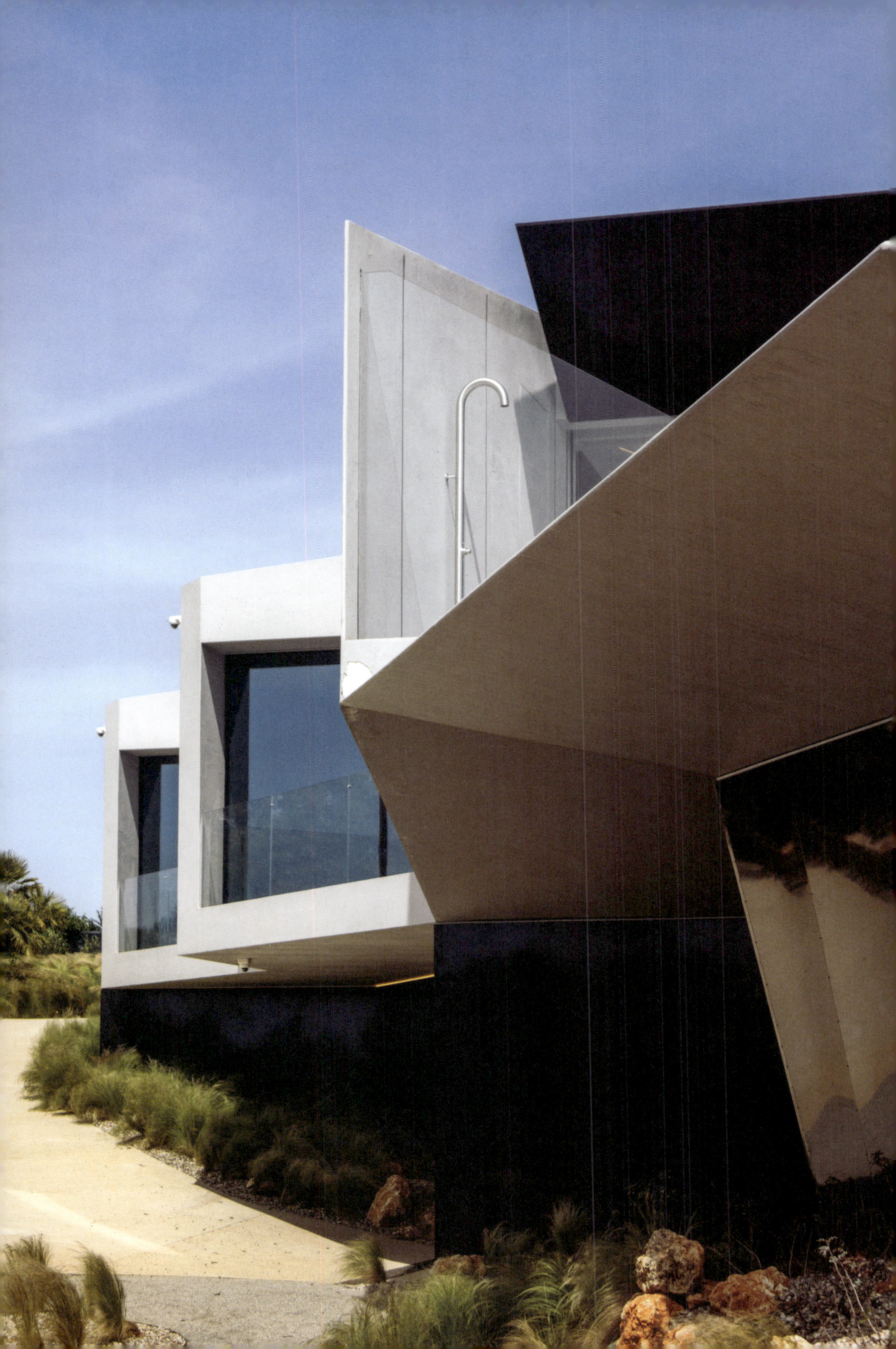

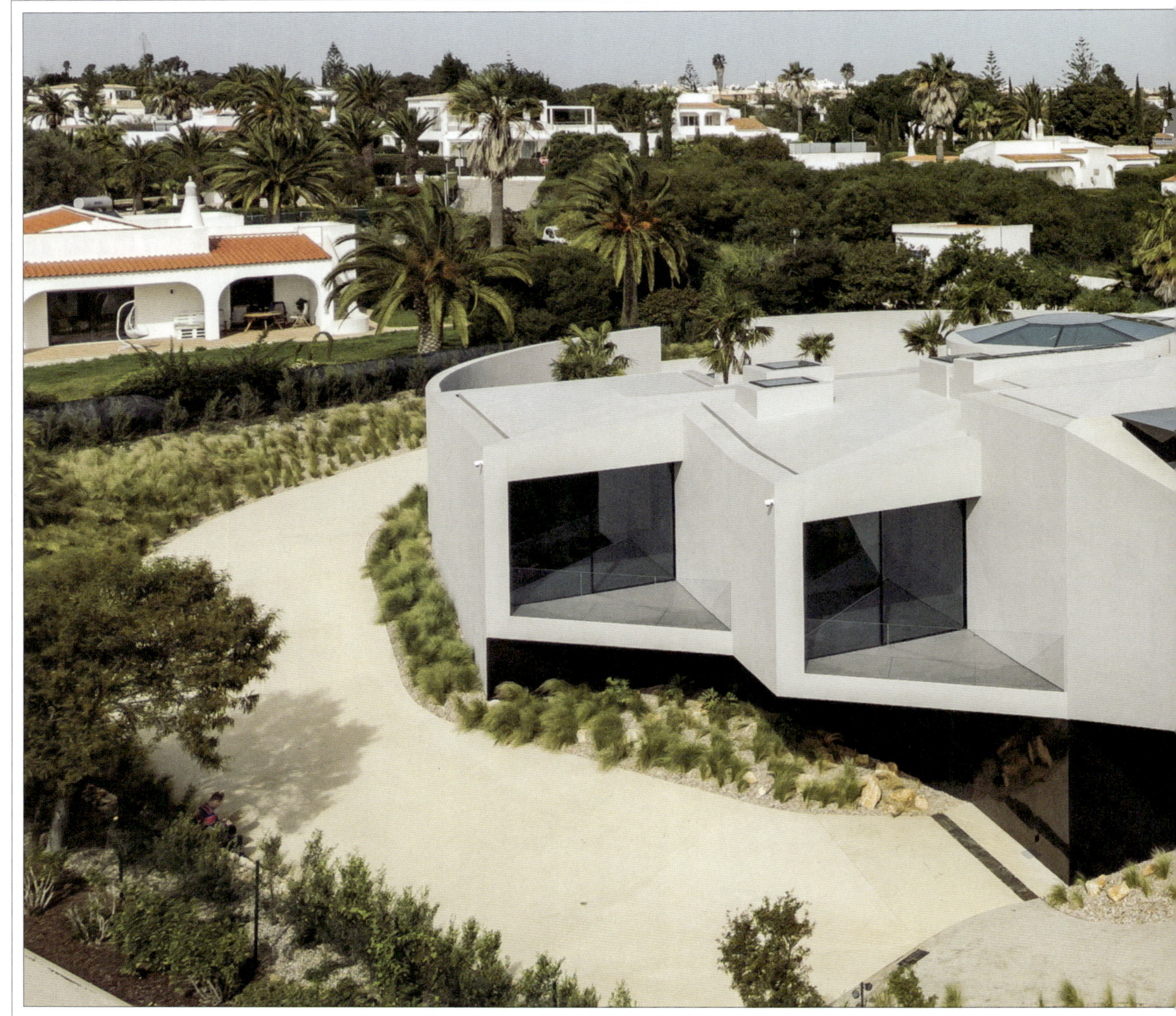

Along the dramatic coasts of Carvoeiro, Portugal, where Atlantic winds sculpt limestone cliffs into otherworldly formations, a $10.2 million dollar villa rises like something from a distant galaxy. Sky Base One, the latest masterwork from Bespoke Architects, challenges every preconception about residential design by fusing science fiction aesthetics with ancient Taoist philosophy, creating a home that feels simultaneously grounded and poised for flight.

"All [of it] started with the client's desire to create a villa inspired by science fiction cult cinema," explains British-born architect John Wilson, who leads the Carvoeiro-based practice. But this wasn't merely about creating a themed residence. "Learning the philosophy behind this cult series led us into a journey of self-development rooted in traditional Chinese Taoism, guiding us to understand how nature balances itself and the essence of things."

The result defies easy categorization. Sky Base One appears to hover above its narrow coastal plot, its darkly colored base contrasting dramatically with the upper levels that seem to defy gravity. The design incorporates fractal geometry and the golden ratio, creating a peaceful, proportional aesthetic that feels both mathematically precise and organically integrated with its dramatic setting.

John and his team members—including Alexandre Mendes, Elisabete Cardoso, Paulo Matias, Mauro Meireles, and Savannah Salgueiro—faced the challenge of maximizing living space and sea views on a relatively narrow plot. Their solution was to elevate the social spaces above the private quarters, creating an architectural hierarchy that enhances both function and drama. Doing so created an exceptional architectural interplay with the raised swimming pool, resulting in a dynamic structure that feels both of this world and otherworldly. Said pool appears to float above the entire landscape, its reflective surface forming a sort of visual bridge between the villa and the endless horizon of the ocean.

At the heart of Sky Base One lies a circular area featuring skylights designed to resemble spacecraft hatches. These windows slope inward from the edges to the center, peaking at the highest point of the form and flooding the interior with dramatic shafts of natural light that shift throughout the day. The centerpiece of this space is a perforated golden cylinder that catches and reflects sunlight, creating an ever-changing interaction of light and shadow.

The journey through the house is carefully choreographed. From the main gate, a rounded blind wall teases the sea's proximity while hiding a secret garden that leads to the entrance. This compression and release of space produces moments of introspection before the dramatic reveal of the house's soaring interiors.

When night falls, Sky Base One undergoes a complete

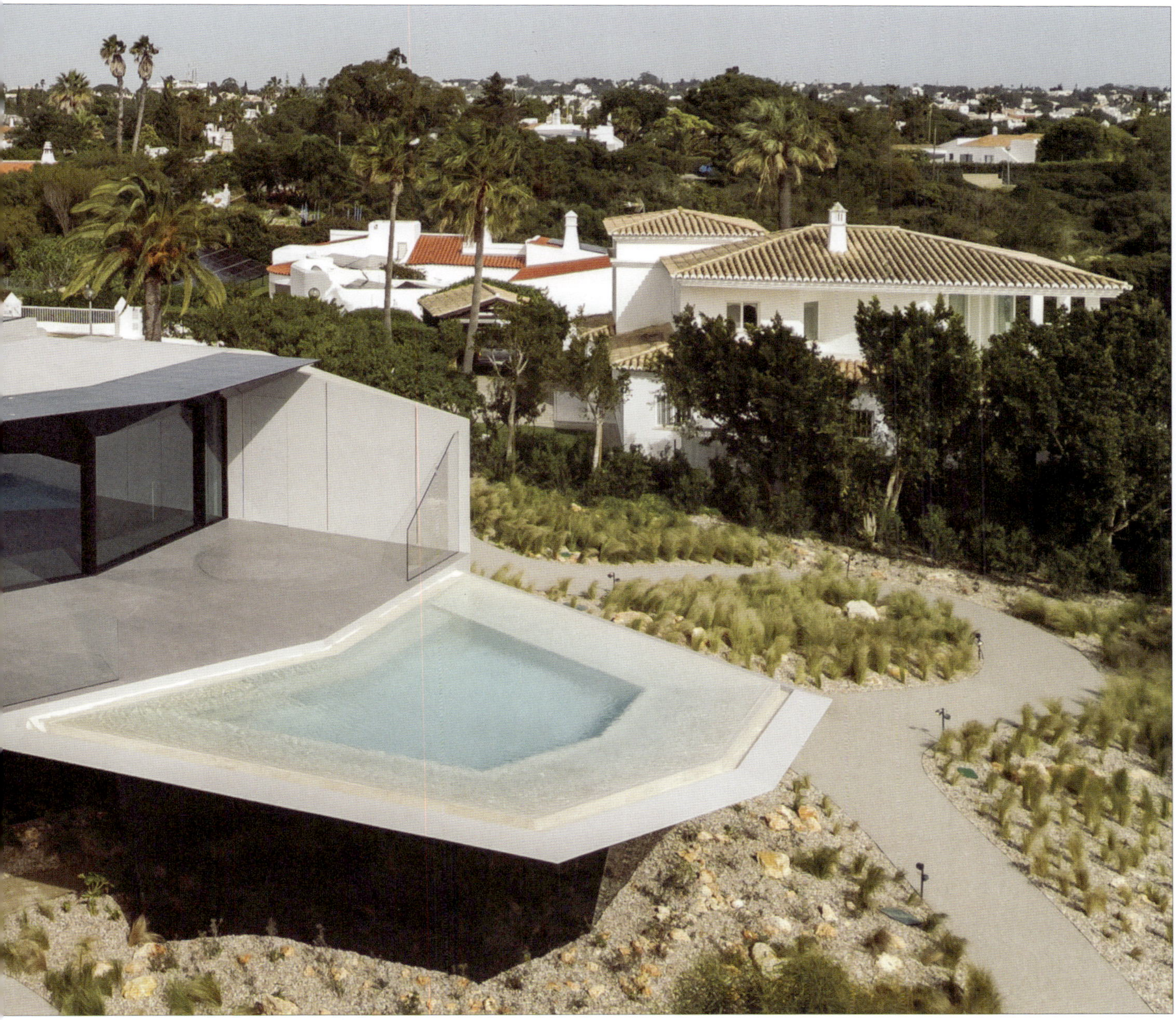

transformation. Strategic lighting elements—including floodlit corridors, descending windows that frame views of the pool, and brass accents throughout—generate what the architects describe as "time warp lights" that turn the villa from something ordinary to something extraordinary. "All of these details are remarkably important in distinguishing Sky Base One from the commonplace," says John. "It seeks to improve the happenings of life, the experience of the house, whether in a group or a party mode."

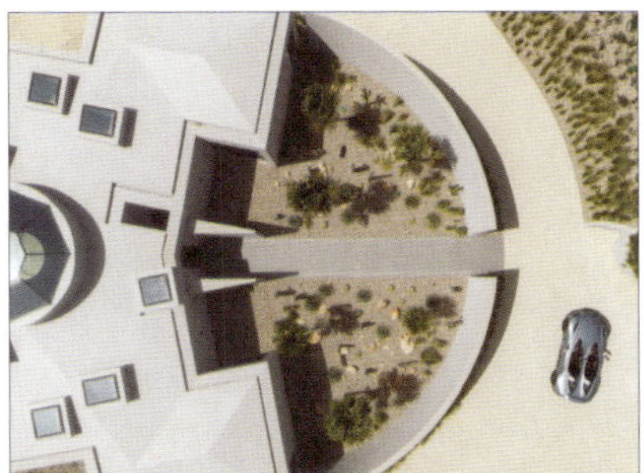

Founded in 2011, Bespoke Architects has established itself as a link between British architectural rigor and Portuguese lifestyle sensibilities. John's practice specializes in unique villa designs, project management, and rural tourism projects across the Algarve, bringing what they describe as "time-tested British practices" to Portuguese projects with distinctive flair. Sky Base One represents the pinnacle of this approach—a place that honors both cutting-edge design thinking and the fundamental human need for spaces that nurture reflection, connection, and wonder. In an era when luxury residential design often defaults to safe conservatism or hollow spectacle, Bespoke Architects has built something genuinely unprecedented: a home that expands the very definition of what domestic architecture can be.

"Sky Base One is not just a residence," John concludes. "It's a place where life unfolds in harmony with the elements, offering a distinctive blend of modern luxury, architectural innovation, and timeless natural beauty." The villa's 6,914 square feet encompass five bedrooms, seven bathrooms, a temperature-controlled wine cellar, and a movie theater room, but these conventional details feel secondary to the house's larger ambition: to create spaces that elevate day-to-day experiences into something approaching the transcendent.

With this villa, John and his team have demonstrated that modern architecture doesn't need to abandon either human comfort or environmental sensitivity. Instead, they've made a template for luxury living that embraces both cosmic inspiration and earthbound wisdom, proving that oftentimes, the most successful contemporary design often emerges from the most unexpected philosophical foundations. For an industry increasingly focused on sustainability and meaningful innovation, Sky Base One offers a compelling vision: architecture that expands consciousness while respecting place, tradition while embracing transformation, and the everyday while reaching toward the sublime.

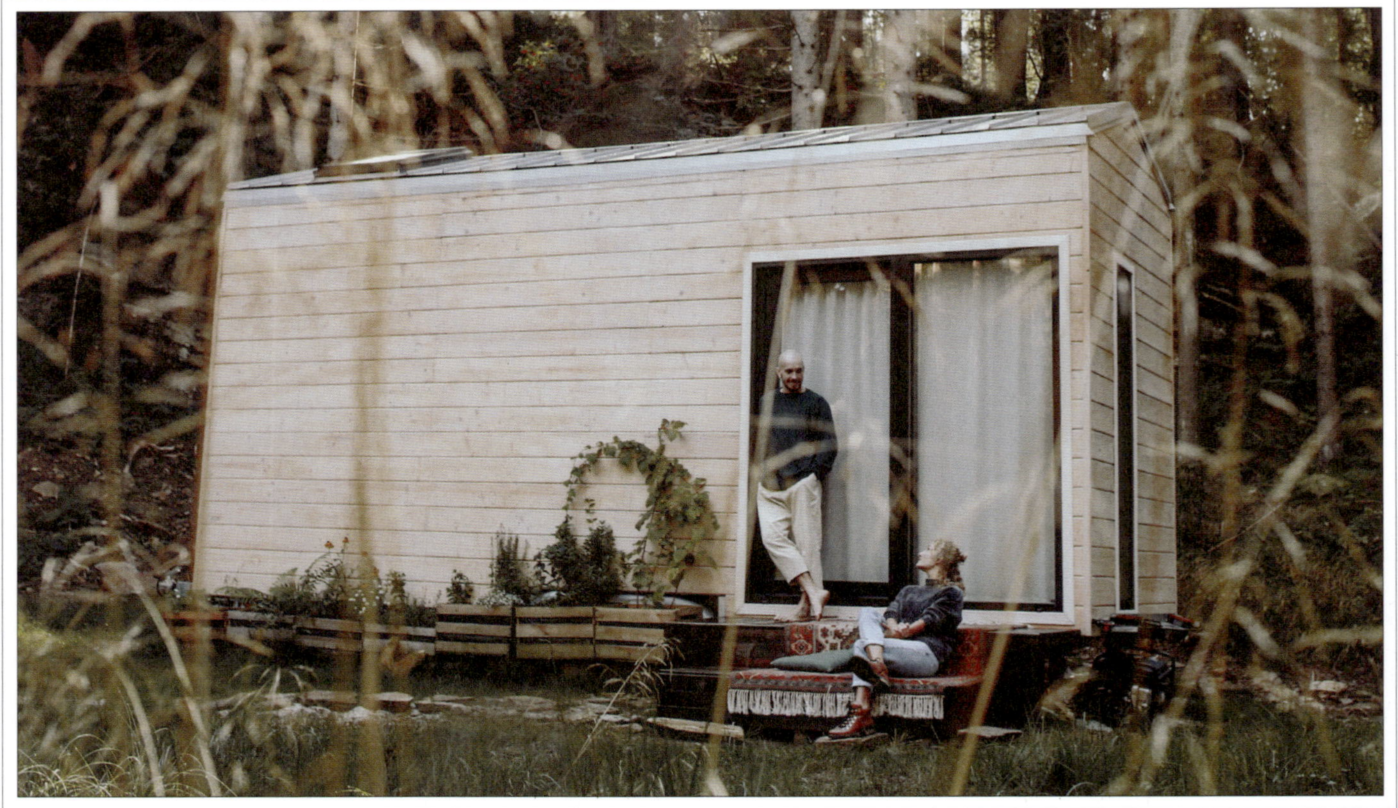

Projekt Datscha. Photo by Magda Tracz.

When Anna Busch met Jakob in Graz, Austria, five years ago, their connection transcended romance—it was philosophical alignment. Anna traveled constantly, everything fitting into a backpack. Jakob was an extreme minimalist who questioned purchasing even socks or plates. This meeting of minds sparked Projekt Datscha, a 194-square-foot mobile cabin that represents an authentic design philosophy made tangible.

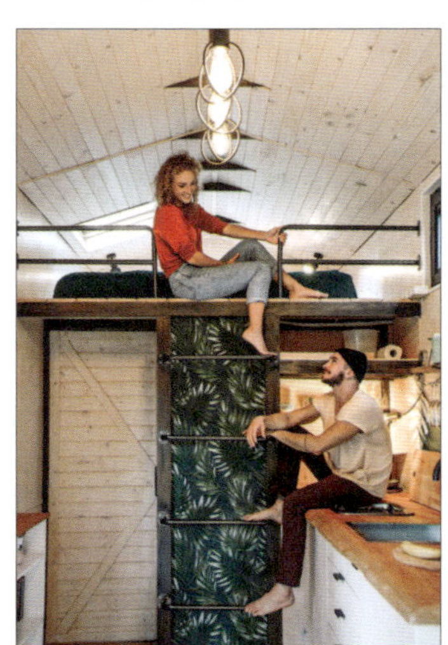

Working with co-architect Monika Binkowska, the Busches faced immediate challenges. To qualify for road transport, the build had to meet truck trailer requirements: a maximum of 13.1 feet high, 8.4 feet wide, 20.7 feet long, and weighing under 3.5 tons.

"Choosing lightweight materials was our number-one priority," Anna explains. The solution was material intelligence: spruce framing with metal supports capable of withstanding 75-mile-per-hour headwinds, aluminum windows, PIR insulation, and a balsa plywood interior. The exterior uses spruce siding painted semi-transparent white, achieving an untreated appearance that still protects the structure.

Within the limited square feet, the Busches created a complete living environment challenging spatial assumptions. Wood panel floors by Polish company Barlinek, spruce ceilings, and plywood walls with pronounced grain provide visual interest without ornamental excess. Space-saving solutions emerged from necessity. A beechwood dining table built into kitchen cabinetry folds when unused, designed by Anna's cousin Marek. The sleeping loft, accessed by a cast-iron ladder designed by Anna's mother, Barbara, includes a skylight for stargazing—transforming functional basics into experiential luxury. The bathroom includes a full bathtub, proving downsizing needn't sacrifice comfort.

Perhaps Datscha's most significant innovation isn't material or spatial—it's social. The build became community-supported creativity. Anna's father worked daily for three months, teaching construction skills. When they returned to their jobs, Anna's mother helped coordinate weekend building sessions.

"On Instagram, it looks like great fun," Anna observes. "You invite friends over, paint a little, then grill together. It sounds silly, but it's true! We couldn't have done this without family and friends." Indeed, including others transformed an expensive, isolating project into a social experience, strengthening relationships while building a shelter. The $35,000 cost reflects material efficiency and collaborative labor as creative practice.

Currently parked near Lake Attersee in St. Georgen, Austria, the cabin operates as a residence and vacation rental at $125 per night, demonstrating how alternative living becomes a sustainable business. The name—a post-Soviet term for holiday houses "somewhere far away in nature"—connects to broader retreat traditions prioritizing experience over exhibition. "Datscha allows us to be close to nature, giving us peace," Anna reflects. "We need time to recharge away from civilization."

As the Busches plan Datscha 2.0 with complete off-grid capabilities, the original establishes new paradigms: design as a lifestyle choice rather than a professional service, building as a community activity rather than a commercial transaction, and minimalism as an authentic response to excess rather than an aesthetic trend.

For designers questioning their work's environmental and social impact, Projekt Datscha offers compelling alternatives: create less, share more, and prioritize experiences that expand consciousness over carbon footprints. In an industry obsessed with spectacle and scale, Anna and Jakob prove the most radical design statement might be the quietest one. After all, in less than 200 square feet, they've demonstrated that luxury isn't about the size—it's about the alignment between values and lifestyle, creative vision and daily practice, and individual satisfaction and community connection.

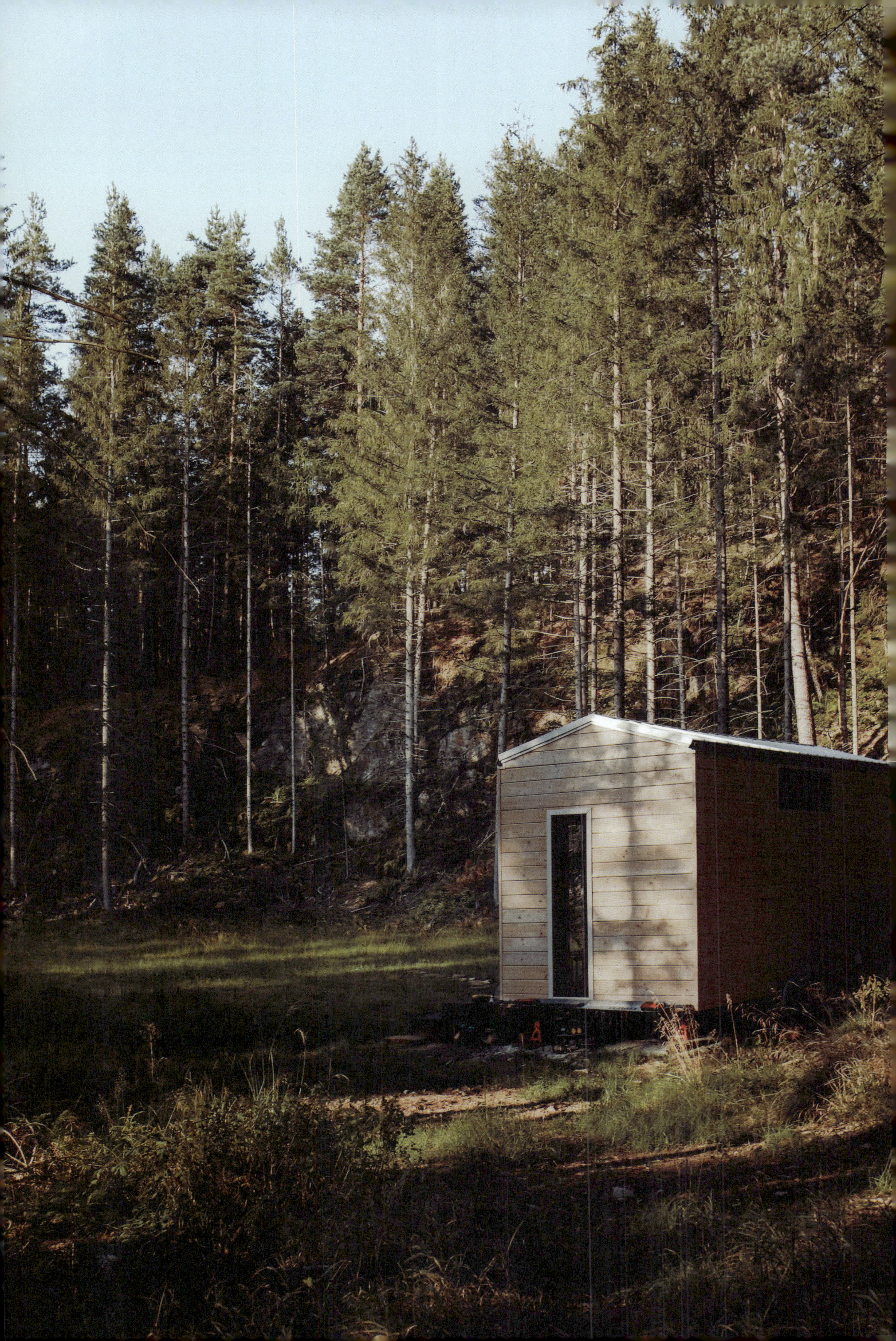

EDUCATION

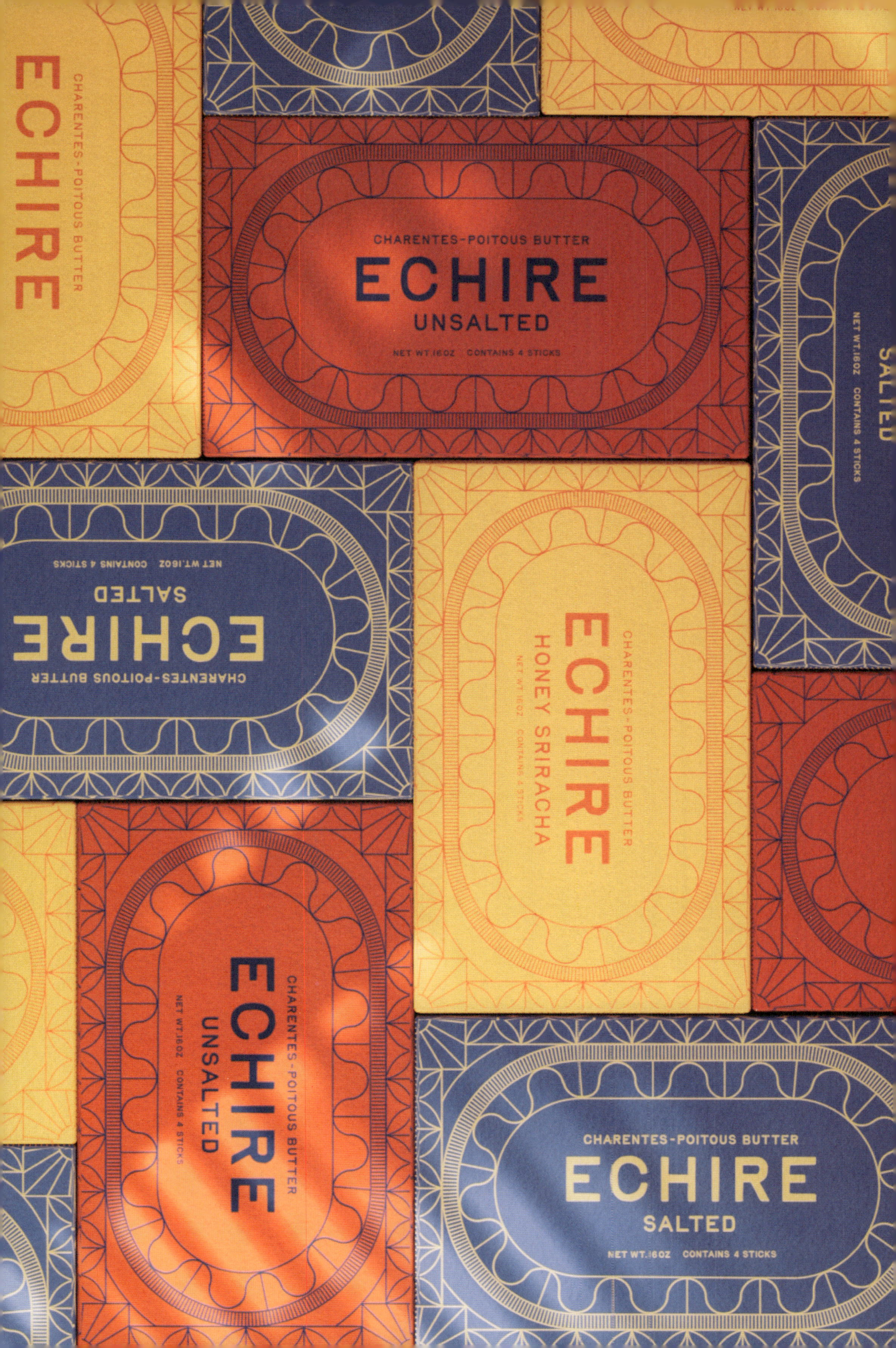

CHARENTES-POITOUS BUTTER
ECHIRE
UNSALTED
NET WT.16OZ CONTAINS 4 STICKS

CHARENTES-POITOUS BUTTER
ECHIRE
SALTED
NET WT.16OZ CONTAINS 4 STICKS

Linda Reynolds (Brigham Young University): Boundaries Encourage Innovative Outcomes

FOR OVER THREE DECADES, LINDA'S EXAMPLE HAS TAUGHT THOUSANDS OF STUDENTS AND COLLEAGUES THAT DESIGN IS ALL-ENCOMPASSING.

Katrina Peterson, *Former Student & Art Director, Actual Source*

LINDA'S THOUGHTFUL AND THOROUGH REMARKS ALLOWED ME TO UNDERSTAND THE WORLD OF DESIGN AND GAIN A LOVE FOR IT.

Chloe Jackson, *Student, Brigham Young University*

LINDA REYNOLDS INTRODUCED ME TO SEMIOTICS AND THE BOUNDLESS POTENTIAL OF DISTILLING MEANING INTO SIMPLIFIED FORMS —A LESSON THAT HAS PERMANENTLY SHAPED MY WORLDVIEW AND DESIGN PRACTICE.

Christian Sant, *Former Student & Designer, 77type.com*

LINDA IS TRULY ONE OF A KIND. SHE LEADS AND INSPIRES WITH SOULFUL PASSION AND HUMBLE STRENGTH. TO SEE THE WORLD THROUGH HER EYES WOULD BE THE GREATEST GIFT.

Grace Graviet, *Former Student & Freelance Graphic Designer*

LINDA MAKES YOU FEEL VALUED AND CAPABLE. HER SHARP EYE, STEADY GUIDANCE, AND KIND CRITIQUES CHANGED HOW I SEE MYSELF AND DESIGN.

Brinlee Kelly, *Freelance Graphic Designer, Gimme Beauty*

LINDA IS EVERYTHING I ASPIRE TO BE. HER DESIGN SERVES AS A TESTAMENT TO HER LIMITLESS TALENT AND BEAUTIFUL SOUL.

Kiera Helquist, *Former Student & Digital Designer, Horizon Sports & Experiences*

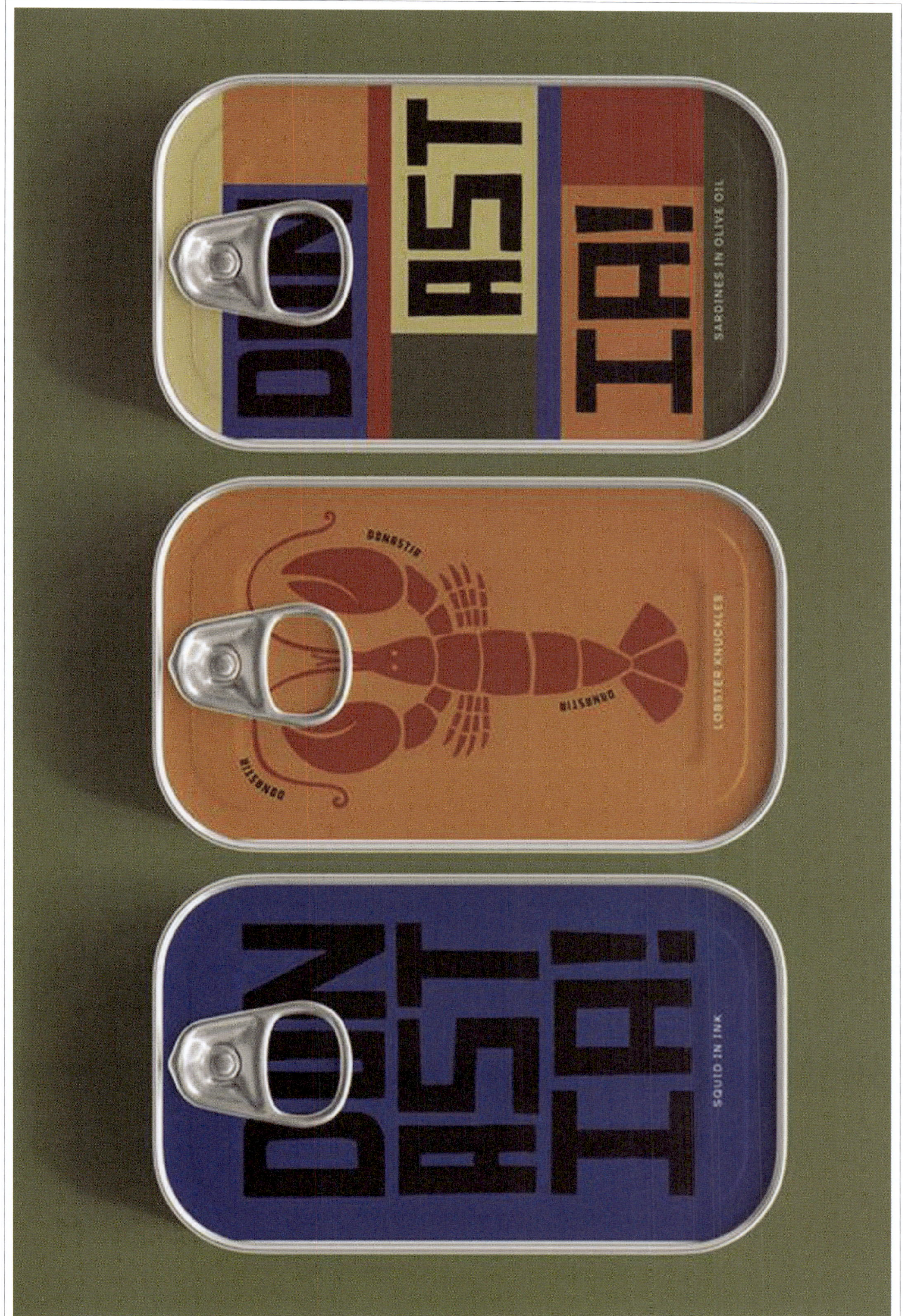

(Page 127) Echire, New Talent Annual 2025. Professor: Linda Reynolds. Gold-winning student: Katie Javadi
(Above) Donastia!, New Talent Annual 2025. Professor: Linda Reynolds. Gold-winning student: Katie Javadi

Introduction by Brent Barson *Professor & Department Chair of Graphic Design, Brigham Young University*

Linda Reynolds is a totally committed and immensely talented university professor. She is committed to her students' learning and success in and outside of the classroom and to the design discipline as a whole. Professor Reynolds has an abiding interest in service learning and social practice and has mentored multiple decades' worth of students in design initiatives for community, national, and international organizations. Her work has been consistently recognized throughout her career by the highest, most respected design publications. She was recently honored in the Communication Arts Design Annual with a Best in Show award for her "No Justice, No Peace" poster.

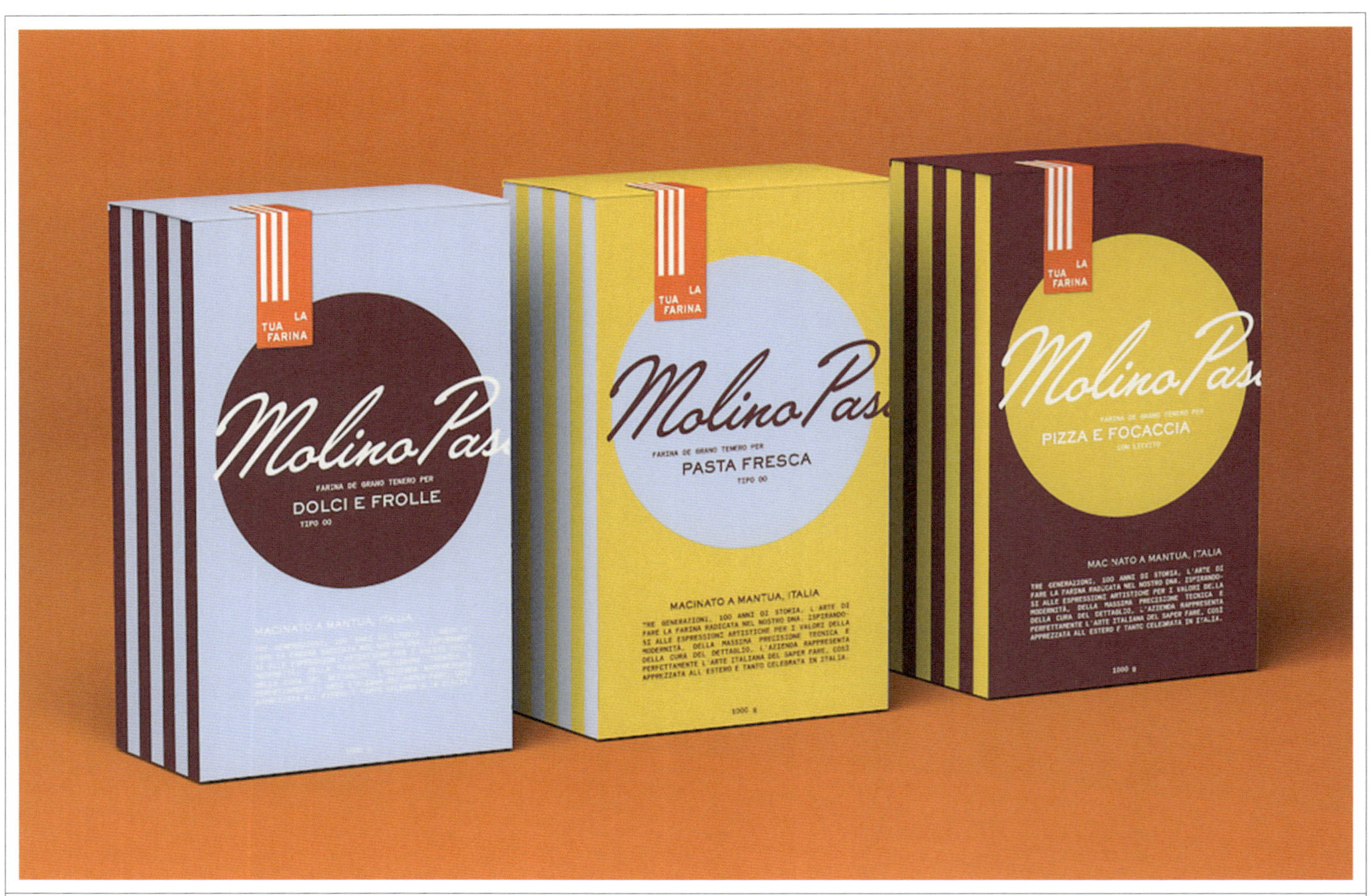

Molino Pasini Flour, New Talent Annual 2025. Professor: Linda Reynolds. Gold-winning student: Grace Graviet

LINDA CREATES MAGICAL EXPERIENCES IN HER TEACHING. SHE EXUDES LOVE FOR HER STUDENTS, FOR DESIGN, AND FOR EXCELLENCE IN EVERY FORM.

Doug Thomas, *Professor, Brigham Young University*

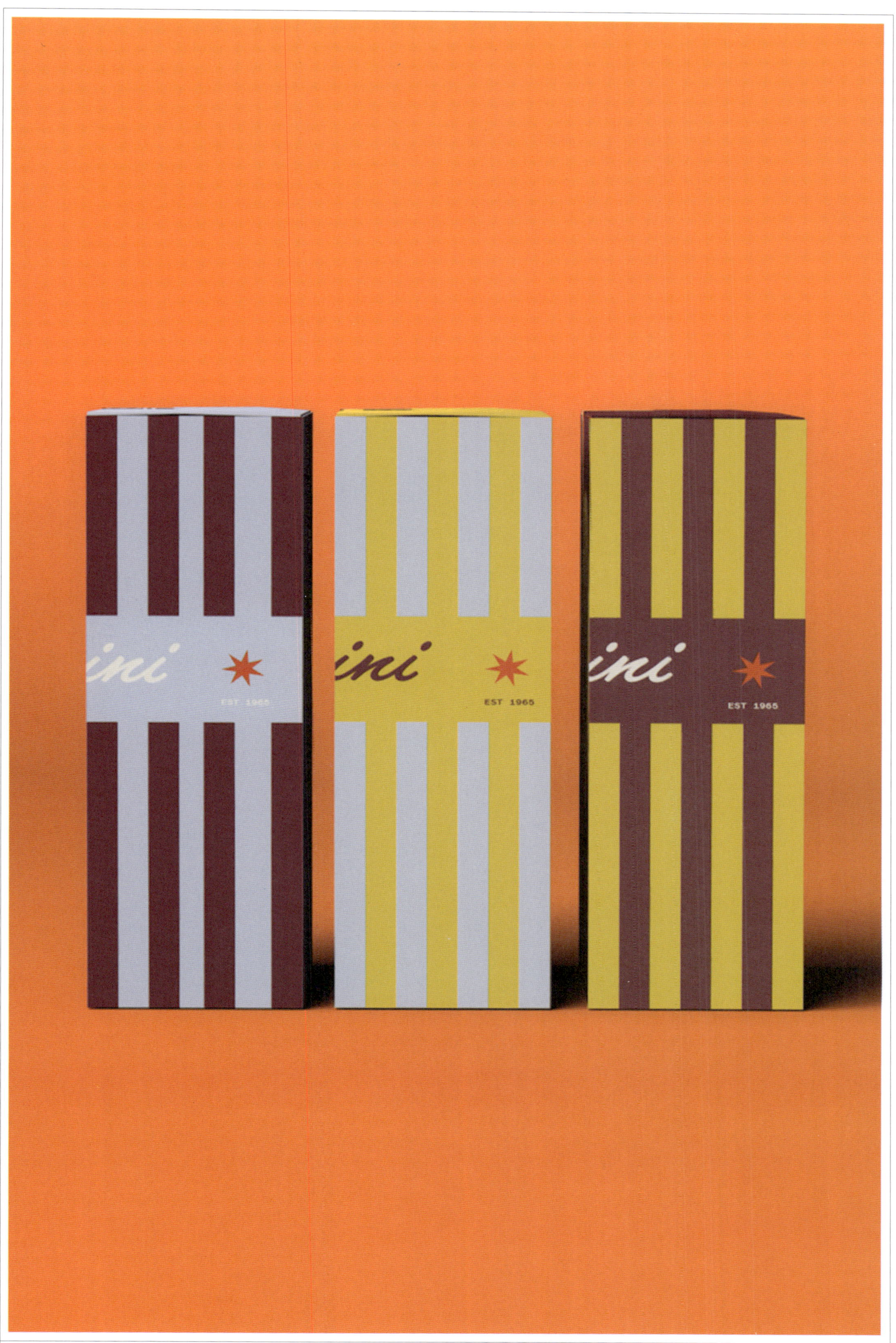

Molino Pasini Flour, New Talent Annual 2025. Professor: Linda Reynolds. Gold-winning student: Grace Graviet

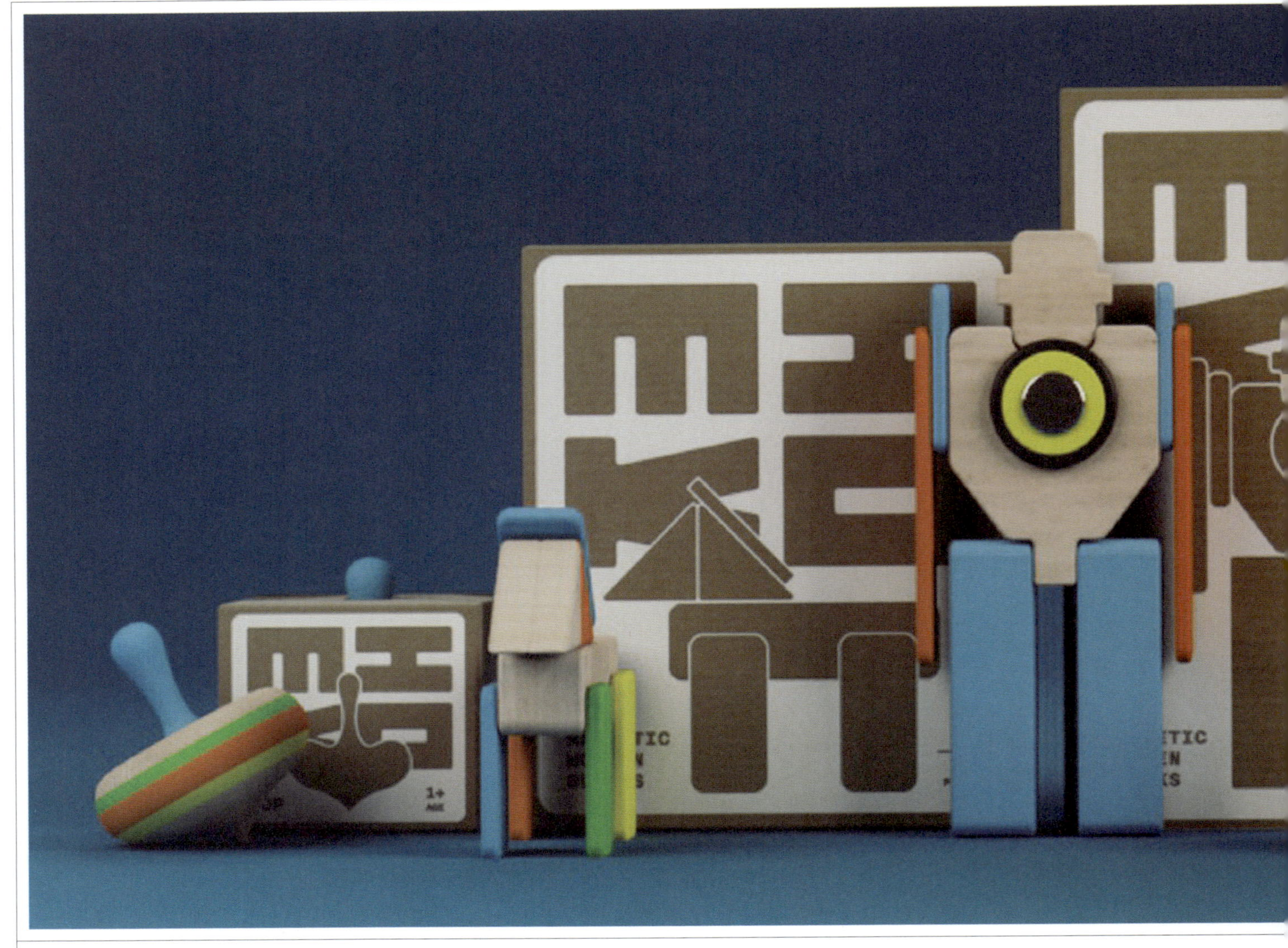

Tell us about your educational background—where did you study, and what led you to design?
I've always loved making art. One day, while walking past my high school art teacher's desk, I noticed a copy of *Communication Arts*. That moment marked my introduction to graphic design. I completed my undergraduate studies at BYU and later earned my master's in graphic design at the University of Utah.

What drew you to teaching, and how did that path unfold?
Becoming a professor was never on my radar—it wasn't something I had considered as a career path. I pursued an MFA not to teach but because I wanted to learn and think more deeply and critically about graphic design. I earned it while working full-time and raising four young children.

Midway through the program, the department chair reached out about an open faculty position. I initially said no—I loved being an art director. But a few months later, he called again. The posting was closing, and if I had any interest, now was the time. Something shifted. That moment changed everything.

Becoming a BYU faculty member has been life-changing for me. I'm often overwhelmed with gratitude for the blessings that have come from it. I love BYU, especially the students and the faculty I work alongside.

What courses do you teach at BYU, and which one holds special meaning for you?
I teach across all levels of our curriculum: branding, typography, senior-level design lab collaboration, packaging, product design and entrepreneurship, and alternative processes (including experimental typography, silkscreen, and letterpress). I also teach a general education course for the university.

While I love all these classes, Alternative Processes in Graphic Design holds special meaning for me. Working with analog methods fosters creativity by encouraging experimentation, risk-taking, and a break from conventional design practices. Students produce unique, tangible outcomes that stand out in an oversaturated digital landscape. It's a course that pushes the boundaries of traditional design and brings a refreshing perspective to their work and portfolios.

What is your teaching philosophy in one sentence?
Everything I know I've learned through curiosity and hard work.

What kinds of assignments do you find most effective, and is there a favorite you return to often?
I'm drawn to assignments that involve systems thinking. From the very first course in our program, students are encouraged to think through complexity. Systems thinking is a throughline in nearly every course I teach.

I also believe in the power of constraints—whether it's limiting time, methods, media, or conceptual scope. In my experience, boundaries encourage more innovative and focused outcomes.

Can you share a student project that really stood out—and why?
We recently collaborated with the CASE Agency in NYC, the BYU AdLab, and our Design Lab. Students developed brand identity systems and tailored ad campaigns for a client serving an underrepresented audience. The work included everything

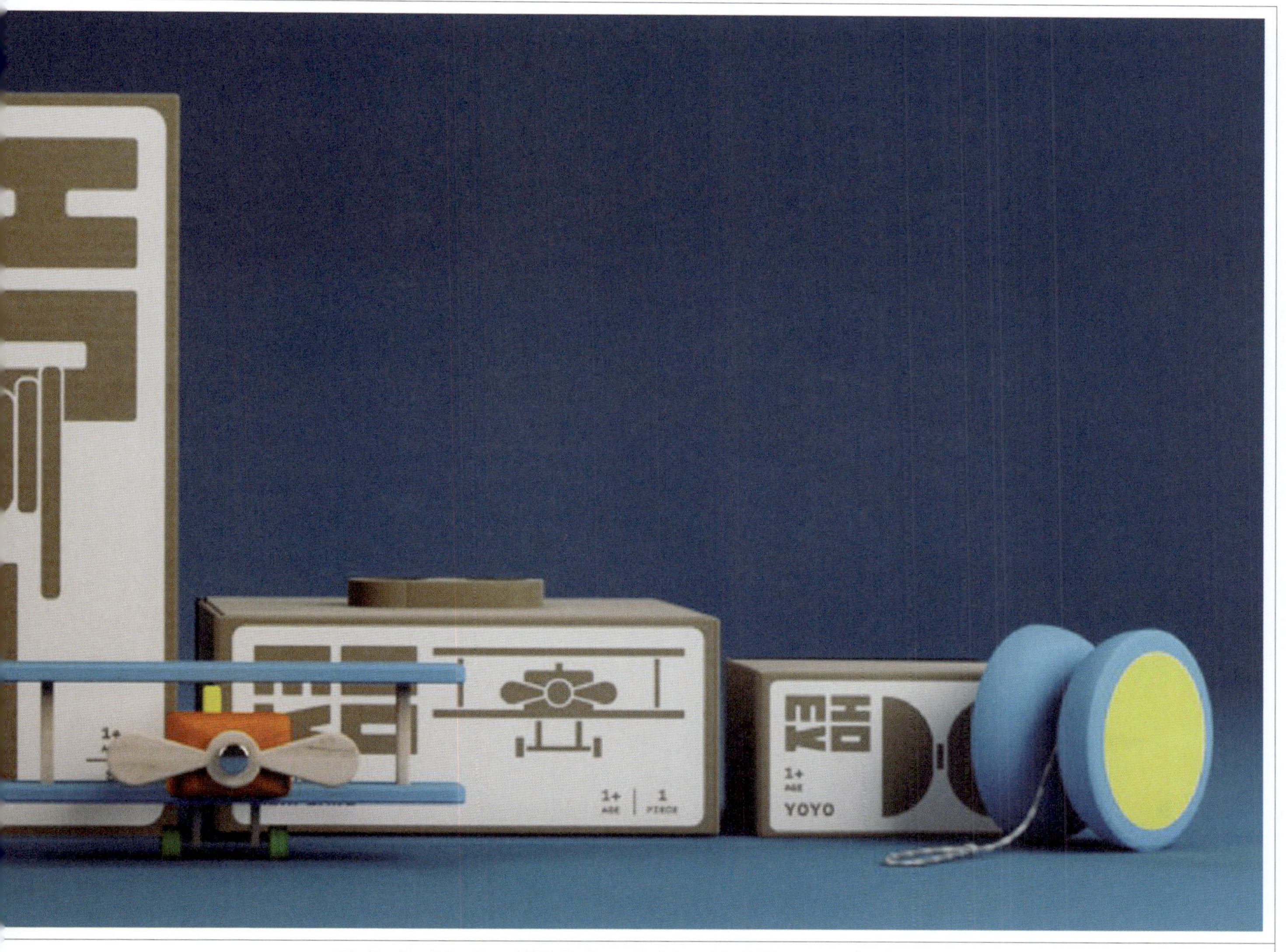

Miko Toy, New Talent Annual 2025. Professor: Linda Reynolds. Gold-winning student: Tavia Borrowman

from packaging and digital design to strategic brand platforms and advertising assets.

Throughout the semester, students received mentorship and feedback from CASE's creative directors, and many traveled to NYC to present their work. This project exemplified the power of collaborative, project-based learning and nurtured real relationships across disciplines and campuses. It was a transformative experience for everyone involved.

What do you do to bring real-world trends and cultural shifts into your classroom?
For years, we have run a senior-level Design Lab course that brings students into direct collaboration with clients, ranging from nonprofits to industry partners. This fall, we are going to expand the course into a multidisciplinary format that will include students from graphic design, illustration, photography, animation, and UX/PX.

This shift mirrors how problems are solved in the real world—rarely within a single discipline. It's a highly relevant evolution of our curriculum and offers students deeper engagement with today's interconnected challenges.

How do you adapt your approach to different types of learners?
Mentorship is a major part of my teaching. I spend significant time one-on-one with students, helping them refine and assess their work. That proximity allows me to tailor my feedback and adapt to their individual learning styles. Students also have a great deal of autonomy in shaping their creative and research direction, which supports a more personalized educational experience.

Can you tell us about one of the most rewarding teaching experiences you've had?
The CASE collaboration stands out—not just for the caliber of work but for the depth of mentorship, interdisciplinary collaboration, and professional growth it offered our students. It was real, high-stakes learning, and the transformation was visible.

When a student is struggling and needs help, how do you get them back on track?
We work hard to build a culture where every student feels they matter. Listening—both to what's said and unsaid—is crucial. If a student stops attending, that's often the first sign of deeper challenges. We reach out immediately—by phone, text, email—whatever it takes.

Our program is small: There are just 50 BFA students in a university of 35,000. That allows us to build a strong, supportive community. Our goal is to ensure every student feels known, valued, and essential.

What are the biggest challenges you face as an educator today?
One of the greatest challenges is understanding how AI will reshape our discipline. I don't fear AI replacing graphic design, but I do worry about our students being replaced by people who know how to use it better. Helping students engage AI ethically and effectively is now part of our responsibility as educators.

How do you stay sharp and up-to-date in your field?
There are clear benchmarks for faculty performance in teaching, scholarship, and service, even post-tenure. We're expect-

ed to stay active in professional practice. I regularly submit commissioned and self-authored work to top-tier design publications like Graphis for peer review.

BYU also makes sure to provide excellent support for faculty development, including funding for research, travel, workshops, and conferences.

What parting words of wisdom do you share with your students at the end of each semester?
I tell them: "You will serve the world with expertise—and with a purpose that aligns with your faith."

Can you highlight a few of your former students now doing exciting things in design?
Katrina Peterson of Actual Source, Kevin Cantrell of Kevin Cantrell Studio, and Christian Sant of 77type.com are doing incredible work and making real contributions to the field.

What's your take on emerging tech like AI, and how is it showing up in the classroom?
We're actively integrating AI into our curriculum. That includes tools for image and layout automation, generative design, and machine learning-enhanced editing. Students are already using AI for many things, such as iterations, sketches, UI, branding, and visual experimentation.

We're also updating our learning rubrics to include ethical considerations and design strategy. Our goal is to ensure students leave with both creative fluency and critical awareness of these emerging tools.

How does BYU's Mormon affiliation influence its academic approach, especially in the arts?
BYU's mission is built on a "double heritage"—academic excellence and spiritual purpose. Our students will graduate into a complex visual culture equipped with powerful tools and deep knowledge. We expect them to make responsible, inspired choices and to communicate with both clarity and compassion.

We hope to shape designers who elevate culture and who encourage contemplation, connection, and truth.

What are some other standout departments at BYU, and how does design interact with them?
The BYU Sandbox program is a hands-on, two-semester experience where students build and launch tech startups. It's an incredible space for entrepreneurship and product development. The College of Fine Arts and Communications also offers funding to support cross-department collaboration, and our award-winning animation program is nationally recognized for its industry-level training and interdisciplinary approach.

How does the design program at BYU prepare students for post-graduate success?
We've had strong success placing students in top internships, full-time positions, and graduate programs. Our alumni are thriving across the country and around the world.

What sets BYU apart from other design schools?
Our students could succeed anywhere. But I believe they come to BYU because they're seeking something deeper—a learning experience that aligns with their values and invites spiritual growth. That shared commitment creates a unique sense of purpose, unity, and creative excellence.

What advice do you give to prospective applicants?
Our program is incredibly competitive: We accept only 20 students per year. I would encourage interested students to reach out. We're happy to answer questions and walk them through the application process.

Can you name a few projects or clients you have worked with that have shaped your creative identity?
While I still take on client work, self-authored projects have become increasingly meaningful. One project of mine that stands out is a poster I created in response to George Floyd's murder. It was a protest piece—black paper, cut by hand at my kitchen table. I posted copies around my community. Though I was alone, I felt connected to others across the country with a shared sense of purpose.

The act of making that poster forced me to confront my own silence. I realized that while I considered myself a strong supporter of civil rights, I simply wasn't doing enough. That moment reshaped not just my creative identity but also my personal one as well.

One design-related book or thinker you always recommend?
I have been interested in the idea of "gifts" and how this aligns with a favorite quote of mine from the German-born American abstract painter and designer Josef Albers, which is: "To distribute material things is to divide them. To distribute spiritual things is to multiply them."

To my mind, in the first part of Josef's quote, he is referencing the reductive nature of dividing objects in the physical world in a way to deemphasize their importance and attention in our lives (and I agree with Josef—that is true). But I know from my learning that there is an inherent spirituality when we give our physical means and possessions—no matter how small—to a person in need. There is a sacredness in the division of the material when it is given in love to others.

In the second part of his quote, Josef emphasizes the intangible, expansive, and multiplying effect of giving gifts of the spirit—service, time, support, encouragement, forgiveness, and faith. My experiences in teaching serve as a powerful example of this idea, demonstrating how a student can obtain knowledge through the education of his mind and heart. We all have gifts to share with each other and the world. I hope students will always use their gifts to serve others with all their might, mind, and heart.

Brigham Young University www.designdept.byu.edu

WE HOPE TO SHAPE DESIGNERS WHO ELEVATE CULTURE AND WHO ENCOURAGE CONTEMPLATION, CONNECTION, AND TRUTH.

Linda Reynolds, *Professor, Brigham Young University*

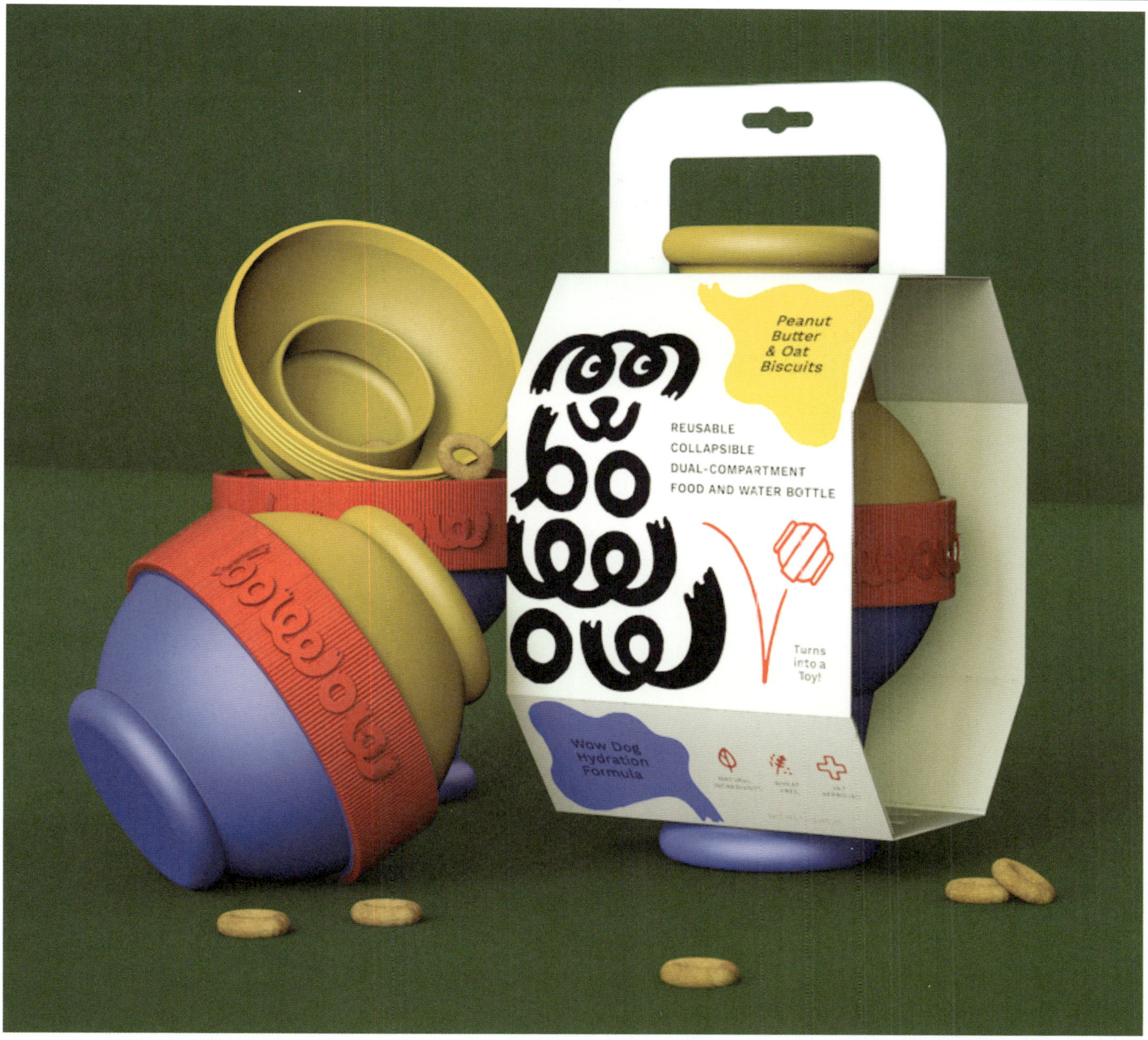

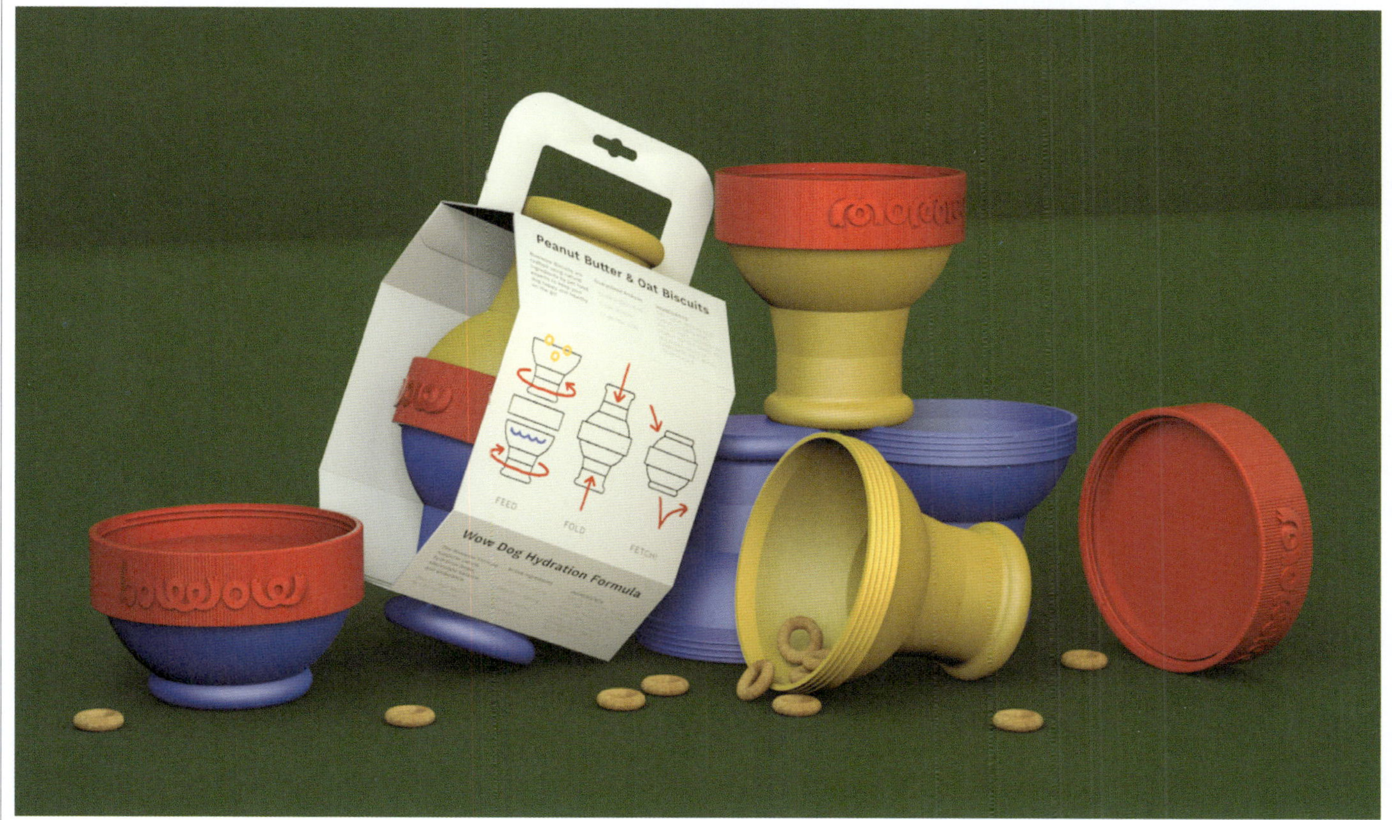

Bowwow, New Talent Annual 2025. Professor: Linda Reynolds. Gold-winning student: Elle Babcock

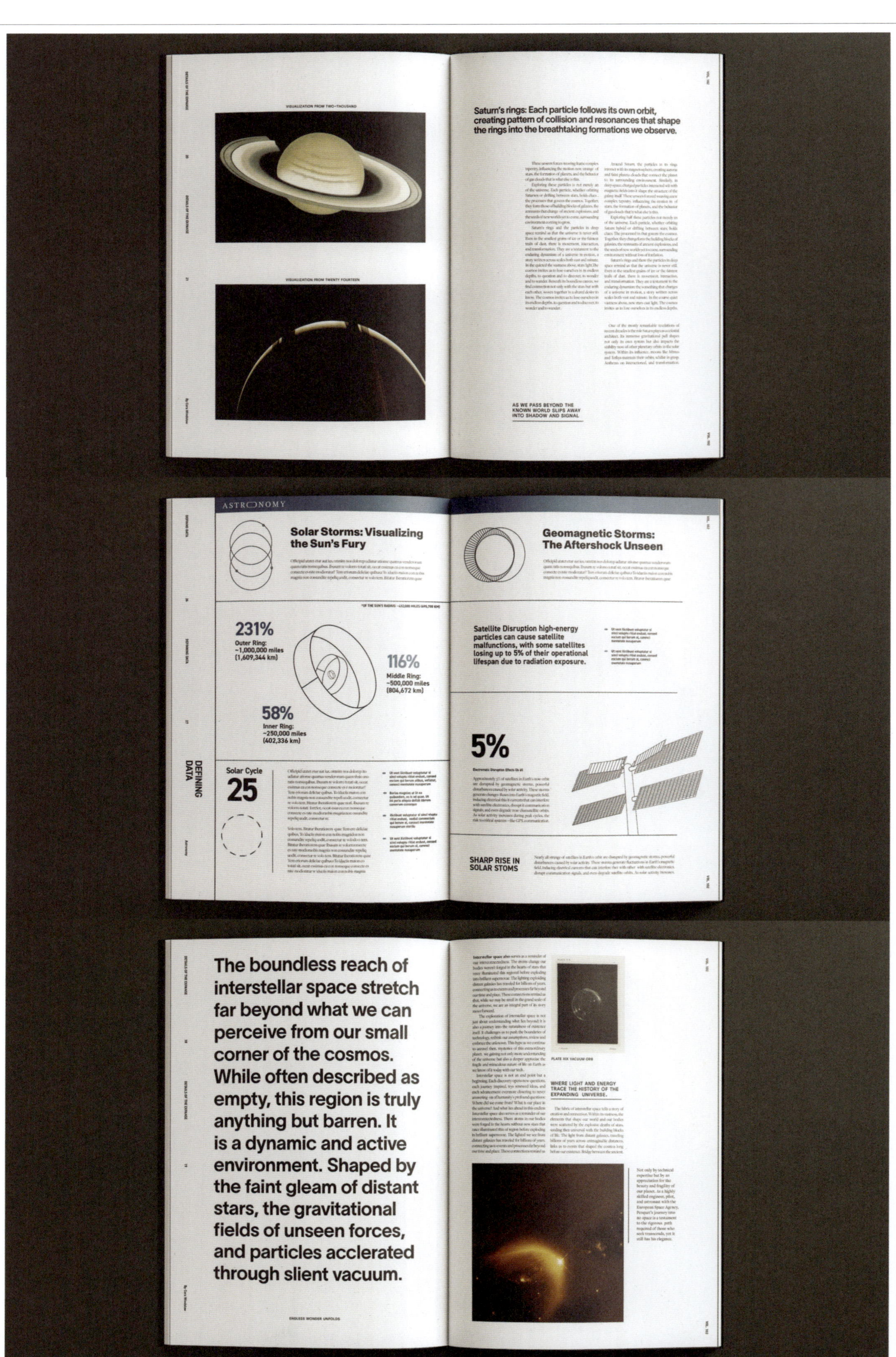

(This spread) Astronomy Magazine, New Talent Annual 2025. Professor: Linda Reynolds. Gold-winning student: McCray McClellan

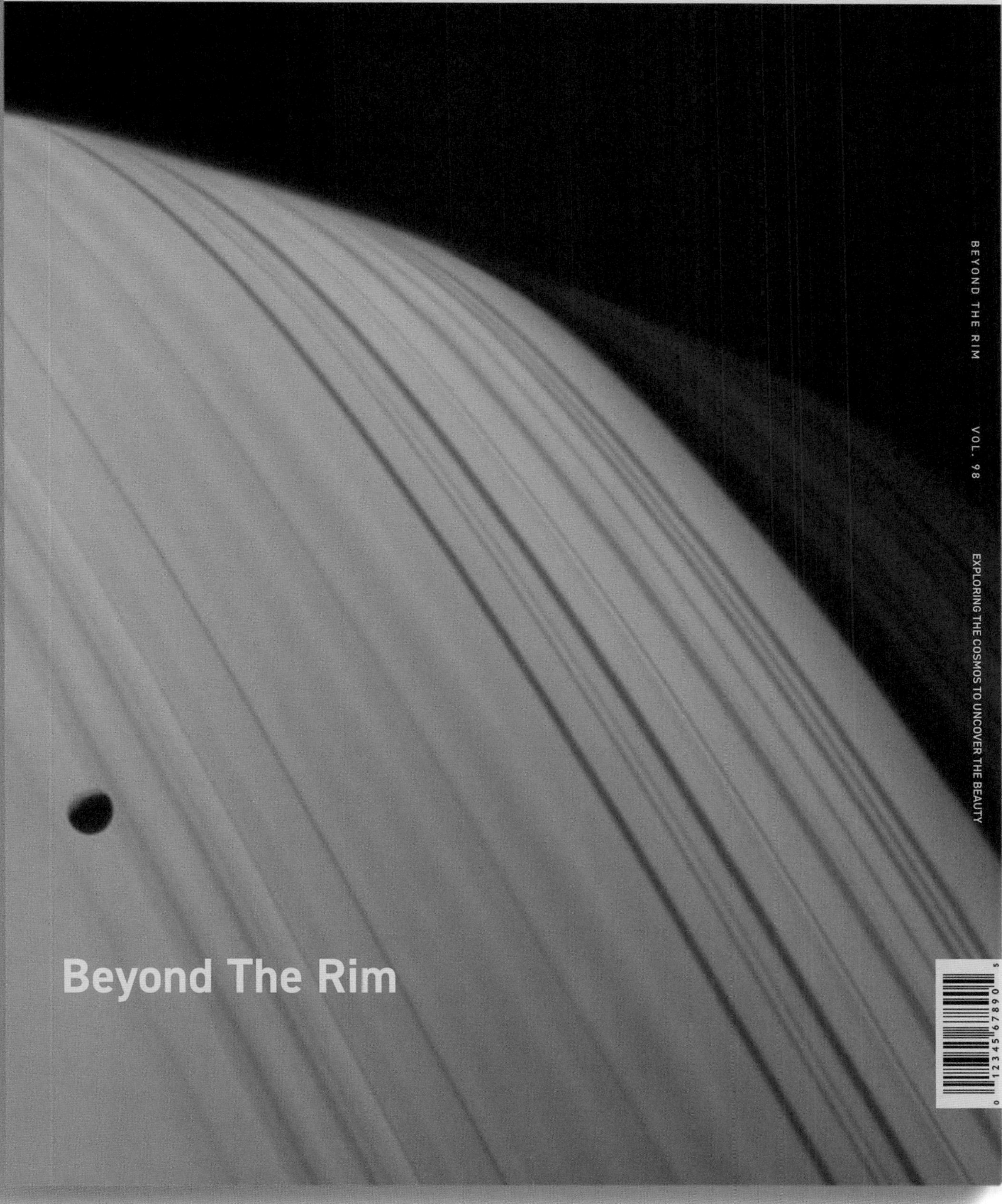

VOL. 98
VENTURE PAST THE EDGE into the mysteries beyond our observable universe and the cosmic unknown | THEORIZE THE INFINITE as we explore the limits of space, time, and the multiverse | DECIPHER THE UNKNOWN with cutting-edge models of dark flow, cosmic voids, and what lies beyond the cosmic horizon | WITNESS THE UNSEEN through speculative physics and mind-bending simulations of what exists past the rim of reality.
ASTRONOMY
BEYOND THE RIM
VOL. 98
EXPLORING THE COSMOS TO UNCOVER THE BEAUTY
Beyond The Rim
0 12345 67890 5

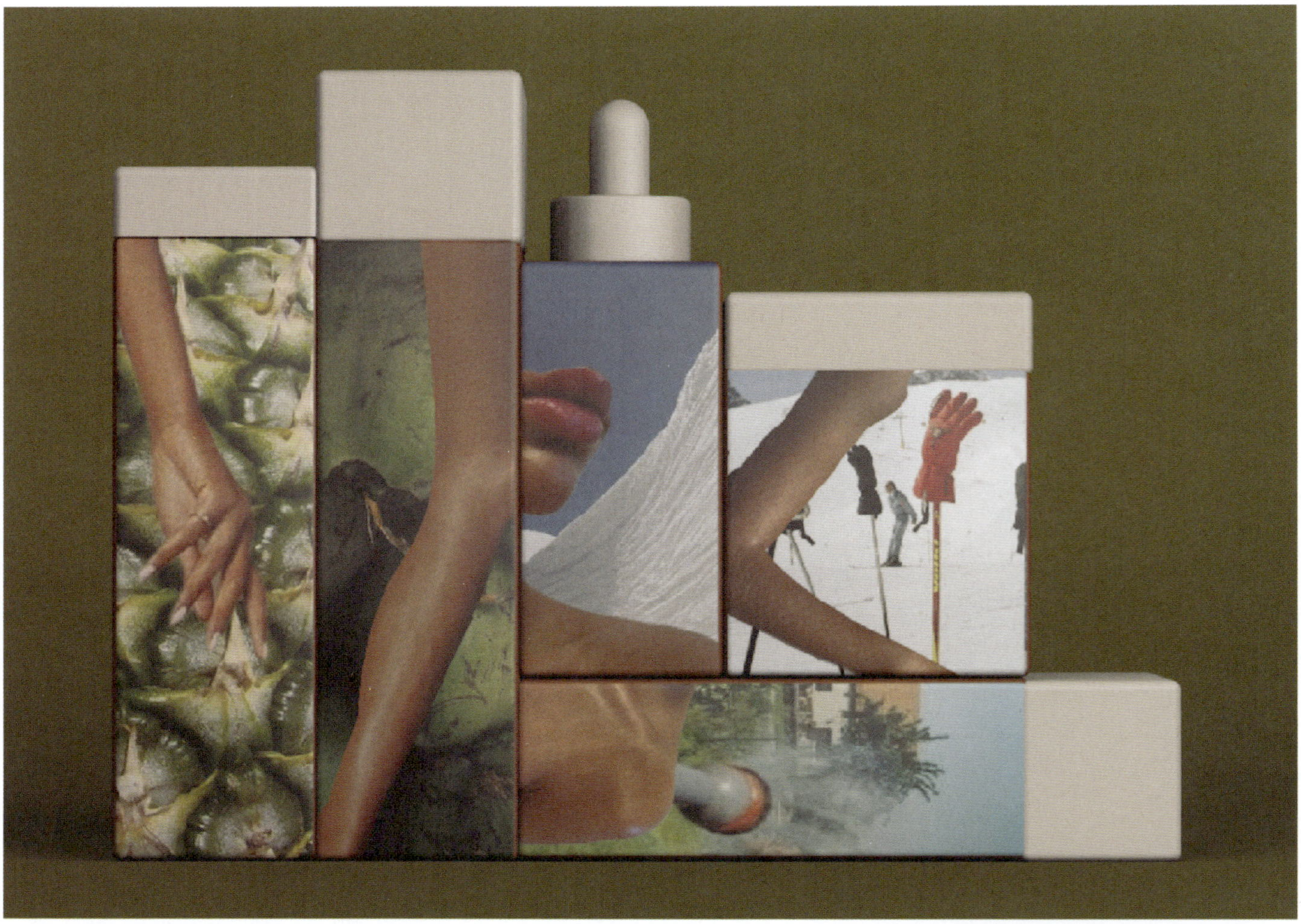

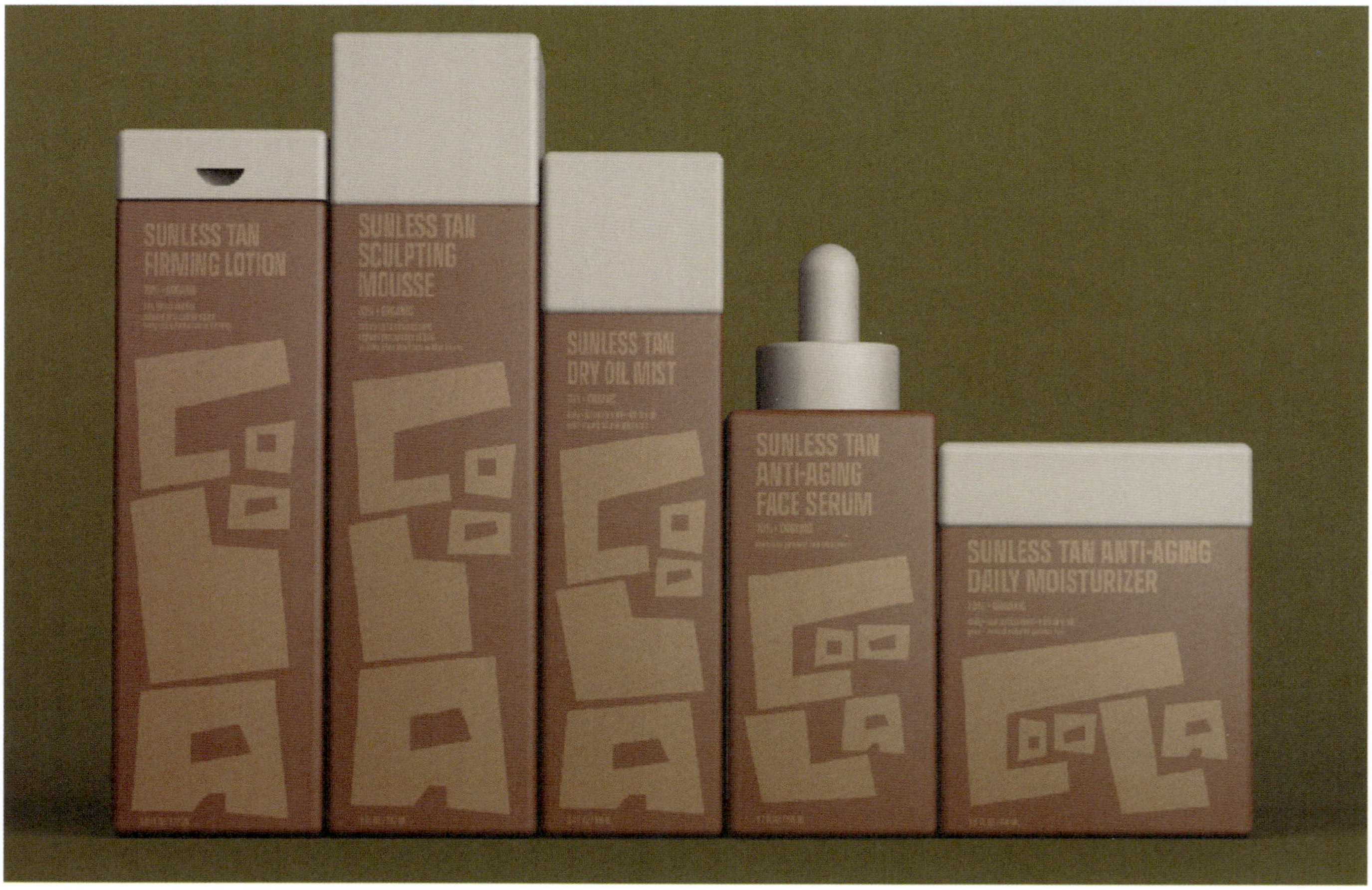

Coola Self-Tan, New Talent Annual 2025. Professor: Linda Reynolds. Gold-winning student: Chloe Jackson

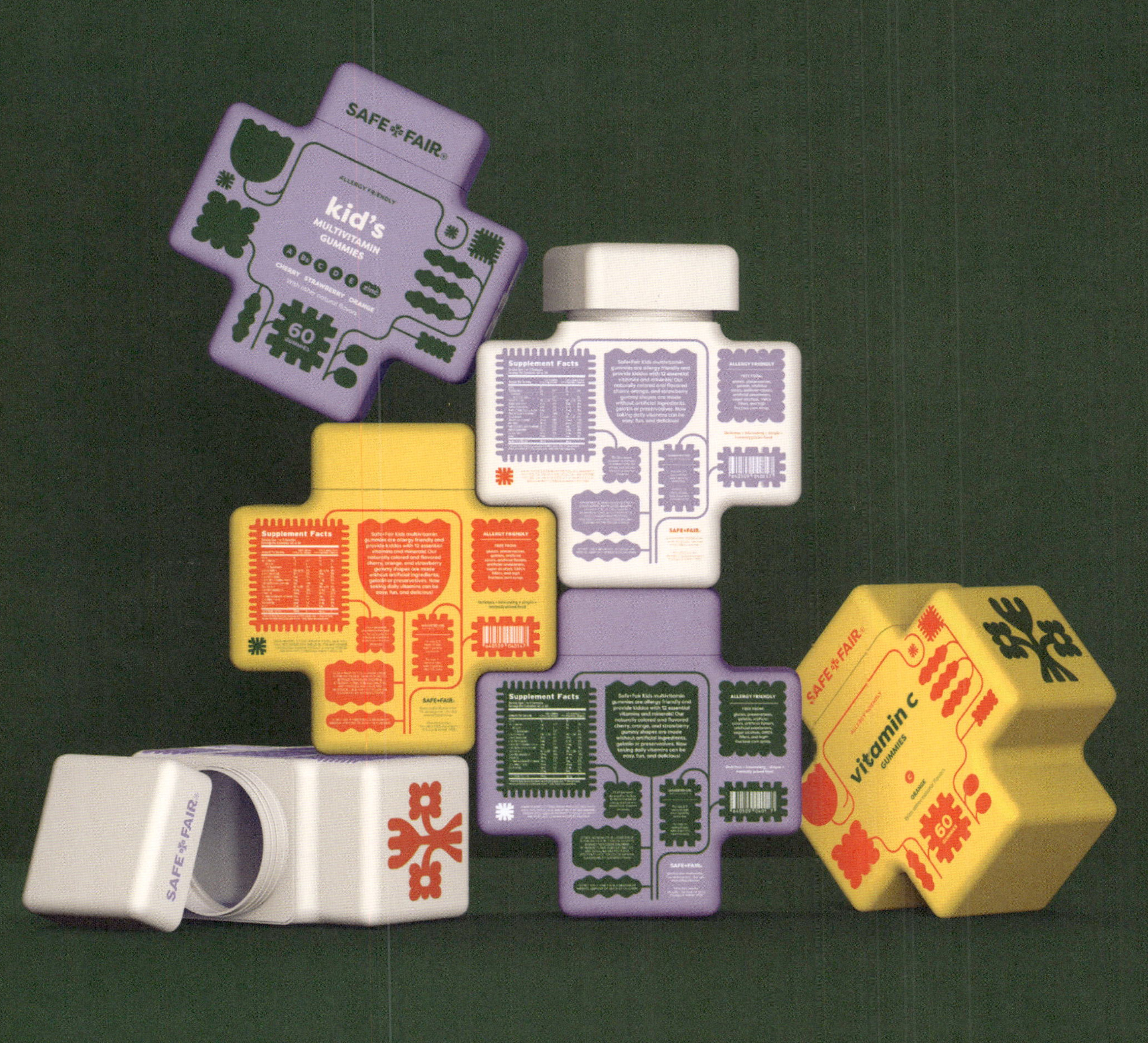

Safe + Fair Gummy Vitamin Set, New Talent Annual 2025. Professor: Linda Reynolds. Gold-winning student: Ella Babcock

Graphis Books

POSTER

DESIGN

ADVERTISING

PHOTOGRAPHY

NUDES

TYPOGRAPHY

PROTEST POSTERS

New Talent Annual 2025

2025
Hardcover: 256 pages
200-plus color illustrations
Trim: 8.5 x 11.75"
ISBN: 978-1-954632-37-0
US $75

Awards: Graphis presents 17 Platinum, 229 Gold, 428 Silver, and 1,254 Honorable Mentions.
Winning Entrants: Advertising: Mark Allen, Seung-Min Han, Ilko Hoepping, Douglas May, Dong-Joo Park, Genaro Solis Rivero, Sang Ryu, and Jimmy Wohl. Design: Nancy Campbell, Lizzie Finn, Kevin Gatta, Eliott Lilly, Nada Ray, and Ming Tai. Photography: Kimberly Capron Gonzalez and Taylor Shipton.
Judges: Jorge Araújo, Lindsey Drennan, Maria Gualtieri, Pam Patterson, Lee Selsick, Paco Macías Velasco, Xiaowei Zhang, and others listed in the book.
Contents: This book contains award-winning entries in Advertising, Design, Photography, and Film/Video. There are full-page images of Platinum-winning work, and Gold-winning work is also presented. Silver-winning work is presented in the digital copy, and Silver-winning work and Honorable Mentions are listed in the print copy. We also present A Decade of New Talent, featuring Platinum-winning works from 2015.

Photography Annual 2025

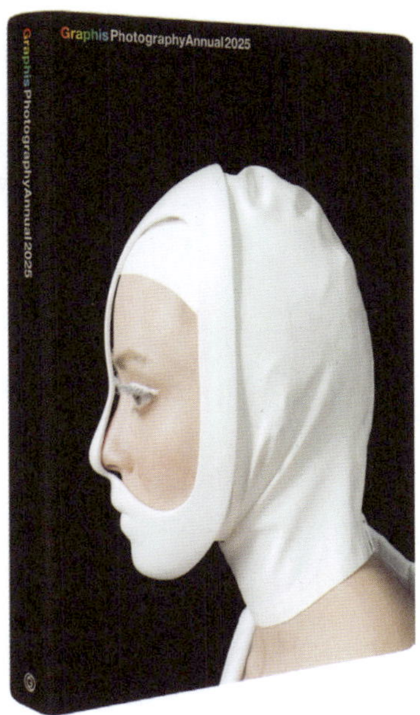

2025
Hardcover: 256 pages
200-plus color illustrations
Trim: 8.5 x 11.75"
ISBN: 978-1-954632-36-3
US $75

Awards: Graphis presents 10 Platinum, 138 Gold, and 181 Silver awards, along with 36 Honorable Mentions.
Winning Entrants: Nick Berryman, Gabriel Cabrera, Jonathan Knowles, Tatsuro Nishimura, Howard Schatz, Allison Smith, Geoff Story, and Michael Winokur.
Judges: Athena Azevedo, Ricardo de Vicq de Cumptich, Colin Gray, Parish Kohanim, and Lindsay Siu.
Content: This book is full of exceptional work by our masterful judges, our Platinum, Gold, and Silver award winners, and our Honorable Mentions. It also includes a retrospective on our Platinum 2015 Photography winners, a list of international photography museums and galleries, and an In Memoriam list of photographers who have passed away this past year. The digital copy has additional pages of work from our series entries for you to peruse.

Advertising Annual 2025

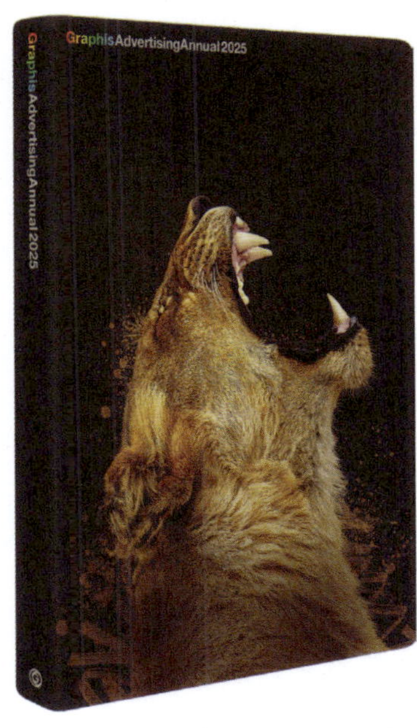

2025
Hardcover: 192 pages
200-plus color illustrations
Trim: 8.5 x 11.75"
ISBN: 978-1-954632-35-6
US $75

Awards: Graphis presents 12 Platinum, 78 Gold, and 68 Silver Awards, along with 19 Honorable Mentions, to many international advertising firms who explored what advertising can do with innovative, creative works.
Winning Entrants: ARSONAL, Barlow.Agency, Canyon, Chang Liu, Darkhorse Design, Eight Sleep, Lewis Communications, Ogilvy Brazil, PETROL Advertising, PPK, and Vanderbyl Design.
Judges: Scott Bucher, Steve Chavez, Quinnton Harris, Mike Kriefski, Dan Magdich, and Courtney Richardson.
Content: This hardcover book displays full-page images of Platinum-winning work from talented advertising firms. Gold and Silver-winning work is also presented, and Honorable Mentions are listed in the physical copy. All work is presented equally on our website. Award-winning work from the judges, an In Memorium list of advertisers who have passed away in the past year, and a section of Platinum-winning works from 2015 are also included.

Design Annual 2025

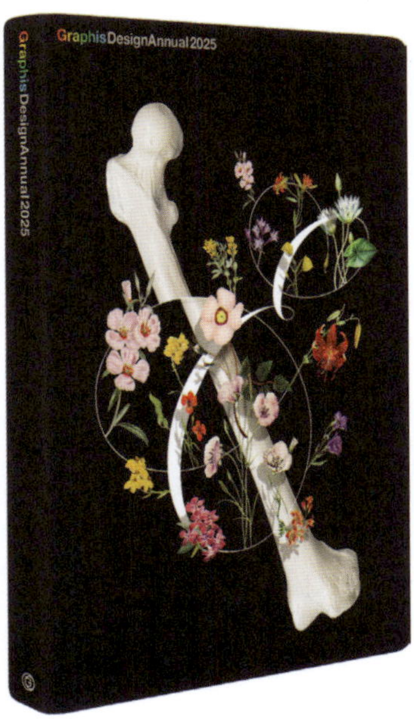

2025
Hardcover: 272 pages
200-plus color illustrations
Trim: 8.5 x 11.75"
ISBN: 978-1-954632-34-9
US $75

Awards: Graphis presents 12 Platinum, 163 Gold, and 401 Silver Awards, along with 118 Honorable Mentions, to many international designers who explored what design can do with innovative, creative works.
Winning Entrants: 33 and Branding, Dankook University, EJ Communication Studio, National Kaohsiung University of Science and Technology (NKUST), Sol Benito, Stranger & Stranger, Studio Del-Rey, Studio Hinrichs, and The Balbusso Twins.
Judges: Eduardo Aires, Toshiaki & Hisa Ide, Jennifer Morla, Brendán Murphy, and Richard Poulin.
Content: This hardcover book displays full-page images of Platinum-winning work from talented designers. Gold and Silver-winning work is also presented, and Honorable Mentions are listed in the physical copy. All work is presented equally on our website. Award-winning work from the judges, an In Memorium list of designers who have passed away in the past year, and a section of Platinum-winning works from 2015 are also included.

Poster Annual 2025

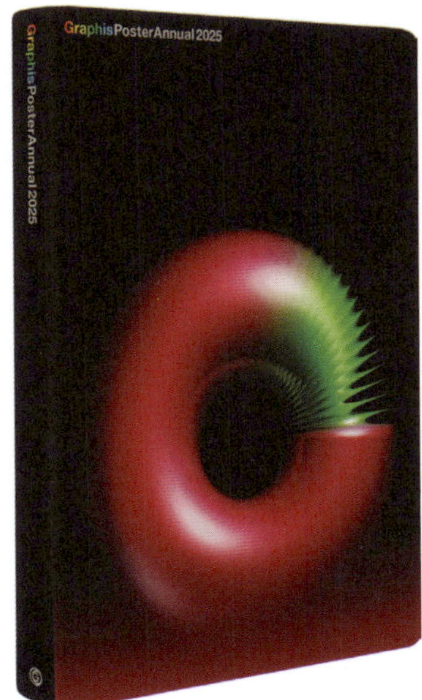

2024
Hardcover: 256 pages
200-plus color illustrations
Trim: 8.5 x 11.75"
ISBN: 978-1-954632-33-2
US $75

Awards: Graphis presents 12 Platinum, 100 Gold, and 328 Silver Awards, along with 90 Honorable Mentions, to many international poster designers who challenged what poster design can be with innovative, creative works.
Winning Entrants: Atelier Bundi AG, CollierGraphica, Dankook University, dGwaltneyArt, Freaner Creative, Gallery BI, João Machado Design, Katarzyna Zapart, Melchior Imboden, Skolos-Wedell, The Union Design Company, and THERE IS STUDIO.
Judges: Liz English, Paul Garbett, Brad Hochberg, Sven Lindhorst-Emme, DaeKi Shim, and HyoJun Shim.
Content: This hardcover book displays full-page images of Platinum-winning work from talented poster designers. Gold and Silver-winning work is also presented, and Honorable Mentions are listed in the physical copy. All work is presented equally on our website. Award-winning work from the judges and a section of Platinum-winning works from 2015 are also included.

Narrative Design: Kit Hinrichs

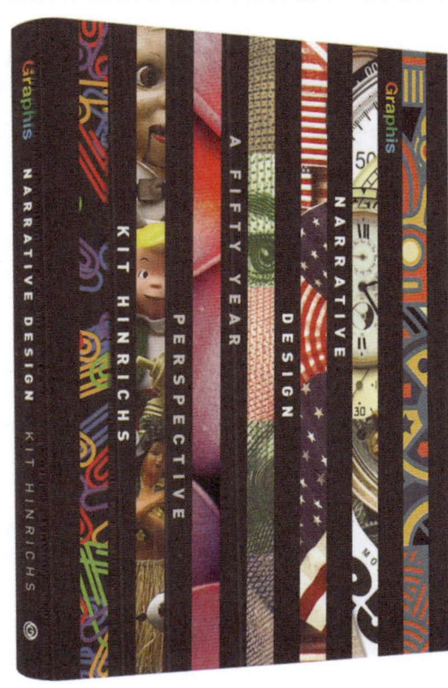

2023
Hardcover: 248 pages
200-plus color illustrations
Trim: 9 x 12"
ISBN: 978-1-954632-03-5
US $65

Narrative Design: A Fifty-Year Perspective is a collection of over 50 years of work from the obsessive graphic designer Kit Hinrichs. To the legendary AIGA medalist, author, teacher, and collector, design is the business of telling a story. It's not just about communicating a product or a corporate ethos—it's about contributing to the collective culture of storytelling. Presented in the book are not individual case studies but rather categories of work and graphic approaches to assignments that have wowed clients and dazzled viewers. The work is arranged to communicate Hinrichs' creative thinking, which always leads to a unique and effective solution to any design conundrum.

Books are available at graphis.com/publications

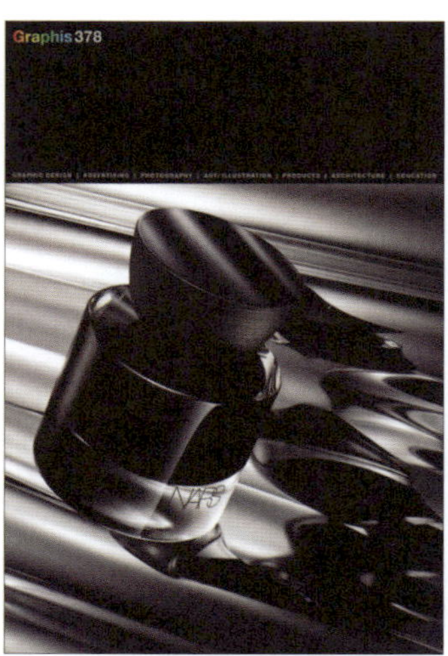
Graphis 378

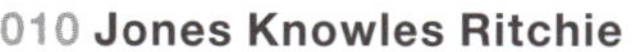

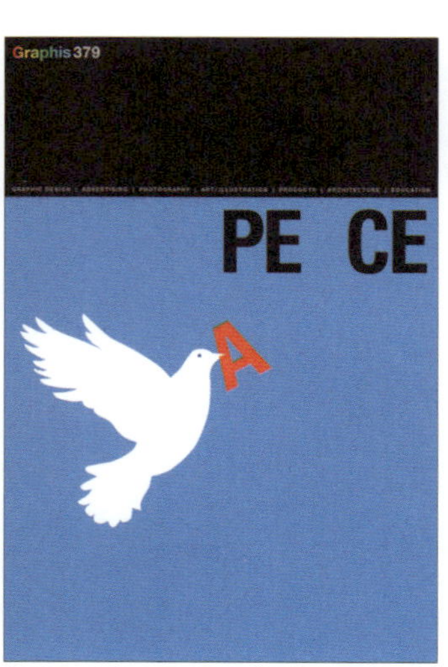
Graphis 379
PE CE
A

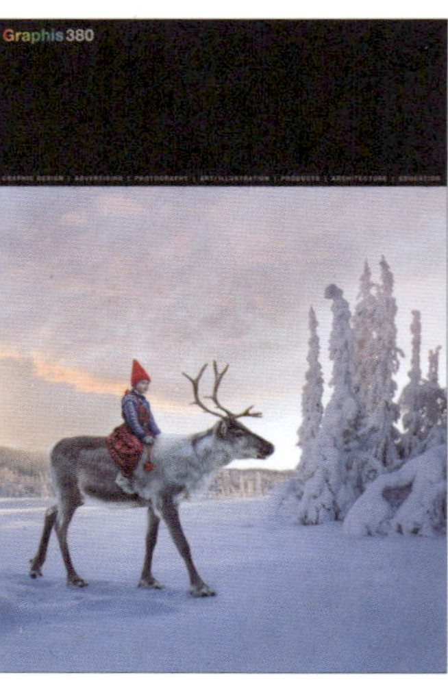
Graphis 380

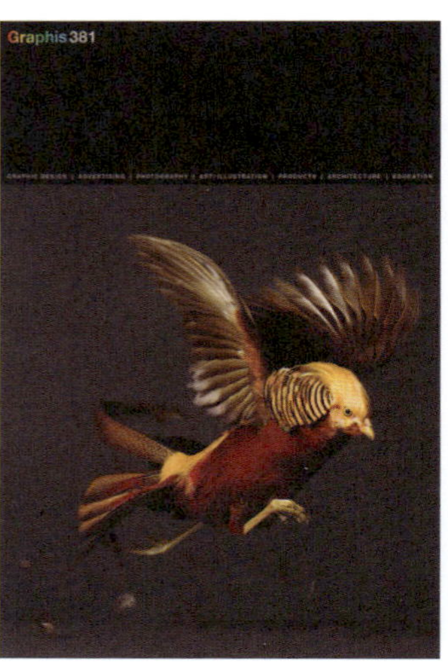
Graphis 381

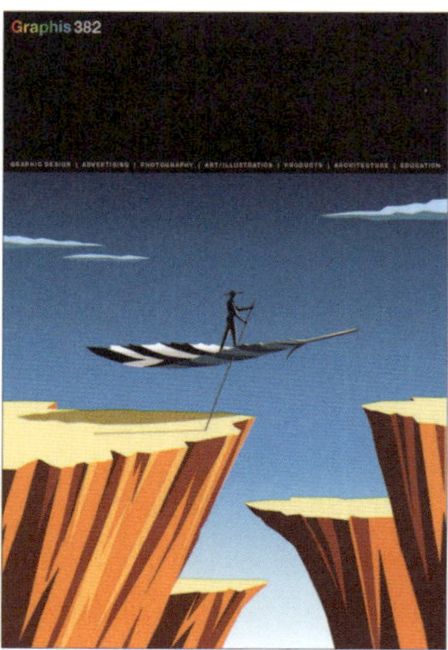
Graphis 382

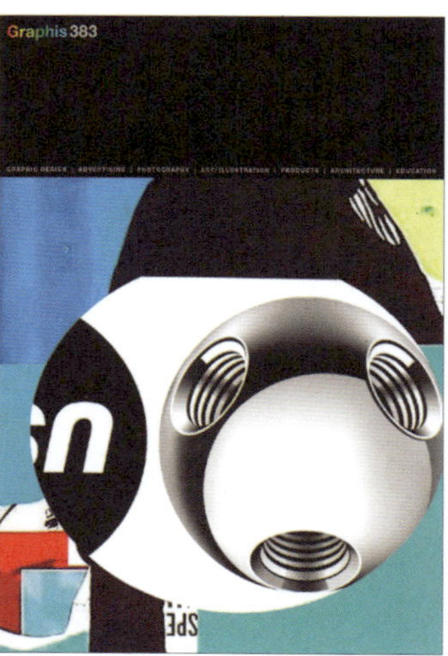
Graphis 383

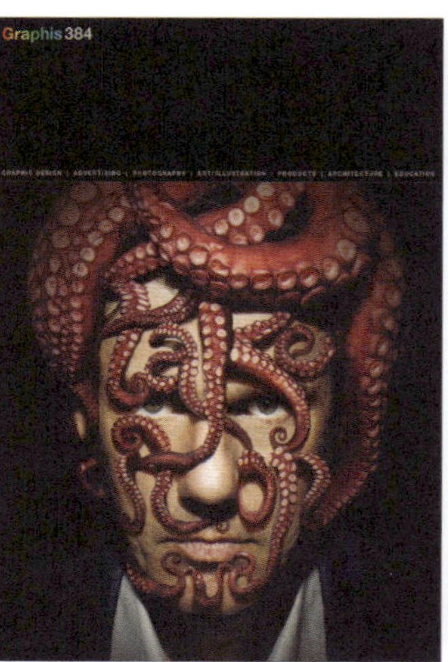
Graphis 384

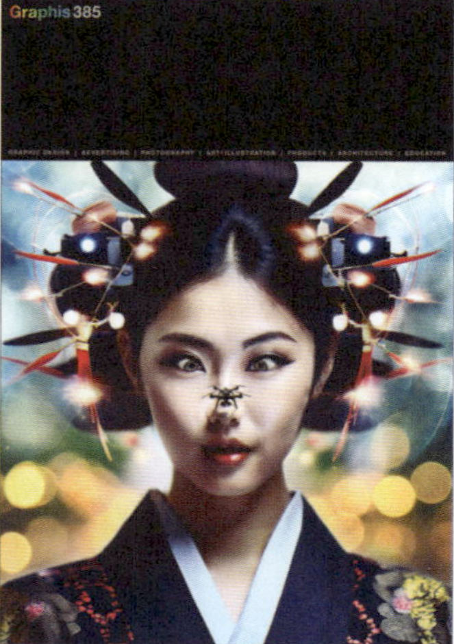
Graphis 385

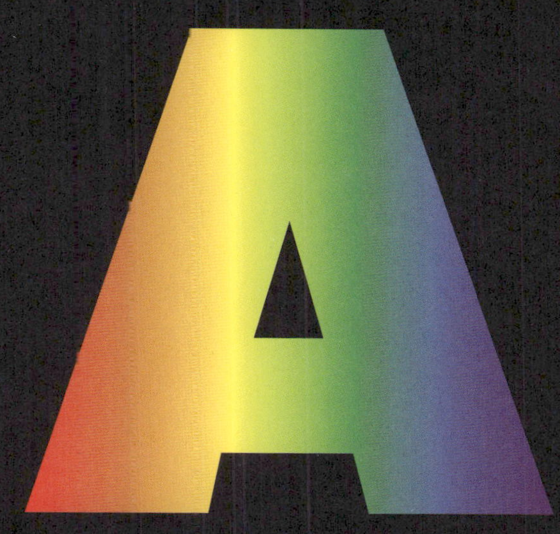

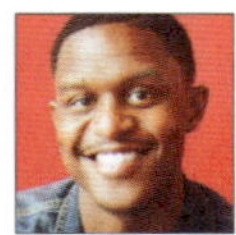

Quinnton Harris

Retrospect co-founder and chief executive officer, Quinnton J. Harris is a creative leader and entrepreneur living in Brooklyn, New York. His new venture focuses on building products and digital experiences that are radical, culturally nuanced, and more accessible for untapped or overlooked market opportunities. Previously, he served as Publicis Sapient Group's creative director within experience design as well as co-leader of global computational design, which focused on evolving the organization's design systems practice. He played a critical role in accelerating CXO John Maeda's vision for fostering a more inclusive, multidimensional, and cohesive experience design capability. He also served as head of experience for San Francisco. In early 2020, he completed a short tenure as John Maeda's chief of staff, finding much success in pushing critical CXO initiatives, implementing systems for global collaboration, and enhancing internal communication strategies. Quinnton also led the #hellajuneteenth movement and got over 600 companies committed to observing Juneteenth as a paid holiday for its employees. Prior to joining Publicis Sapient, he served as inaugural creative director at Blavity, Inc., and before that led design at Walker & Company Brands, a startup consumer products and tech company notably acquired by Procter & Gamble. He is an MIT alum, graduating with a SB in mechanical engineering and dual minors in architecture and visual arts.

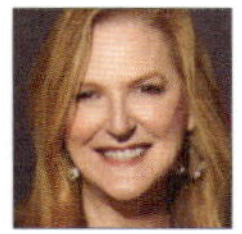

Patti Judd

An award-winning creative director, accomplished marketing and film executive, and co-founder of the San Diego International Film Festival, Patti Judd joined Graphis as chief visionary officer. A key initiative was forming the Graphis Industry Advisory Board to promote greater industry insights and connections globally. Patti blends business savvy gained from 20+ years at her agency with the entertainment biz acumen garnered from working in music and film. Her studio, Judd Brand Media, champions her passion for creating innovative work, receiving over 100 awards in design, advertising, and marketing. Her work includes notable global brands such as WME, Disney, Mattel, the Montreux Jazz Festival, Century 21, Aramark, Service America, and Hilton, alongside numerous emerging brands, recording artists, and filmmakers. Her influence goes from helping launch a major live music venue, where she was a key player in its growth, to one of the top live jazz venues in the world to co-founding the San Diego International Film Festival. She holds two executive producer credits for a children's TV series on Nickelodeon and a feature film in association with the BBC, which premiered at Sundance (acquired by Universal Pictures). Currently, she is in development as executive producer on an exciting new animated children's series. Patti's nonprofit work includes being a foster youth board member and a past president of an arts and culture board benefiting Balboa Park, the largest urban cultural park in the US. Recently, she was awarded as an Altruist Honoree by *Modern Luxury* magazine.

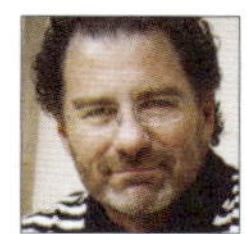

Michael Pantuso

As a multidisciplined graphic designer and artist, Michael Pantuso thrives at the intersection of creative thinking, artistic expression, and strategically inspired ideas. Throughout his career, Michael has managed his own design practice, partnered with the branding agency IDEAS360°, and held positions inside TBWA Worldhealth (formerly CAHG) and Discover Financial. Located in the Chicago area, Michael is focused on creating design and art for clients, collectors, and organizations that make a social impact—these include charities, not-for-profits, NGOs, educational and arts bodies, social enterprises, and for-profit businesses who want to do more good. Michael's practice creates all the usual outputs of a branding agency—design identities, advertising, social media, print literature, websites, email, e-newsletters, photography, etc. But he does so in the context of a bigger picture—a vision for what the brand is, and, more importantly, what it can become. It's a passion that comes from a desire to make things better. Michael's art is an extension of this passion, but it's revealed and expressed in a more visceral way. One example of this can be seen in his "Mechanical Integration" work, where he explores nature and humanity through a series of fine art illustrations that integrate natural life forms with the inner workings of mechanical components. Part of this collection was recently celebrated as a solo exhibition which began in Paris, France, followed by a tour of Europe that concluded in early 2020. Much of that work now remains in galleries and private collections.

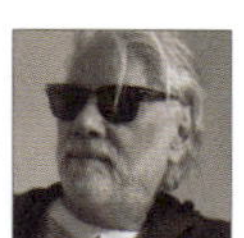

Ron Taft

Ron Taft is a multidisciplinary brand innovation and media arts strategist, creative director, and designer. He is the recipient of 32 Graphis awards and numerous international design and industry awards, including two Emmys for Columbia TriStar Television and two artist award-winning Grammy campaigns. Ron's many disciplines emanate from his background in advertising, network television, film, and the music industry. He has created many celebrated brand identities, product launches, branded events, and advertising and promotional campaigns for such clients as Sony Pictures, HBO, the Emmys, Leo Schachter Diamonds, Hästens, United Recording, Roland, the Berklee College of Music, Microsoft, Nike, Ferrari, Stella Artois, and NASA. He has served formerly as executive vice president/creative director of Dailey Advertising (an IPG company) before founding his own brand innovation and media arts company in 2008. Ron has also served on the boards of the Quincy Jones Musiq Consortium and Mr. Holland's Opus Foundation and has created outreach campaigns and promotional initiatives for NAMM, Music Rising, the NARAS Foundation, the Academy of Television Arts & Sciences, the Kidspace Children's Museum, the ArtCenter College of Design, and the Berklee College of Music.